DIASPORA MISSIONS TO INTERNATIONAL STUDENTS

ENOCH WAN (EDITOR)

DIASPORA MISSIONS TO INTERNATIONAL STUDENTS
Enoch Wan (Editor)   Copyright © 2019 by Western Seminary Press.   All Rights Reserved.

Cover designed by Esther Yong

This book is part of a series on Diaspora Studies

Published by the Center of Diaspora and Relational Research (CDRR)
Western Seminary Press
5511 SE Hawthorne Blvd., Portland, OR 97215, USA

Printed in the United States of America

First Printing: June 2019

ISBN-978-1-949201-17-8

✳ ✳ ✳

For more information on CDRR at Western Seminary or Enoch Wan, please visit the following sites:
https://www.westernseminary.edu/outreach/center-diaspora-relational-research
https://www.enochwan.com
https://www.globalmissiology.org

ISBN
978-1-949201-17-8

WESTERN SEMINARY
Center for Diaspora
and Relational Research

Table of Contents

CONTRIBUTORS

Stacey Bieler
Served on InterVarsity/USA for six years, the last two as an ISM specialist with Chinese scholars at UCLA. She co-wrote *China at Your Doorstep* (IVP) with Dick Andrews and co-wrote and edited *Chinese Intellectuals and the Gospel* (P&R) with Sam Ling. She wrote *"Patriots" or "Traitors"? A History of American Educated Chinese Students* (Routledge). She has co-edited three volumes of short biographies, *Salt and Light: Lives of Faith that Shaped Modern China* with Carol Hamrin. She has served on the ACMI board, in the international student ministry at University Reformed Church, East Lansing, MI, and has been active in Community Volunteers for International Programs (CVIP) at Michigan State University for thirty years.

Dennis C. Bradford, PhD
Dennis C. Bradford has graduate degrees from Eastern University and Capital Bible Seminary, his PhD is from Capital Seminary & Graduate School/Lancaster Bible College. He serves on the board of Jacksonville State University's International House. Previously, he served on the board of DayBreak Ministries, Washington, DC, as Adjunct Instructor with Washington Bible College, and as Extension Campus Coordinator at Birmingham Theological Seminary. Dennis is a former U.S. Army officer, who resides near the University of Alabama Huntsville, and worships at The Village Church, PCA.

Leiton E. Chinn
Leiton has been mobilizing the Church in North America and globally for over 40 years, including serving as President of the Association of Christians Ministering among Internationals [students] (ACMI) and the first Lausanne Movement's Catalyst for International Student Ministry. He is an ISM advocate with the World Evangelical Alliance Missions Commission, the Table Coalition, the Ethnic America Network, and other mission networks.

Lisa Espineli Chinn (MA in Communications - Wheaton College)
Served for 14 years as the National Director of International Student Ministry (ISM) of InterVarsity/USA (2000-2014). Books published: a) *Think Home*, b) *Back Home*, c) *Coming to America/Returning Home to Your Country*. In 2010, she was awarded the prestigious Hugh Jenkins Award for Excellence in Community Programming by NAFSA: Association of International Educators. Co-founder of *T.I.P.S.*– Truro International Programs and Services.

Sam Green
Sam and his wife Courtney lead a ministry focused on making disciples among internationals in New York City. Sam holds a Bachelor of Science degree in math and computer science from Union University, three graduate degrees in finance and accounting from the University of Illinois and University of Michigan, and is currently working on an MDiv. From 2003-2005, he served in East Asia. Sam and Courtney have had internationals from over 50 nations in their home, have been married for 12 years, and have two young children, Elijah and Elizabeth.

William Murrel (MSt. University of Oxford, 2011; PhD, History, Vanderbilt University, 2018)
Serving currently as Director of Every Nation Seminary (a global seminary based in Manila that will launch in 2021) and his research focus is "History of Christianity and Islam" He co-authored *The Multiplication Challenge: A Strategy to Solve Your Leadership Shortage* (2016).

Katie J. Rawson
Katie Rawson is currently ISM Senior Resource Developer for InterVarsity Christian Fellowship. She first became involved in ISM while doing research in Paris, where she was involved with InterVarsity's sister movement, the GBU. After getting her doctorate in French at UNC-Chapel Hill, she came on InterVarsity staff as an ISM specialist at North Carolina State University, where she started a student-led fellowship as part of an already existing ministry begun by a volunteer. After eight years she went to CA, where she planted a fellowship among Chinese scholars at UCLA and eventually completed a DMiss at Fuller Seminary, researching evangelizing East Asian students in the United States. Katie then returned to North Carolina and led a team of IV ISM ministers in the Carolinas and VA for eleven years. She authored *Crossing Cultures with Jesus: Sharing Good News with Sensitivity and Grace* in 2015.

Christopher D. Sneller
Currently serving as the Director of Innovation at Bridges International (Cru's international student ministry) and a Lecturer in Missional Theology at Houston Baptist University.
After obtaining seminary degrees at Covenant Theological Seminary (MO) and Dallas Theological Seminary (TX), he completed a PhD in historical theology from King's College London (UK). His dissertation, supervised by Professor Alister McGrath, examined how Union Theological Seminary (NY) impacted Christianity in twentieth-century China. He has worked cross-culturally in East Asia, North America, and Western Europe.

Florence PL Tan (MABS, ThM, DMin. - Dallas Theological Seminary (DTS) Fulltime with The Navigators (Nav) for three decades, faculty - Singapore Bible College for 18 years; adjunct teaching: Trinity Western University, Canada; Redcliffe College in Gloucester, UK; DTS, USA; Malyon College, Brisbane, Australia.

Chin John T. Wang
Chin Wang (John) was born in Taiwan and grew up in Argentina. He came to the US in 1987. John has been a pastor of the Chinese and Spanish ministry of First Baptist Church of Flushing and is currently serving as international deputy director for Gospel Operation International, an international and interdenominational mission organization initiated by Chinese churches around the world. He holds an MDiv from Bethel Seminary of the East and a PhD in Intercultural Studies from Trinity Evangelical Divinity School. Prior to his ministry career he was a professional engineer for 14 years. His engineering educational background includes BS, MS, and PhD degrees in civil engineering

CHAPTER 1
INTRODUCTION

Enoch Wan

The Background and Uniqueness of this Book

International student ministry (ISM) has a long history; however, the recently emerged diaspora missiology paradigm for ISM has seldom been employed. This book is an attempt to explore such an approach. In addition to this paradigmatic uniqueness, the choice of a relational perspective is a departure from the popular programmatic orientation of Christian mission and practice. This is not merely another book on ISM; rather its distinctive approach is integrative of two paradigms, i.e. diaspora missiological paradigm and relational paradigm. Readers will find further explanation of this unique approach of integration in Chapter 2.

Purpose

The purpose of this book is to employ the diaspora missiological paradigm for ISM with an emphasis on relational practice for Kingdom ministry in the context of ISM. There are two assumptions behind this purpose statement: paradigmatically ISM should not be formulaic, as in traditional missiology and, second, the ministerial approach should be relational. This point will be further explained in Chapter 2.

Definition of Key-Terms

Diaspora Ministry — serving the diaspora in the name of Jesus Christ and for His sake in these two ways: (1) ministering to the diaspora, i.e., serving the diaspora, and (2) ministering through the diaspora, i.e., mobilizing the diaspora to serve others (Wan 2014:5).
Diaspora Missiology Paradigm (DMP) — a missiological framework for understanding and participating in God's redemptive mission (*missio Dei*) among diaspora groups(Wan 2014:6).[1]
Diaspora Missions — Christians' participation in God's redemptive mission to evangelize their kinsmen on the move, and through them to reach out to natives in their homelands and beyond.[2]

---

[1] See "The Seoul Declaration on Diaspora Missiology," accessed March 25, 2010, http://www.lausanne.org/documents/seoul-declaration-on-diaspora-missiology.html.
[2] Enoch Wan, "Global People and Diaspora Missiology," presentation at Plenary session, Tokyo 2010—Global Mission Consultation, Tokyo, Japan, May 13, 2010.

Managerial Missiology Paradigm (MMP) — the framework of engaging in the academic study of missiology by uncritically adopting the secular management paradigm and proposing the practice of Christian mission accordingly (Wan 2014:6).

Managerial Mission Practice — ways and means of practicing Christian mission in the same manner of secular management in business that might be "biblical" and secularly contextual; but definitely not "scriptural" (Wan 2014:6).[3]

Ministry — rendering witness/service to people in the name of Jesus Christ, for His sake, by His power, and to His glory (Wan 2014:7).

Mission — a process by which Christians (individuals) and the Church (institutional) continue on and carry out the *missio Dei* of the Triune God ("mission") at both individual and institutional levels, spiritually (saving soul) and socially (ushering in *shalom),* for redemption, reconciliation, and transformation ("missions") (Wan 2014:7).[4]

Missions — ways and means of accomplishing "the mission" which has been entrusted by the Triune God to the Church and Christians (Wan 2014:7).[5]

Missiology — the systematic and academic study of missions in the fulfillment of God's mission (Wan 2014:7).

International student ministry (ISM) — Christians relationally carrying out *missio Dei* and Christian ministry to students from other countries, internationally.

Paradigm of relational realism — a conceptual framework for understanding reality based on the interactive connections between personal beings/Beings. (Wan & Hedinger 2017:14).

Relational missiology/ministry — Systematic study of mission (missiology) and the practice of Christian service (ministry) based on relational paradigm.

Relational Missionary Training — missionary training developed from the perspective of the paradigm of relational realism (Wan & Hedinger 2017:14).

The Organization of The Book

There are eleven chapters altogether in this book, covering various aspects

---

[3]Enoch Wan, "A critique of Charles Kraft's use/misuse of communication and social sciences in biblical interpretation and missiological formulation," Accessed Dec 20, 2013, http://ojs.globalmissiology.org/index.php/english/article/viewFile/120/346
[4] Enoch Wan, "'Mission' and *'Missio Dei'*: Response to Charles van Engen's 'Mission Defined and Described,'" in *MissionShift: Global Mission Issues in the Third Millennium,* ed. David J. Hesselgrave and Ed Stetzer, (Nashville: B & H Publishing Group, 2010d), 41-50.
[5] Enoch Wan, "Rethinking Missiological Research Methodology: Exploring a New Direction," *Global Missiology,* October 2003b, www.GlobalMissiology.org

of ISM. Following this introductory chapter, Chapter 2 covers theoretical and theological issues of definition of Christian "mission" and the diaspora missiological paradigm.

- Chapters 3 and 5 are case studies of individuals and personal reflection. Without footnote or bibliography, therefore light reading. Chapter 4 is a theological and biblical study that is foundational for subsequent chapters.
- Chapter 6 and Chapter 7 form a unit covering the history and development of ISM. Chapter 8 presents the helpful and insightful "Five Thresholds in Cross-cultural Evangelism." We acknowledge the generous permission of InterVarsity Press for its inclusion in this book.
- Chapter 9 provides helpful guides for local congregations to engage in ISM among unreached people groups. Chapter 10 presents case studies in the practice of diaspora mission.
- This book is a collection of contributions from seasoned ISM workers with a cumulative total of years with ISM being century-long. There are also stimulating and challenging concepts and insights that will serve our readers well

CHAPTER 2
DIASPORA MISSIOLOGY AND INTERNATIONAL STUDENT MINISTRY (ISM)

Enoch Wan

Introduction

The purpose of this chapter is to give an overview of diaspora missiology for the sake of applying it to "international student ministry" (ISM) which is a reference to Christian ministry among internationals (foreign passport holders with a student or work visa) within an academic context. The theoretical framework as explained in this chapter is foundational to the whole book. This chapter begins with a review of the popular view of Christian "mission" and a proposed relational alternative. An overview of the diaspora missiology paradigm is presented for its application **relationally** to ISM among foreign students and researchers.

Below are definitions of several key terms, along with the embedded assumptions:

Mission — a process by which Christians (individuals) and the Church (institutional) continue on and carry out the *missio Dei* of the Triune God ("mission") at both individual and institutional levels spiritually (saving souls) and socially (ushering in *shalom**) for redemption, reconciliation, and transformation ("missions")[6] (Wan 2014:7).

*• *"shalom"* is the context of total wellness in which created humanity can reach his/her full potential and properly respond to God and His message relationally (Jer. 29:7, 1 Tim. 2:1-5).

Missions — ways and means of accomplishing "the mission" which has been entrusted by the Triune God to the Church and Christians (Wan 2014:7).[7]

Relational missiology — the practical outworking of relational theology in carrying out the *missio Dei* and fulfilling the Great Commission.

Missio Dei — the Triune God pressing Himself out thus showing forth His nature of love, communion, commission (sending), and glory.

---

[6] Enoch Wan, "'Mission' and *'Missio Dei'*: Response to Charles van Engen's 'Mission Defined and Described,'" in *MissionShift: Global Mission Issues in the Third Millennium*, eds. David J. Hesselgrave and Ed Stetzer, (Nashville: B & H Publishing Group, 2010d), 41-50.
[7] Enoch Wan, "Rethinking Missiological Research Methodology: Exploring a New Direction," *Global Missiology*, October 2003b, www.GlobalMissiology.org

Paradigm — the perceptual perspective, conceptual framework, or scientific model of reality (Wan 2003:1).[8]

Traditional/popular Missiological Paradigm — the conceptual framework and methodological practice of Christian organizations such as AD 2,000, Missio Nexus, American Society of Missiology, Evangelical Missiological Society, and Lausanne Congress of World Evangelization.

There are several assumptions behind the above definitions as listed below:

- Traditional missiology paradigm has its focus on program and performance with formula and matrix.[9]
- Popular pattern of Christian ministry and mission practice are extremely functional and pragmatic, either de-emphasizing or bracketing out the vertical linkage with the Triune God (in contrast to the Pauline conviction that it is "…in Him we live, and move and have our being…" — Acts 17:22-31).
- Christian faith and practice are essentially "relational" first, then existentially "functional."
- Paradigmatically, ISM should not be formulaic as in the popular missiological paradigm, and its ministerial approach should be relational.
- Methodologically, missiological research is to be interdisciplinary,[10] including the "STARS" approach of 5 steps in sequence and with priority: 1. Scripturally Sound, 2. Theologically Supported, 3. Analytically Coherent, 4. Relevantly Contextual, 5. Strategically Practical (see Appendix 1).

---

[8] Enoch Wan, "The Paradigm of 'relational realism,'" *Occasional Bulletin*, 19, No. 2, 2006.

[9] see Chapter 7 of Wan 2014 for the critique of "managerial missiology."

[10] See previous publications on interdisciplinary research below:

- Enoch Wan, "Rethinking Missiological Research Methodology: Exploring a New Direction," *Global Missiology*, October 2003, www.GlobalMissiology.org
- Enoch Wan, "The Paradigm and Pressing Issues of Inter-disciplinary Research Methodology," *Global Missiology*, January 2005.
- Enoch Wan, "Research Methodology for Diaspora Missiology and Diaspora Missions," presented at the Regional EMS Conference – North Central, February 26, 2011b, Trinity Evangelical Divinity School, Deerfield Illinois.
- Enoch Wan, "Inter-disciplinary and Integrative Missiological Research: the 'What,' 'Why,' and 'How,'" July 2017, **www.GlobalMissiology.org**
- Edward Rommen and Gary Corwin, eds., "A Critique of Charles Kraft's Use/Misuse of Communication and Social Sciences in Biblical Interpretation and Missiological Formulation," in *Missiology and the Social Sciences: Contributions, Cautions, and Conclusions*, (Pasadena, CA: William Carey Library, 1996) 121-164.
- Enoch Wan and Mabiala Kenzo, "Evangelical Theology, Postmodernity, and the Promise of Interdisciplinarity," *Global Missiology*, January 2006, www.globalmissiology.org

The Popular Definition and Prevalent Theology of Christian Mission

More often than not, "Christian mission" is defined as "the Great Commission" with the favorite text — Matthew 28:19-20. Combined with Acts 1:8 and Matthew 24:14, the popular view in summary form is as follows:

- THE GREAT COMMISSION: (DOING for God)
  What to do? (making disciples)
  How? (going, baptizing, teaching)
  Where? (Jerusalem, Judaea, Samaria, end of the earth)
  When? (now to the end of the age)

The two quotations below illustrate the popular programmatic/managerial approach in "Christian mission" —

"Mission" is the "total biblical assignment of the church of Jesus Christ. It is a comprehensive term including the upward, inward, and outward ministries of the church."[11]

In the traditional sense the term missionary has been reserved for those who have been called by God to a full-time ministry of the Word and prayer (Acts 6:4), and who have crossed geographical and/or cultural boundaries (Acts 22:21) to preach the gospel in those areas of the world where Jesus Christ is largely, if not entirely, unknown (Rom. 15:20).[12]

The programmatic/managerial way of practicing Christian "mission" is in line with the predisposition of American culture as described in the quotation below:

The foreign visitor in the United States quickly gains an impression of life lived at a fast pace and of people incessantly active. This image reflects that **doing** is the dominant activity for Americans. The implicit assumption that "getting things done" is worth while is seldom questioned…The ramifications of the **doing** assumption impinge upon other values and assumptions of the culture and pervade the language of Americans, as in the colloquial exchanges of greeting: "How're you doing?" "I'm doing fine — how are you coming along?" All aspects of American life are affected by the predominance of **doing**…Kluckhohn's definition of **doing** is compatible with other characteristics of Americans such as the importance of achievement, emphasis on visible accomplishments, and the stress on

---

[11] George W. Peters, *A Biblical Theology of Missions*, (Chicago: Moody, 1972), 11.
[12] J. Herbert Kane, *Understanding Christian Missions*, (Grand Rapids: Baker, 1974), 28.

measurement.[13]

As shown in the comparative table in Appendix 2, the left column shows the Ameri-European[14] pattern as follows:

- the cognitive pattern includes: perception — man **separated from nature**, preference — **achievement**, predisposition — **doing/program, effort-optimism**.
- the cognitive process includes: tendency — quantitative, direction — teleological, future.

The above description and analysis can help in explaining the popular view of Christian mission.

In America, there is a common saying: "if it looks like a duck, walks like a duck, and quacks like a duck, it must be a duck." In other words, identity is to be determined by activity, being is dependent on doing as shown in Figure 3.

Relational Understanding of Christian "Mission"

The discussion below follows the five steps of the "STARS" approach, explaining that the proposed relational understanding of Christian mission is being scripturally sound, theologically supported, analytically coherent, relevantly contextual, and strategically practical.

Scripturally sound

The favorite texts of popular understanding of "mission" are as follows:

- Matthew 28:19-20 Therefore go and make disciples of all nations, baptizing them in the name of the Father and of the Son and of the Holy Spirit, and teaching them to obey everything I have commanded you... I am with you always, to the very end of the age.
- Acts 14:21 They preached the gospel in that city [Derby] and won a large number of disciples. Then...Lystra, Iconium, and Antioch.
- Acts 1:8 But you will receive power when the Holy Spirit comes on you; and you will be My witnesses in Jerusalem, and in all Judaea, and in Samaria, and unto the uttermost part of the earth.
- Matthew 24:14 And this gospel of the kingdom will be preached in the whole world as a testimony to all nations, and then the end will come.

The key verse for the Great Commission is Matthew 28:19-20 and it is

---

[13] Edward C. Stewart, *American Cultural Patterns: A Cross-cultural Perspective*, (Chicago: Intercultural Press, 1972), 36.

[14] "Ameri-European" is focusing on American culture with European background, whereas Sino-Asian is focusing on Chinese culture with Asian background.

to be carefully examined in light of the narrative structure of the entire book.[15] There are various ways to understand the structure of Matthew, one being to see all the action revolving around Jesus' five main discourses:

Narrative—chapters 1-4
I—First Discourse—Sermon on the Mount—chapters 5-7
Narrative—chapters 8-9
II—Second Discourse—Missionary Discourse—chapter 10
Narrative—chapters 11-12
III—Third Discourse—Parables of the Kingdom—chapter 13
Narrative—chapters 14-17
IV—Fourth Discourse—Teachings on the Church—chapter 18
Narrative—chapters 19-23
V—Fifth Discourse—Eschatology and Parousia—chapters 24-25
Narrative - chapters 26-28.

The disciples were systematically and relationally trained in Kingdom-orientation (vertical) by Jesus in two stages: each concluded with an imperative, i.e. "the Great Commandment" (horizontal) of Matthew 22:37-38 and "the Great Commission" (vertical + horizontal) of 28:16-20.

Instead of the popular view of equating "mission" with the Great Commission of making disciples of all nations by going, teaching, baptizing, "mission" is God relationally (vertical) loving and sending His Son to redeem and reconcile His own with Himself (vertically upward; not merely doing ministry horizontally). God's own should be a witness to God's abundant grace and unmerited favors to serve and glorify Him.

Historically, bearing witness to God was carried out by diasporic individuals/groups (e.g. Joseph in Egypt, Daniel and friends in Babylon, Israelites in foreign lands during their exile, scattered Christians of the early NT church) and witnesses sent by God (e.g. OT prophets, John the Baptist, apostles and Christians of the NT[16]). There is no explicit reference to their efforts in making disciples for the Kingdom; yet they all faithfully bore witness to God, including the list in Hebrew 11. Therefore, bearing witness to God is scripturally sound; instead of simply "biblical" (i.e. selectively focusing on two passages: Matthew 28:19-20 — dialogical and Acts 14:21 — descriptive).

---

[15] This discussion is based on the forthcoming title, *Missionary Preparation in the Gospel of Matthew in light of 28:16-20* by Enoch Wan and Rob Penner in the CDRR "Relational Research Series."

[16] It is worth noting: "you are My witnesses" is found in favorite texts of the popular view of Christian "mission" (see the Lukan accounts: Lk 24:48 and Acts 1:8); yet being ignored or underplayed.

Theologically supported

The popular action-oriented and programmatic approach of Christian mission has a misguided emphasis on the secondary — DOING; instead of BEING. The correct way is sequential: BEING precedes DOING; nevertheless with both. In the definition (beginning of this chapter) on "mission" above, a key element is the pattern of interaction within the Triune God and the key concept is *"missio Dei"* as shown in the figures below.

Figure 1 — Interaction: Sending and Submission within the Trinity

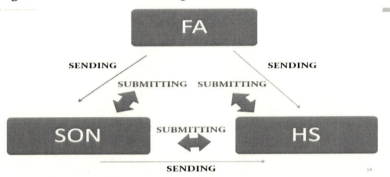

Figure 2 — *Missio Dei* **within the Trinity**

FATHER	❖ Desires many to be saved (1 Timothy 2:4, 2 Peter 3:9, Ezekiel 18:23, Matthew 23:37) ❖ Designed the plan of salvation for His own (OT & NT)
SON	❖ Being sent by the Father & sends Christians likewise (John 17:18, 20:21) ❖ There is mutual glorification between the Father and the Son (John 17:1) ❖ Jesus the Son shares the heart of the Father (so should God's children), desiring many to be saved (1 Tim. 2:4, 2 Pet. 3:9) ❖ Obedient to the Father & glorifies the Father (John 17:4, 1 Pet. 4:11) ❖ Like Jesus, Christians are to be in touch of the Father's heartbeat & be obedient/glorifying the Father (John 17:4)

FATHER	❖ Desires many to be saved (1 Timothy 2:4, 2 Peter 3:9, Ezekiel 18:23, Matthew 23:37) ❖ Designed the plan of salvation for His own (OT & NT)
HOLY SPIRIT	❖ The FA & Son: a) sent by both; b) witnessing of & c) glorifying both (John 16:14) ❖ Bears witness to the Son & the Father (John 15:26) ❖ Holy Spirit & Christians: a) regenerates/sanctifies Christians (Titus 3:4-7, 1 Pet. 1:2) b) indwells & empowers Christians to be witnesses & to glorify God (Acts 1:8 (John 14:17, 1 Cor. 6:19–20) c) helps Christians to bear fruit (Gal. 5:22-23)

Mission does not begin in history with Eve, Abraham, or Israel. Theologically, "mission" is "*missio Dei* intra-Trinity" (within the Triune God: the Father, the Son, and the Holy Spirit). The following quotation is helpful for our critical review on Christian mission:

In eternity past, God the Father gave to His Son a chosen people and commissioned His Son to redeem them by the help of His Spirit (Luke 22:29, John 6:37–40, Heb. 9:14). This is the foundation of mission — it begins with the Triune God. What unfolds in the history of redemption in relation to mission was first established in the covenant of redemption between the Persons of the Trinity.[17]

"Mission" as *missio Dei* is intrinsic within the Trinity then extended to Christians as stated by Jesus Christ, "…as the Father sent Me, so send I you" (John 20:21). There is a consistent interactive pattern from the Triune God to redeemed/reconciled humanity with the characteristic of reciprocity for sending and submission, witnessing and glorifying.

Analytically coherent

The popular view of Christian "mission" is usually narrow in focus — doing (making disciples) without the sequential base of "being." In other words, pragmatic precedes ontology: however, without existence there cannot be function. The focus on performance without personhood is logically wrong; though in conformity to a secular orientation.

---

[17] Jonathan Gibson, "A 7-Point Biblical Theology of Mission," October 03, 2016, accessed Feb. 1, 2019, https://faculty.wts.edu/posts/a-biblical-theology-of-mission/

Figure 3 — Two columns: A and B

1. A		2. B	
3.	Being	4.	Doing
5.	Personhood	6.	Performance
7.	Messenger	8.	Methodology
9.	Identity	10.	Activity
11.	Witnessing	12.	Winning
13.	Vertical relationships	14.	Horizontal relationship
15.	Faithfulness	16.	Fruitfulness

Some observations of the popular view of "mission" from the above figure:

- **doing** (b) precedes **being** (a) / (a) determined by (b);
- **performance** (b) precedes **personhood** (a) / (a) is dependent on (b);
- **activity** (b) precedes **identity** (a) / (b) determines (a);
- **fruitfulness** in the eyes of man (b horizontal) is more important than **faithfulness** to God (a - vertical) / (b) horizontal is greater than (a).

According to the figure above, there are two patterns, three possibilities and one correct:

2 patterns	3 possibilities	A		B
either-or (wrong)	(wrong)	X		
		X		
both-and (right)	(half-right)	B	+	A
			A	+ B

As explained in prior publications,[18] the both-and "Trinitarian

[18] Enoch Wan

- "Christ for the Chinese: A Contextual Reflection," *Chinese Around the World*, November 2000.
- "Practical contextualization: A case study of evangelizing contemporary Chinese," *Chinese Around the World*, March 2000:18-24.
- "Theological contribution of Sino-theology to global Christian community," *Chinese Around the World*, July 2000.

paradigm" is derived from the doctrine of the Trinity (i.e. God is first ONE then THREE; He is both ONE and THREE).[19] When we say "God is first ONE then THREE" in that the doctrine of Trinity had been gradually unfolding in human history. God revealed to mankind in the OT as Jehovah – the Father within the Trinity. It was not until NT times that the Son and the H.S. had been made known. The Three Persons are equal in power, honor and authority, i.e. "in essence One;" but revealed to mankind as Father, Son, HS, i.e. "existence 3."

As shown in the figure below, the Triune God is one in essence; three in existence.

Figure 4 — The Trinity

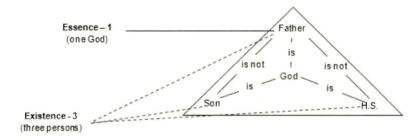

We can then list out the main ideas in two points as follows:

- TRIUNE GOD: God is **one** (essence) and **three** (existence).
- TRINITARIAN PARADIGM:[20] God is **both** one **and** three; but **first** one **then** three.

The Trinitarian paradigm **("both-and"** with **priority**: one-then-three) is correct, for there is only ONE God Who exists in THREE Persons. This both-and pattern is theoretically the same in the Chinese concept of Tai-je (

- *Sino-theology: A survey study*, (Ontario, Canada: Christian Communication Inc. of Canada, 1999, in Chinese).
- "Christianity in the eye of traditional Chinese," *Chinese Around the World,* July 1999:17-23.
- "Critique of Traditional Western Theology," *Chinese Around the World,* October 1999:19-25.

[19] Enoch Wan, "Critiquing the Method of Traditional Western Theology and Calling for Sino-Theology," *Global Missiology,* October 2003, www.globalmissiology.net

[20] Based on the Trinitarian paradigm ("both-and" with priority), three books have been published:
- Enoch Wan and Mark Hedinger, *Relational Missionary Training,* (CA: Urban Loft, 2017).
- Enoch Wan, *Sino-theology: A Survey Study* 《中色神學網要》, (Canada: Christian Communication Inc., 1999, in Chinese).
- Enoch Wan, *Theology of Unmerited Favor*, 《恩情神學》, (Hong Kong: TienDao Publisher, 2016, in Chinese).

太極 = Yang + Yin; but Yang precedes Yin) contextually.[21] The both-and pattern is theoretically the same as the cognitive process of being "holistic/correlational" as seen of the Sino-Asian pattern in Appendix 2.

The integrated approach ("**A + B**" in the table below) in Christian ministry/mission is neither dichotomist nor dualistic; rather, "both-and," including **being** and **doing**, personhood and performance, witnessing and making disciples, the fulfilment of the Great Commission and the practice of the Great Commandment of loving your neighbor. We summarize it in the figure below:

Figure 5 — Relational Paradigm & Popular Missiological Paradigm

#	(A) Relational Paradigm Great Commandment + Great Commission	(B) Popular Missiological Paradigm (Great Commission)
1.	BEING: vertically God works **in us** →	DOING: horizontally God works **through us**
2.	PERSONHOOD: Christians being **in Christ** →	PERFORMANCE: Christians doing **for Christ**
3.	MESSENGER: saved/shepherd/sent **by Him**→	METHOD: making disciples **for Him**
4.	WITNESSING: by life & living **(to serve)** →	WINNING: strategize to win the lost **(to save)**
5.	VERTICAL: Triune God & His own →	HORIZONTAL: enterprising & managerial
6.	RELATIONAL: vertical + horizontal →	FUNCTIONAL/PROGRAMATIC: (vertical) horizontal
7.	PROCESS: open-ended and unpredictable, convergence of tri-systems[17] (i.e. theo-/angelic/human) without "excluded middle" →	PROGRAM: structured plan & procedure, lip service to vertical, secularized with "excluded middle"[18]

From the table above we can list out the characteristics of the relational paradigm in summary format:

- Relational paradigm is sequential from A → B.
- It is processual from the left column → to the right column; not programmatically obsessed with outcomes of the right column. It is not formulaic nor the mere pragmatism of the right column.
- It is integrative of both A and B.

Contextual and practical

The popular approach in Christian ministry and missions is non-integrated due to its underlying cognitive processes: a) methodologically causative and b) operationally dialectic with duality (see figure in Appendix 2). The following descriptions are helpful for this kind of cultural understanding:

> It has often been observed that Americans draw a **distinction** between the subjective and the objective. They also clearly separate "we" from "they" and "our group" from "their group." This **differentiation** (which is not confined to the "we" versus "they" dichotomy) reflects the tendency of English-speaking peoples to make twofold judgments: this is particularly applicable to Americans. The language itself

---

[21] Enoch Wan, "Critiquing the Method of Traditional Western Theology and Calling for Sino-Theology" *Global Missiology*, 2004, **www.globalmissiology.org**

provides a precedent for it in its clear **differentiation** of subject and predicate… (Stewart 1972:28).

The propensity to make these kinds of judgments is interrelated with the American tendency to see the world in terms of black or white, and in the American character at any rate, it is related to a **predisposition to action**. That is in part due to the fact that the dichotomies which Americans set up are unequal: one element is usually valued more than the other. This characteristic can be seen in the following **dichotomies**: work-play, good-evil, peace-war, military-civilian, right-wrong, successful-unsuccessful, and man-nature. These **polarities** simplify the view of the world, predispose to action, and provide Americans with their typical method of evaluating and judging by means of a comparison (Stewart 1972:29; emphasis added).

A case in point is the seminal work of the late David Hesselgrave: *Paradigms in Conflict: 10 Key Questions in Christian Missions Today* (MI: Kregel Publications. 2005). There are ten chapters in the book dealing with the following dichotomistic pairs: sovereignty and free will, restrictivism and inclusivism, common ground and enemy territory, holism and prioritism, incarnationalism and representationalism, power encounter and truth encounter, amateurization and deprofessionalization, form and meaning, countdowns and prophetic alerts, the kingdom of God and the Church of Christ. Missiological paradigms, therefore, are explained and discussed in 10 dichotomist pairs.

From the above figure, it is obviously clear that the practice of Christian "mission" is to be an integration of both columns and to be holistic as shown in the figure below. It is not a choice of either saving souls spiritually or serving people in multiple ways: socially, financially and spiritually.

Figure 6 — Integrated approach of holistic Christian missions in practice

Integrated Holistic Christian Missions: Practice

Practice:
Vertically: God's grace & love received, then
Horizontally: charity & sharing with others

GOAL:
• Reconciliation
• Redemption
• Transformation

Horizontal

VERTICAL

evangelism/discipleship
friendship / partnership

The dual-track (of the Great Commandment and the Great Commission) is required for the engine (holistic ministry/missions) to operate. Sharing God's grace and mercies in charity and sharing the Gospel of salvation for spiritual conversion are not to be compartmentalized.

Figure 7 — Holistic Christian missions/ministry in process

Integrated Holistic Christian Missions: Process

The above figure shows **the process of holistic approach** = **witness** (being/personhood) + **the Great Commission** (doing/performance/making disciples).

We need to strive to maintain relational integrity as a reflection of the perfect partnership within the Trinity as shown in the figure below.

Figure 8 — Partnership in light of the Trinity[22]

PRINCIPLES	PRACTICE OF MINISTERIAL PARTNERSHIP
1. relationship	know, confer, plan with one another
2. unity	spiritual unity leading to unity of goal
3. diversity	difference in gifting and distinct roles
4. interdependence	not self-sufficient
5. love	self-sacrificial love within the Trinity and beyond
6. peace	harmony; freedom from anxiety and inner turmoil
7. joy	Christians are to be joyfully serving God and others

The Relational Paradigm is not only theoretically coherent and consistent; it is living out relationally the essence of Christian faith both

---

[22] Enoch Wan, "Partnerships Should Mimic the Trinity," *Faith Today*, July/August 2010:27.

vertically and horizontally. Relationship is so essential to Christianity, like the chicken in the chicken soup: genuine, tasty, and nutritious.

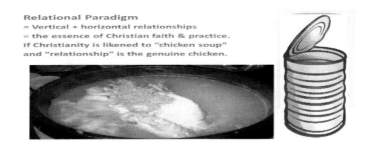

Relational Paradigm
= Vertical + horizontal relationships
= the essence of Christian faith & practice.
If Christianity is likened to "chicken soup"
and "relationship" is the genuine chicken.

We hereby are calling all Christians and all churches to rediscover and revitalize "relationship" in faith and practice. All our action and activity, performance and productivity are to anchor on the vertical relationship with the Triune God 24/7 for enlightening, enablement, empowerment, renewal, and revival.

Summary of this portion:

BEING (Christians witnessing)
- *Imago Dei* — image bearer of the Creator (Gen. 1:26-28, 9:1-7)
- Blessings to nations — Abrahamic covenant (Gen. 12:1-7)
- Light to the nations — Children of Abraham (Gen. 17:1-14) & Israel = God's elect of the OT are to be "light to the nations" (Isa. 42:6, 49:6 cf. Matt. 4:16)
- God's children in the NT (4 identities: chosen people, a royal priesthood, a holy nation, God's special possession, 1 Pet. 2:9) — "...declare the praises of Him Who called you out of darkness into His wonderful light" OR "new humanity" (Col. 1:15, 3:9-11, Eph. 2:14-16, Gal. 3:28)
- The "sent ones" such as Romans 10:14-15 (x4 rhetorical questions; Eph. 4:11-13 "...evangelist...").

DOING — popular understanding: the Great Commission (make disciples)
- *missio Dei*: both Triune God & Christian
- Being (personhood/witnessing) + Doing (performance/disciple-making)
  As the Son bearing witness to the Father and HS bearing witness to the Father and the Son, His redeemed children are to be **primarily His witnesses**, as listed below:

- The disciples — "…You are My witnesses…" (Luke 24:45-49) and those at Christ's ascension — "you… will be My witnesses…" (Acts 1:8)
- Lazarus at the banquet with Jesus as a **witness** of His resurrection power leading many to faith, the Jews plotted to kill him because his **being** there was a powerful **witness;** though **doing** nothing (John 12:9-11)
- The dying penitent thief accepted Christ as Lord and Master and received assurance from Jesus Christ of a place in paradise (Matt. 27:38, Luke 23:32-43, Mark 15:27); he was a powerful **witness** of God's unmerited redeeming grace; without **doing** anything other than acknowledging Jesus as Lord, he is a witness of God's unmerited favor bestowed upon an unworthy individual, without disciple making.

In light of the "relational approach" (vertical + horizontal, like **the cross**) within the "relational realism paradigm,"[23] we can summarize Christian "mission" with a relational framework as follows: In contrast to the obsession with doing/performance/outcomes as is the popular programmatic/managerial mission position, an integrated understanding (as reflected in the definition of "mission") is:

Christian Mission = Being (God working in us) + doing (God working through us)
(vertical) *(primary)*   (horizontal) *(secondary)*

Christian Ministry =
- Serving **in Christ's name** (motivation)

---

[23] For further reference on "relational realism," see previous publications listed below:
Enoch Wan, "The Paradigm of 'relational realism,'" *Occasional Bulletin,*
Evangelical Missiological Society, Spring 2006, 19:2, 1-4.
Enoch Wan, *Relational Theology: An Exploratory Study,* (Hong Kong: TienDao Publisher, 2015, in Chinese).
- Enoch Wan and Narry Santos, "Missio-relational Reading of Mark," *Occasional Bulletin,* Evangelical Missiological Society, Spring, 2011, 24:2.
- Enoch Wan, "Missio-relational Reading of Mark," EMS Audio interview, http://www.emsweb.org/home
- _____, "Relational Tree," Published in "Relational Study," www.GlobalMissiology.org January 2011.
- _____, "A Missio-Relational Reading of Romans," *Occasional Bulletin*, Evangelical Missiological Society, Winter 2010.
- Rethinking the Great Commission for the African Context: "A Proposal for the Paradigm of Relational Missiology" (Part I), *Global Missiology*, April 2019, www.globalmissiology.org

- Doing this **for His sake** (attitude)
- Operating **by His guidance**/power/enablement/empowerment/gifting (operational dynamics)
- Best stewardship **for His glory** (ultimate goal).

The major ideas are as follows:
- Following Christ's example means carrying out God's mandates (vertically received: Luke 4:16-21, Isa. 61:1-3, Phil. 2:7-9) as a servant (ministering to others horizontally).
- Instead of relaxing, surrounded by material blessings, or looking for economic, political, or religious programs to accomplish God's work, believers and churches must recognize their own weakness and total dependence on God. They must look to Him to triumph in (being) and through them (doing). The challenge for the church today is: to be God's people (centripetally vertical) amidst others (horizontally) and to proclaim God's message to others (horizontally) to the praise of His glory (centrifugally vertical).
- We believers (including what we do/say and how we relate to others horizontally) are to be for the sake of God's name (vertically). Selfish agendas (programmatic) cannot replace our total dependence on God (vertical relation) in ministry.
- "Just as God established Israel as His chosen vehicle to bless all nations" (first vertical then horizontal), in Christ He is creating a new people "to live in the sight of the nations for the sake of the nations…. This is the story of which we are part…this is the mission in which we are called to participate."[24]
- "Mission does not begin in history with Eve, Abraham, or Israel, rather in eternity with God the Father, the Son, and the Holy Spirit. In eternity past, God the Father gave to His Son a chosen people and commissioned His Son to redeem them by the help of His Spirit (Luke 22:29, John 6:37–40, Heb. 9:14). This is the foundation of mission—it begins with the Triune God. What unfolds in the history of redemption in relation to mission was first established in the covenant of redemption between the persons of the Trinity."[25]
- When engaging in ministry (doing **horizontally**), we are to anchor in the **vertical** relationship: i.e. in Christ's name (motive), for His

---

[24] Adapted from Christopher J. H. Wright, *The Mission of God: Unlocking the Bible's Grand Narrative*, (Grand Rapids: IVP Academic, 2006).

[25] Jonathan Gibson, "A 7-Point Biblical Theology of Mission," October 3, 2016, accessed February 1, 2019, https://faculty.wts.edu/posts/a-biblical-theology-of-mission/

sake (attitude), by His guidance/power/enablement (operational dynamics), for His glory (ultimate goal).

Christian mission

= *missio Dei* (relational Triune God) + relational ministry
"grace & love" from God to man, man reconciling to GOD
= vertical + horizontal relationships, i.e. the essence of Christian faith & practice)

- In the USA, when a conversation comes to a serious point, the general introduction is "sorry, nothing personal!"
- God, when relating to mankind, renders everything "personal" (e.g. Incarnation, indwelling of Holy Spirit).
- God, out of HIS love, grace, and by design, "everything is personal" without apology.

An Overview of Diaspora Missiology

Diaspora missiology is a new missiological paradigm, supplementing the "popular missiological paradigm."[26] It informs the Church on how to participate in God's mission locally and globally in view of the new demographic reality of diaspora phenomenon in the 21st century.

Demographically people often moved spatially due to educational advancement, economic improvement, famine, war, political and religious oppressions; yet the number of people moving on large scales and at high rates has increased significantly since the last century. Consequently, this brought about an unprecedented number of diasporas thus the emergence of "diaspora missiology" to cope with this new demographic reality. Diaspora missiology as "the systematic and academic study of the phenomenon of diaspora in the fulfillment of God's mission" (Wan 2007).

Popular missiological paradigm and diaspora missiological paradigm

The figures below are a comparison of the "popular missiological paradigm" with "diaspora missiology paradigm."

---

[26] Popular missiology is represented by organizations such as the Missio Nexus, American Society of Missiology, and Evangelical Missiological Society (Wan 2011, 97-98).

Figure 9 — "Popular missiology" vis-à-vis "diaspora missiology" — 4 elements[27]

#	ASPECTS	POPULAR MISSIOLOGY ←→ DISPORA MISSIOLOGY	
1	FOCUS	Polarized/dichotomized -"great commission" ←→ "great commandment" -saving souls ←→ social Gospel -church planting ←→ Christian charity -paternalism ←→ indigenization	-Holistic Christianity with strong integration of evangelism with Christian charity -contextualization
2	CONCEP-TUALIZA-TION	-territorial: here ←→ there -"local" ←→ "global" -lineal: "sending" ←→ "receiving" -"assimilation" ←→ "amalgamation" -"specialization"	-"deterritorialization"[28] -"glocal" -"mutuality" & "reciprocity" -"hybridity" -"inter-disciplinary"
3	PERSPECTIVE	-geographically divided: foreign mission ←→ local, urban ←→ rural -geo-political boundary: state/nation ←→ state/nation -disciplinary compartmentalization: e.g. theology of missions / strategy of missions	-non-spatial, - "borderless," no boundary to worry, transnational & global -new approach: integrated & interdisciplinary
4	PARADIGM	-OT: missions=gentile-proselyte -coming -NT: missions=the Great Commission going -Modern missions: E-1, E-2, E-3, or M-1, M-2, M-3, etc.	-New reality in the 21st Century – viewing & following God's way of providentially moving people spatially & spiritually -moving targets & move with the targets

---

[27] Enoch Wan, "Diaspora Missiology," Originally published in *Occasional Bulletin*, of EMS, Spring 2007:8, posted in "Featured Article" July 2007, www.globalmissiology.org

[28] "Deterritorialization" is the "loss of social and cultural boundaries" due to the large-scale diaspora.

Figure 10 — Comparing popular missiology & diaspora missiology in ministry[29]

#	ASPECTS	POPULAR MISSIOLOGY ←→ DIASPORA MISSIOLOGY	
1	MINISTRY PATTERN	OT: calling of gentile to Yahweh (coming) NT: sending out disciples by Jesus in the four Gospels & by the H.S. in Acts (going) Modern missions: -sending missionary & money -self-sufficient of mission entity	-new way of doing Christian missions: "mission at our doorstep" -"ministry without border" -"networking & partnership" for the Kingdom -"borderless church,"[30] "liquid church"[31] -"church on the oceans"[32]
2	MINISTRY STYLE	-cultural-linguistic barrier: E-1, E-2, etc. Thus various types M-1, M-2, etc. -"people group" identity -evangelistic scale: reached→←unreached -"competitive spirit" "self-sufficient"	-no barrier causing worry -mobile and fluid -hyphenated identity & ethnicity -no unreached people -"partnership,"[33] "networking" & synergy

Popular missions is polarized or dichotomized in focus and territorial with a sharp distinction between here and there spatially; and movement is lineal, meaning it goes one way. It is fixated with geography and unilineal in direction. In contrast, diaspora missions focuses on holistic missions and contextualization, integrating evangelism and social concern, Great Commandment with Great Commission, evangelism and social action. It is de-territorialized and simultaneously local and global conceptually (thus "glocal mission"). In perspective, it is borderless; not geographically divided. It is transnational and global.[34]

---

[29] Enoch Wan, "Diaspora Missiology," Originally published in *Occasional Bulletin,* EMS, Spring 2007:9.
[30] David Lundy, *Borderless Church,* (Los Angeles: Authentic Media, 2005).
[31] Peter Ward, *Liquid Church,* (Carlisle: Paternoster, 2002).
[32] A church was founded by the chief cook's brother Bong on board the container vessel Al Mutannabi, November 2002, (see Martin Otto, *Church on the Oceans*, UK: Piquant, 2007, 65). From personal communication of March 29, 2007, a staff worker reported that "Last week I met the second cook on another ship, and I was very happy to see that the second cook already started planting a church..."
[33] "Partnership" is defined as "entities that are separate and autonomous but complementary, sharing with equality and mutuality." More discussion on "partnership" in another section.
[34] Wan and Tira, "Diaspora Missiology and Mission in the Context of the 21st Century," 4.

Two kinds of diaspora ministry and four types of diaspora missions/ministry (ISM)

According to the figure below, there are two kinds of diaspora ministry: ministering to the diaspora and ministering along the diaspora (Wan 2014:129). "Ministry to the diaspora" (including ISM) is non-diaspora Christians who participate in the Great Commission through proclaiming the good news and practicing good deeds — focusing on the diaspora by using the strategy of missions "*to*" and "*through*" the diaspora.

Kingdom orientation is essential in motivating and mobilizing Christians individually and collectively for Kingdom ministry. Key is the understanding that "a person with Kingdom-orientation is someone who embraces the perspective, sentiment, and motivation of the Kingdom at heart and in action."[35] "Ministry along the diaspora" is mobilizing diaspora Christians as individual "Kingdom workers" (**KW**) to partner with others to fulfill the Great Commission (i.e. collaborate Kingdom-partners (**KP**)) beyond their own diaspora people — focusing on other diaspora and non-diaspora peoples by using the strategy of missions "*by & beyond*" and "*with*" the diaspora. On the basis of Kingdom-orientation, ISM organizations (e.g. IFES, Cru, ISI, etc.) and local congregations can network in operation (of **KW**) and partner in sharing resources (as **KP**).

There are four types of diaspora missions in practice, as listed below:

Missions *to* the Diaspora (ISM) — reaching the diaspora groups with forms of evangelism or pre-evangelistic social services, then discipling them to become worshipping communities and congregations.

Missions *through* the Diaspora (ISM) — diaspora Christians reaching out to their kinsmen through networks of friendship and kinship in host countries, their homelands, and abroad.

Missions *by* and *beyond* the Diaspora (ISM) — motivating and mobilizing diaspora Christians for cross-cultural missions to other ethnic groups in their host countries, homelands, and abroad.

Missions *with* the Diaspora/ISM — mobilizing non-diasporic Christians individually and institutionally to partner with diasporic groups and congregations.

---

[35] Enoch Wan, *Diaspora Missiology: Theory, Methodology, and Practice*, 2nd ed. (Portland: IDS-USA, 2014), 198.

Figure 11 — Diaspora Ministry and Missions (including ISM) (Wan 2014:8)

DIASPORA MISSIOLOGY (ISM)	DIASPORA MINISTRY (ISM)			
	Type	ministering **to** the diaspora		ministering **along** the diaspora
	Means	the Great Commandment as pre-evangelistic and holistic		the Great Commission — imperative and inclusive
	Recipient	focusing on diaspora: serving the diaspora by ministering — social and spiritual dimensions		focusing beyond diaspora: mobilizing diaspora Christians to serve other diaspora people or non-diaspora
	DIASPORA MISSIONS (ISM)			
	Type	missions *to* the diaspora	missions *through* the diaspora	missions *by* & *beyond* the diaspora	missions *with* the diaspora
	Means	motivate & mobilize diaspora individuals & congregations to partner with others: the Great Commission, i.e. evangelistic outreach, discipleship, church planting and global missions			
	Recipient	focusing on diaspora		focusing beyond diaspora	
		members of diaspora community	kinsmen in homeland & elsewhere; not cross-culturally	cross-culturally to other ethnic groups in host society & beyond	partnership between diaspora and others in Kingdom ministry

Diaspora missiology in action for ISM

The scope of diaspora missiology covers all kinds of diaspora (i.e. people moved away from their homeland), e.g. international students, refugees, migrants, immigrants, victims of human trafficking, international displaced persons, etc. The discussion below will focus on diaspora missiology in action in the context of ISM.

Diaspora missiology in action for ISM

Daniel and his friends received a Babylonian royal education against their will because of their exile from their homeland. Contemporary international students have a totally different scenario: they choose their destination and eagerly acquire language and customs of the host society. In such a transition, these are open to change linguistically and socio-culturally. In such a state of mind and in the process of acculturation, they are receptive to changes, including in the religious/spiritual dimension. Though being a relative new paradigm, about a decade-long,[36] diaspora missiology is very relevant to ISM.

Unlike the popular missiology which has a strong distinction between outreach locally (called "evangelism") and internationally (called "mission"), in diaspora missiology there is not a territorial distinction; rather integrated "glocal missions" (i.e. global in scope, local in action and in sequence).[37] ISM, practicing "global missions" in terms of reaching those enrolling in nearby campuses with the Gospel, is part and partial of fulfilling the Great Commission[38] due to the sequential four types of approach listed earlier.

It is also a way of practicing "missions at our doorstep" with the advantage listed below:

---

[36] For a brief review of the short history of diaspora missiology, see Enoch Wan, "Diaspora missiology and beyond: paths taken and ways forward," in *Diaspora Missions: Reflections on Reaching the Scattered Peoples of the World,* Michael Pocock and Enoch Wan, eds., (Pasadena, CA: William Carey Library, 2015).

[37] Sadiri Joy Tira, "Glocal Evangelism: Jesus Christ, Magdalena, and Damascus in Greater Toronto Area," *Lausanne World Pulse,* June 2010, accessed September 26, 2018, **http://www.lausanneworldpulse.com/perspectives-php/1291/06-2010**

[38] "Local churches, and some denominations, have been discovering the great value of ministry to internationals on campus. Their members are volunteer missionaries right at home and often using their homes. 'Glocal' (global/local) missions is not only for adults, but for whole families, from children to grandparents…" as explained by Leiton & Lisa. See Leiton Edward Chinn & Lisa Espineli Chinn, "Agents of diaspora missions in and from the academic world," in *Scatted and Gathered: A global compendium of diaspora missiology*, Sadiri Joy Tira and Testsunnao Yamamori, eds., (Regnum Books International, 2016) 235.

Figure 12 "Missions to the Diaspora (ISM)" = "Mission at Our Doorstep" (Wan 2014:184)

NO	YES
-No visa required	-Yes, door opened
-No closed door	-Yes, people accessible
-No international travel required	-Yes, missions at our doorstep
-No political/legal restrictions	-Yes, ample opportunities
-No dichotomized approach	-Yes, holistic ministries
-No sense of self-sufficiency or unhealthy competition	-Yes, powerful partnership

Relational missiology for ISM

The popular approach in Christian mission is formulaic and programmatic in practice. Managerial/programmatic mission practices are ways and means of practicing Christian mission in the same manner as secular management in business and these ways and means appear obsessed with programmatic details. In contrast, relational missiology/ministry is the "systematic study of mission (missiology) and the practice of Christian service (ministry) based on relational paradigm."

"Paradigm of relational realism" is a reference to "a conceptual framework for understanding reality based on the interactive connections between personal beings/Beings. (Wan & Hedinger 2017:14). The following table shows the differences between the two approaches.

Figure 13 – Popular Programmatic/Managerial Missiology and "Relational Missiology"

ASPECTS	PROGRAMMATIC MISSIOLOGY	MANAGERIAL/ENTREPRENEUR MISSIOLOGY	RELATIONAL MISSIOLOGY
#1 – FOCUS	-Program-oriented • Confident in program planning • Mindful of principle and details of program	-Market-oriented • Commodification of Christianity & consumerism thus "mercenary" instead of "missionary" • Recipient of Gospel as customers Entrepreneurship: • Efficiency & outcome based • Profiting in relationship	-Relation-oriented: • Focusing on both vertical and horizontal relationship with priority • Convergence of systems: Triune God, angel, human being
	- Emphasis: • Focusing on horizontal relationship with a low (or no) view of vertical • Subscribe to critical realism		-Emphasis • Focus on horizontal, even more on vertical • Subscribe to "Relational realism"
#2 – CONCEPTUALIZATION	• Effort-optimism: what counts is trying hard and long enough • Packaging: event & action	• Instrumentalism (functionalism): felt needs approach, receptor-oriented • Pragmatism: measurable success & outcome-base	• Multi-level • Multi-contextual • Multi-dimensional
#3 – PERSPECTIVE	- Performance-based; empirical; impersonal - "Babel Complex" (Gen. 11, man-centered)		- Relationally nurturing - Glorify God, first and foremost
	-Management and entrepreneur studies		-Interdisciplinary approach
#4 – ORIENTATION	-Extremely proactive -Concrete in planning; careful scheduling and detailed planning of event	-Emulating the secular business management model Humanistic and impersonal Managerially statistical and strategic	-High touch, people-oriented, networking -Reciprocity and strategic - Kingdom partnership
	-Dichotomy: "the Great Commandment" vs "the Great Commission" saving souls vs serving human/social needs		-Holistic Christianity: integrating "the Great Commandment" & "the Great Commission"

Ontologically, the relational paradigm is that in which "relational 'reality' is primarily based on the 'vertical relationship' between God and the created order and secondarily 'horizontal relationship' within the created order."[39] The philosophical element of the relational paradigm is based on "relational realism"[40] and the methodological element is based on "relational theologizing."[41] Theologically, the relational paradigm is grounded on the fact that man was created in the image of God and his existence (ontologically) is solely dependent on God at all times (Gen. 1:26-27, Rom. 11:36, Heb. 1:3). His ability to know (epistemologically) and his undertaking in missions (*missio Dei*) are all dependent on God, Who is the great "I AM" (Exod. 3), as stated in the following three statements (Wan 2007:3):

---

[39] Enoch Wan, "The Paradigm of 'Relational Realism,'" *Occasional Bulletin*, EMS, 19, no. 2, 2006:1.

[40] Enoch Wan, "The Paradigm of 'Relational Realism,'" *Occasional Bulletin*, EMS, 19, no. 2, Spring 2006:1-4.

[41] Enoch Wan, "Relational Theology and Relational Missiology," *Occasional Bulletin*, EMS, 21, no. 1, Winter 2007:1-7.

- "'I AM' therefore i am" ontologically[42]
- "'I AM" therefore 'i know'" epistemologically
- "'I AM' (*missio Dei*) therefore 'i am'" missiologically.[43]

These three statements are in contrast to the rationalist's maxim of Descartes—"I think therefore I am" (Wan 2006:2).

In view of the global diaspora phenomenon, the rise of churches from the majority World (covered elsewhere[44]) and the emerging diaspora missions in the 21st century, we need a new paradigm to formulate an appropriate strategy to support diaspora KW in the fields based on the "diaspora missiology paradigm" and the "relational paradigm."

Figure 14 Relational Paradigm: Synthesizing Diaspora Missiology & Diaspora Missions for ISM[45]

RELATONAL PARADIGM		DIASPORA MISSIOLOGY & DIASPORA MISSIONS (ISM)
5 ELEMENTS	**5 RELATIONAL ASPECTS**	
PARTICIPANTS • Triune God & Christians carry out the Great Commission • resistant: Satan, fallen angels	**RELATIONAL NETWORK** • Triune God is the originator of relationship; the center and foundation of all networks • two camps: God, obedient angels & Christians ← → Satan	• not programmatic, not entrepreneur, not outcome-based • strong emphasis on relational dimensions between person Being (the triune God) and beings (of humanity and angelic reality) • recognizing the dimension of spiritual warfare

---

[42] The "I AM" is God's self-identification and "i am" (lower case) is an intentional designation for man in contra-distinction to "I AM."

[43] Our Triune God is characterized by love, communion, commission (sending), and glory. Also see Kevin Daugherty, "Missio Dei: The Trinity and Christian Missions," Evangelical Review of Theology, 31, April 2007; John A. McIntosh, "All Things New: The Trinitarian Nature of the Human Calling" in *Maximus the Confessor and Jurgen Moltmann*, (Oregon: Pickwick Publications, 2014), https://books.google.ca/books?isbn=1630875465

[44] Enoch Wan, *Missions from the Majority World: Progress, Challenges, and Case Studies,* Enoch Wan and Michael Pocock, eds., (Evangelical Missiological Society Series Book 17, William Carey, 2009).

[45] Wan 2014:196

RELATONAL PARADIGM		DIASPORA MISSIOLOGY & DIASPORA MISSIONS (ISM)
5 ELEMENTS	**5 RELATIONAL ASPECTS**	
PATTERN (→sending) • Father → the Son & together→ H.S. • Father → the Son → Christians (John 17:18), Christians obeying • H.S. sending: Acts 10:19, 13:2 Christians empowered	**RELATIONAL DIMENSIONS /CONTEXT** • vertical dimension to God • horizontal dimensions within the Church & beyond • multi-context: divine, angelic, human; changing human contexts due to globalization, diaspora movement, etc.	• vertical dimensions, e.g. "relational accountability" • "glocal" missions in the globalized context[46] • non-spatial, "borderless," no boundary to cause worry, transnational • different approach: integrated ministry & interdisciplinary study of Missiology • learn new demographic reality of the 21st Century & strategize accordingly with good stewardship
PRACTICE • Christians participating in God's mission, carrying out the "Great Commission"	**RELATIONAL REALITY** • God: reconciling the world to Himself in Christ through Christians • Satan & fallen angels at enmity with God and His followers	• new reality in the 21st Century • viewing & following God's way of providentially moving people spatially & spiritually • moving targets & move with the targets (diaspora)
POWER • God's love transforms Christians and compels them in carrying out His mission	**RELATIONAL DYNAMICS** • doing missions out of love for God and compassion for the lost • empowered by the H.S.	• micro: love, compassion, Christian hospitality • macro: partnership & networking • holistic Christianity with strong integration of evangelism with Christian compassion & charity
PROCESS • God: plan of salvation provided & the Church carrying	**RELATIONAL INTERACTION** • God's calling, Christ's commissioning, H.S. empowering	• "Great commission" + "great commandment" • diaspora mission: ministering **to** and **through** and **by/beyond** & **with** the diaspora[47]

[46] Chinn and Chinn 2016:235
[47] Excellent missiological strategy as explained below by China and Chinn 2016:234:

RELATONAL PARADIGM		DIASPORA MISSIOLOGY & DIASPORA MISSIONS (ISM)
5 ELEMENTS	**5 RELATIONAL ASPECTS**	
out God's mission	• Christians obedient to God, • Satan resisting God's mission	• relational accountability • strategic stewardship and partnership

The popularity of social media is symptomatic of the starvation for relationship of contemporary people due to multiple factors, e.g. broken marriage, dysfunctional
family, high mobility, etc.[48]

Figure 15 - Popular vs Relational Christian Ministry for ISM

Ministry Aspects	Popular (Programmatic/Managerial)	Relational Ministry for ISM
Ministry Purpose	Services for recognition, promotion, job description & satisfaction	Vertical & horizontal relationships, spiritual modeling
Ministry Focus	• Measurable goals • Program & performance with quantifiable outcome	• People, process, & relationship • Personal face-to-face interaction
Ministry strategy	Systematic transmission of services, such as evangelism, accomplishments, etc.	• Relational modeling • Relational teaching • Relational serving
Ministry Evaluation	Numerical results, performance & productivity of minister	• Spiritual qualities • Spiritual fruit of ministry
Ministry Concerns	• Packaged plan • Expected outcomes	• Vertical: Triune God • Horizontal people & process
Ministry Principles	Systematic transmission of knowledge and skills	• Relational modeling • Servanthood
Ministry Style	Performance & productivity	• Vertical & horizontal relationship • Spiritual maturity: knowledge, skills
Ministry Procedures	Organizational growth Franchising & global expansion	• Kingdom orientation • Partnership for God's glory[46]

The figure above lists various aspects of the relational approach in Christian ministry (including purpose, focus, strategy, evaluation, concerns, principles, style, and procedures) which are in distinct contrast to the popular approach (i.e. programmatic/managerial) in ministry. The

"Traditionally, the focus of ISM is that of welcoming and reaching students from other countries coming to a host nation. But there is another trend of student mobility with untapped missiological implications. That is the accelerating growth of Study Abroad programs which offers a broad and natural highway for expanding diaspora ministry in the academic community. It is an underdeveloped but potentially high-yield mission strategy, involving the deliberate mobilization, training, and sending of national Christian students to study abroad as Christ's missional agents, a kind of 'reverse ISM.'"

[48] Enoch Wan, "Mission Amid Global Crises: Holistic Missions to Diaspora Groups," paper presented at EMS Canadian meetings, March 8, 2019 at Tyndale University College & Seminary, Toronto, Canada, 2019:8.

practical way of carrying out what is listed at the right column in the table above can be found in the two tables below: Figure 16 — ISM service: the "CORRECT" approach and Figure 17 — 4 Stages & 10 procedures in implementation: working with diaspora in ISM cyclically.

Figure 16 — ISM service: the "CORRECT" approach[49]

#	APPROACH	CATEGORY
1.	Compassion: love and grace from God (vertical: downward)	Motive
2.	Obedience: (vertical: upward) - submit to the Lordship of Christ - obey the great commandment & the Great Commission	Means
3.	Relationships of grace: grace received and given (vertical→horizontal)	
4.	Reality of community: (vertical→horizontal) - grace transformed community mobilized to serve others	
5.	Empowerment: (vertically endowed for serving horizontally) - Sent by the resurrected Christ (Matt. 28:18-20, John 17:18) - Empowered by the H.S. with gifts to serve others (Acts 1:8, 1 Cor. 14)	
6.	Christian multiplication: (vertical & horizontal) We labor; God grants the growth (1 Cor. 3:1-9) - multiplication of believers (Acts 2-8) - the multiplication of kingdom growth (Acts 8:6, 12, Eph. 4:11-12, Heb. 6:14)	Mission
7.	The full-circle: (vertical & horizontal) - cyclical multiplication & Kingdom expansion (2 Tim. 2:2, Micah 4:1-2, 7:11-12)	

---

[49] Enoch Wan, "The Practice of Diaspora Missions in Local Congregation: From Beginning to Base1," *Global Missiology*, January 2017:16, www.GlobalMissiology.org

Figure 17 — 4 Stages & 10 procedures in implementation: working with diaspora in ISM[50]

STAGES (x 4)	PROCEDURES (x 10)	
	PRINCIPLE	PARTICULAR
PRE-	1. Preliminary understanding	Types of diaspora: refugee, migrant, immigrant, international student, etc.
	2. Profiling	Learning the "7Ws" e.g. where?
	3. Probing	Figuring out how & where to start?
PRACTICE-	4. Initial contact	Store, camp, campus, prison, etc.
	5. Regular contact	Systematic and intentional contact
	6. Engaging	Hosting, reciprocating, etc.
POST-	7. Nurturing relationship	Cultivating long-term relationships for Kingdom purposes
	8. Co-laboring	Working "through the diaspora"
	9. Partnership	Working "with the diaspora"
PERPETUAL (CYCLICAL)	10. Alternating: to/through/by & beyond/with	-Systematic coaching & mentoring -Periodic evaluation & strategizing -Alternating between: to/through/by & beyond/with

---

[50] Enoch Wan, "The Practice of Diaspora Missions in Local Congregation: From Beginning to Base1," *Global Missiology*, January 2017:16, www.GlobalMissiology.org

Conclusion

This chapter provides the theoretical framework for the entire book with contributions from various authors. Their expertise and field experiences enrich this volume on ISM. Their writings are illustrative historically, theologically, and practically of ISM.

References

"A Critique of Charles Kraft's Use/Misuse of Communication and Social Sciences in Biblical Interpretation and Missiological Formulation." In *Missiology and the Social Sciences: Contributions, Cautions and Conclusions.* Eds. Edward Rommen and Gary Corwin. Pasadena, CA: William Carey Library,1996.

Chinn, Leiton Edward and Lisa Espineli Chinn. "Agents of diaspora missions in and from the academic world." In *Scatted and Gathered: A global compendium of diaspora missiology.* Eds. Sadiri Joy Tira and Testsunnao Yamamori. Regnum Books International, 2016:228-241.

Daugherty, Kevin. "*Missio Dei*: The Trinity and Christian Missions." *Evangelical Review of Theology*, April 2007, 3.

Gibson, Jonathan. "A 7-Point Biblical Theology of Mission." October 03, 2016. https://faculty.wts.edu/posts/a-biblical-theology-of-mission/ (February 1, 2019)

Hiebert, Paul. "The Flaw of the Excluded Middle." file:///C:/Users/ewan/AppData/Local/Temp/p-hiebert-flaw-of-excluded-middle.pdf (May 1, 2019)

Kane, J. Herbert. *Understanding Christian Missions.* Grand Rapids: Baker, 1974.

Lundy, David. *Borderless Church.* Waynesboro, GA: Authentic Media, 2005.

McIntosh, John A. "Maximus the Confessor and Jurgen Moltmann." In *All Things New: The Trinitarian Nature of the Human Calling.* Eugene, OR: Pickwick Publications, 2014.

Otto, Martin. *Church on the Oceans.* UK: Piquant, 2007.

Peters, George W. *A Biblical Theology of Missions.* Chicago: Moody, 1972.

Piper, John. "Let the Nations Be Glad." In *Perspectives on The World Christian Movement: A Reader*, 4th ed. Eds. Ralph Winter and Steven Hawthorne. Pasadena, CA: William Carey Library, 2009.

Pocock, Michael and Enoch Wan, Eds. *Diaspora Missions: Reflections on Reaching the Scattered Peoples of the World.* Pasadena, CA: William Carey Library, 2015.

Stewart, Edward C. *American Cultural Patterns: A Cross-cultural Perspective.* Intercultural Press Inc., 1972, 28.

Tira, Sadiri Joy. "Glocal Evangelism: Jesus Christ, Magdalena, and Damascus in Greater Toronto Area." *Lausanne World Pulse,* June 2010. http://www.lausanneworldpulse.com/perspectives-php/1291/06-2010 (September 26, 2018)

Wan, Enoch. "A Comparative Study of Sino-American Cognitive & Theological Pattern & Proposed Alternative." Symposium on "China-West Cultural Exchange: Retrospect and Prospect." William Carey International University, CA. October 25-27, 2007.

Wan, Enoch. "A Missio-Relational Reading of Romans." *Occasional Bulletin,* EMS, Winter 2010.

Wan, Enoch. "Christ for the Chinese: A Contextual Reflection." *Chinese Around the World.* November 2000.

Wan, Enoch. "Christianity in the eye of traditional Chinese." *Chinese Around the World.* July 1999:17-23.

Wan, Enoch. "Core Values of Mission Organization in the Cultural Context of the 21st Century." "Featured Article" January 2009:6-7. www.GlobalMissiology.org

Wan, Enoch. "Critique of Traditional Western Theology." *Chinese Around the World,* October 1999:19-25.

Wan, Enoch. "Critiquing the Method of Traditional Western Theology and Calling for Sino-Theology." *Global Missiology,* October 2003. www.globalmissiology.net

Wan, Enoch. "Diaspora Missiology." *Occasional Bulletin,* EMS, vol. 20:3 (Spring 2007), 3-7.

Wan, Enoch. *Diaspora Missiology.* 2nd ed. Portland, OR: The Institute of Diaspora Studies, 2014.

Wan, Enoch. "Inter-disciplinary and Integrative Missiological Research: the 'What,' 'Why,' and 'How.'" July 2017. www.GlobalMissiology.org

Wan, Enoch. "Mission Amid Global Crises: Holistic Missions to Diaspora Groups." Paper presented at EMS Canadian Meetings, March 8, 2019. Tyndale University College & Seminary, Toronto, Canada.

Wan, Enoch. "'Mission' and *'Missio Dei'*: Response to Charles Van Engen's 'Mission Defined and Described,'" in *MissionShift: Global Mission Issues in the Third Millennium.* Eds. David J. Hesselgrave and Ed Stetzer. Nashville: B & H Publishing Group, Nashville, 2010d.

Wan, Enoch. "Missio-relational Reading of Mark." EMS Audio Interview. http://www.emsweb.org/home

Wan, Enoch. "Practical contextualization: A case study of evangelizing contemporary Chinese." *Chinese Around the World,* March 2000:18-24.

Wan, Enoch. "Relational Theology and Relational Missiology." *Occasional Bulletin,* EMS, vol. 21:1 (Winter 2007), 1-7.

Wan, Enoch. *Relational Theology: An Exploratory Study.* TienDao Publisher, Hong Kong, 2015 (in Chinese).

Wan, Enoch. "Relational Tree." In "Relational Study," January 2011. www.GlobalMissiology.org

Wan, Enoch. "Research Methodology for Diaspora Missiology and Diaspora Missions." Paper presented at the Regional EMS Conference – North Central, February 26, 2011b. Trinity Evangelical Divinity School, Deerfield, IL.

Wan, Enoch. "Rethinking Missiological Research Methodology: Exploring a New Direction." *Global Missiology,* October 2003b. www.GlobalMissiology.org

Wan, Enoch. "Rethinking the Great Commission for the African Context: A Proposal for the Paradigm of Relational Missiology" (Part I). *Global Missiology,* April 2019. www.globalmissiology.org (May 2019)

Wan, Enoch. *Sino-theology: A Survey Study*《中色神學網要》. Ontario, Canada: Christian Communication Inc., 1999.

Wan, Enoch. "Theological contribution of Sino-theology to global Christian community." *Chinese Around the World*, July 2000.

Wan, Enoch. *Theology of Unmerited Favor*《恩情神學》. Hong Kong: TienDao Publisher, 2016.

Wan, Enoch. "The Paradigm and Pressing Issues of Inter-disciplinary Research Methodology." *Global Missiology,* January 2005.

Wan, Enoch. "The Paradigm of 'Relational Realism.'" *Occasional Bulletin*, EMS, vol. 19:2 (Spring 2006), 1-4.

Wan, Enoch. "The Practice of Diaspora Missions in Local Congregation: From Beginning to Base1." *Global Missiology,* January 2017. www.GlobalMissiology.org

Wan, Enoch and Mark Hedinger. *Relational Missionary Training: Theology, Theory, and Practice.* Skyforest, CA: Urban Loft Publishers, 2017.

Wan, Enoch and Mabiala Kenzo,."Evangelical Theology, Postmodernity, and the Promise of Interdisciplinarity." *Global Missiology,* January 2006. www.globalmissiology.org

Wan, Enoch and Jacky Lau. *Chinese Diaspora Kingdom Workers: In Action and with Guidance.* Portland, OR: CDRR Western Press, 2019.

Wan, Enoch and Michael Pocock Eds. *Missions from the Majority World: Progress, Challenges, and Case Studies.* Evangelical Missiological Society Series Book 17. Pasadena, CA: William Carey Library, 2009.

Wan, Enoch and Narry Santos. "Missio-relational Reading of Mark," *Occasional Bulletin*, EMS, vol. 24:2 (Spring, 2011).

Wan, Enoch and Sadiri Joy Tira, "Diaspora Missiology and Mission in the Context of the 21st Century." *Torch Trinity Journal,* 2010:13, 4.

Ward, Peter. *Liquid Church.* Carlisle: Paternoster, 2002.

Wright, Christopher J. H. *The Mission of God: Unlocking the Bible's Grand Narrative.* Grand Rapids: IVP Academic, 2006.

CHAPTER 3
INTERNATIONAL STUDENTS AND DIASPORA MISSIOLOGY

Chin T. Wang (John) and Sam Green

Introduction

In January 1987, with the blessing of my parents and friends I (John) came to the United States to pursue graduate studies in engineering. I had graduated from the University of Buenos Aires and was admitted to a master's program in engineering at the University of Buffalo. However, I first arrived in New York and stayed in the Big Apple for a few days before heading to school in Buffalo. My sister had been studying at a graduate program in New York for two years prior to my arrival. She brought me to her church in Flushing, introduced me to life in America, and prepared me for the winter in Buffalo. The most memorable image I had was the crowd, the busyness, and the diversity of New York.

I grew up in a Christian home and committed my life to Jesus Christ while in high school. I have been involved in church ministry and occasionally joined the activities of ABUA (Asociación Bíblica Universitaria Argentina, a member of IFES). When I received my University of Buffalo admissions notice, my sister told her friends who went to school in Buffalo about my coming. While I was still in Argentina applying for my student visa, a staff member of International Students, Inc. (ISI) sent me a welcome letter encouraging me to join the ISI campus ministry upon my arrival. When I started school in Buffalo, I left my name at the ISI booth during new student orientation, and the next day the campus minister was at my door. For the next year and a half, while completing my master's degree I participated in campus ministry programs or small groups with ISI, InterVarsity, and a local Chinese church student fellowship. I was nurtured by the campus workers and student leaders, and experienced spiritual growth.

Fanny came from the other end of the world, Taiwan. She also received admissions to come to Buffalo for graduate studies. Although exposed to the gospel in college, she was not a believer. Concerns of going into a foreign environment under the pressure of completing her degree, she was eager to join some other fellow foreign students along the way. By the providence of God, she met two Christian ladies from Taiwan who planned to attend the same program. Together they decided to come to the University of Buffalo and committed to help each other during their time in school. Upon arrival the two ladies brought Fanny to the local Chinese church. After two years of attending that church, Fanny committed her life to Christ. She was also nurtured by those who were involved in ministry among international students.

Fanny and I eventually married. We continued to grow in our commitment to Christ. We went to Chinese Mission conference in 1989, Urbana Missions Conference in 1990, and, at the time we lived in upstate New York, we were also involved in campus ministry among the students. Eventually we moved to New York City and I began my seminary education. After graduation, I became pastor of First Baptist Church of Flashing, a multi ethnic, multilingual, and multi-congregational church with ministry among Chinese, Hispanics, and immigrants from other parts of the world.

This is a story that shows God's grace to His people. The narrative is also marked by the intersection of campus ministry, diaspora missions, and urban ministry. It is campus ministry because it involves not only two international students but also the campus workers and local churches that helped to nurture and prepare them for a greater task in the kingdom. It is diaspora missions because the international students stayed in America and are even now involved in pastoral ministry among the immigrant communities. The focus of ministry at the local church is not only missions to the diaspora, it is also missions through the diaspora and missions by and beyond the diaspora. It is urban ministry in the fact of finally settling in pastoral ministry in New York City, which shows the powerful attraction of megacities like New York. The experience of being a foreign student and an immigrant at the same time, demonstrates unique preparedness for ministries in cities like New York.

Tim Kellert and Michael Kellert talked about the uniqueness of university evangelism: Universities are ideal environments for students to explore and rethink the beliefs of their upbringing, including meaning in life, values, and identity. It is an environment where Christian faith can be presented and compete freely with other religions without social and cultural pressure of being considered impolite. It is rather a place of persuasion, where individuals debate and accept differing explanations of the good, the truth, and the beautiful. This is also the stage of one's life when students have the luxury of time to consider these big questions of life. It is true that college work is demanding. However, once graduated from college, people become even busier and more occupied in pursuing career, marriage, family, with many other goals and responsibilities. College years are a most ideal time for evangelism.

Tim Kellert and Michael Kellert also talked about the strategic priority of campus ministry, especially among international students. Many international students come from countries where open evangelism is not permitted. Yet many of them are eager to come to the West in order to learn and explore new ideas including faith in Christ. As people on the move, international students also tend to be more receptive to the Gospel. It is commonly recognized that many international students return to their home countries and assume positions of influence, some even become heads of governments, or business and academic leaders. The social impact of Christianity can multiply enormously in their countries of origin.

Once graduated, many international students decide to apply for permanent residence and stay. These become part of the diasporic communities in America. Some students with PhD, who are more academically driven, go on to teach and live in college towns across the nation. Others develop successful careers and live in suburbs outside of major cities in America helping increase even more visible ethnic and cultural diversity. Still a large portion of international students are attracted to live in the mega cities like New York after graduation. These find jobs and settle in the city joining existing immigrant communities. As the students and graduates, together with their families, slowly become core members of the local ethnic churches, many participate actively in diaspora mission. The transnational ties, genuine conversion experience, Christian faith, higher educational background, multilingual talents, and ability to adapt to life in America make them uniquely prepared for cross cultural and international ministry. Indeed, they stand for great potential in God's worldwide mission.

The focus of this article is also on gateway cities across America. Taking the example of New York, the Big Apple has some of the best universities in America. The strategic potential of reaching out to international students fits perfectly the narrative of reaching out and training future leaders in other countries in the gospel of Jesus Christ. Students around the world are attracted by the cosmopolitan atmosphere of these gateway cities. They're not only ready to embrace this culturally diverse environment, these will also be exposed to the urban religiosity, especially in a multiethnic environment. In fact, the ethnically diverse landscape of Christian churches in New York provides students a home away from home. However, the support and blessings experienced are mutual. The students and graduates not only receive support in strengthening their spiritual walk and their ethnic identity, their above average educational background also provides much needed social capital to the ethnic churches and their future generations for upper mobility. For those who participate in American churches, they also help increase the level of diversity in all aspects of church life.

The Stories

In 2017, Sam Green, staff worker of International Student Inc. (ISI), conducted interviews with five students with whom he had interacted in the past. Some of these are currently studying in New York. Others have graduated recently. These come from different nationalities and religious backgrounds. Some believed in Christ over the course of their studies in New York. Others continued their religious inquiry. Yet all developed a more positive and enriching attitude toward Christianity. The following paragraphs record their stories:

Ethnography #1: A Buddhist from China

L grew up in a very religious Buddhist family in China. His family is upper-middle class; his hometown is 275 miles south of Beijing with a population of 2.8 million. Growing up in China, L had never met a Christian or seen a Bible. He had heard of other religions, had a negative view of Islam, and a neutral view of Christianity.

In 2014, he moved to the United States to pursue a master's in Business Administration from a university in New York City. The university covered approximately 10% of his tuition with scholarships; the remainder was paid for by his family. He was surprised by the diversity he found in the United States and began to ponder the meaning of his life. L struggled privately with online pornography and was troubled by his shame, desiring to break free. As he was still searching for answers, he visited a Buddhist temple in Manhattan, yet left feeling empty.

After living in the United States for three months, a friend invited him to attend an international student Christmas party, and he agreed to attend after seeing the photos of previous events posted on Facebook. L was invited to join a small group discovery Bible study with three of his friends, meeting every Friday morning at my home. The Bible study began with Creation and moved to the resurrection of Christ. After 10 weeks of Bible study, L wanted to continue even though a couple of his friends decided to stop. He continued in small group Bible study over that summer. One day after reading John 10, L told me he didn't understand verse 18. I asked him what he thought the verse meant, and he told me, it didn't make any sense because the verse says that Jesus can lay His life down willingly and can take it back up again. When I asked why is that confusing, he told me that we all know Jesus died on the cross, so why doesn't he use His power to come back to life? It was at this point he first understood that Jesus had risen from the grave.

L continued in Bible study during the fall semester, and at Christmas he decided to participate in a homestay program with members of my parents' church in Kentucky. During his two weeks in Kentucky, he made a public profession of his decision to give his life to Christ. A few months later, he was baptized at a church in New York. Around this time, he began to share with some of the Christian men in his life that he struggled with pornography, was seeking accountability, and asked for prayer to break free. He said Buddhism never offered him a chance to be forgiven of his sins, and he felt very dirty and shameful until he put his faith in Christ. When he told his parents of his decision, they were not happy with his rejection of Buddhism.

After graduation, L had trouble finding employment in the United States and he decided to move to Beijing to find employment. Three weeks before his flight to China, he met a Christian girl from China at a church, and they started dating. After continuing their long-distance relationship for five months, they decided to move to California and get married. Today they are both active in their church and quick to share their testimonies of how Christ has changed their lives.

Ethnography #2: An atheist from China

N grew up in a working-class family in a village about 450 miles south of Beijing. Everyone in his family was an atheist. Growing up in China, he had never encountered any religious traditions. He had never visited a place of worship or seen a Bible. He knew little about world religions, had neither a positive nor negative view of any religion. After completing his undergraduate degree in China, N married a girl from southern China. They moved to Beijing to look for employment, but because of China's laws governing city residency, he had great difficulty in finding a good job in Beijing as his residency was still officially in his village.

Soon after their first daughter was born, N decided to move to the United States to start a new life. He moved to California to begin a master's program in Computer Science, with plans for his wife and baby daughter to join him in the future. N struggled greatly with speaking English and was told of free English classes at a local church. He began attending regularly, and while at the church some members started to share the gospel with him. After a few months, he was told of an affordable master's program in New York City, and he moved to New York to complete his degree.

I met N on his college campus and invited him to a dinner and Bible study at my home with other international students. He joined us that Friday night and began to regularly study the Bible. A friend also invited him to attend Bible study, although the group hosting the study denied the divinity of Jesus. N continued to study the Bible in both groups, and after almost a year in New York, he went on retreat during Easter weekend. On Easter Sunday 2014, he decided to follow Christ.

A couple of months later, N brought his wife and daughter over from China. He had already been sharing with her and immediately began encouraging her to study the Bible in a group. She studied the Bible off and on for the next two years and eventually decided to make Jesus Lord of her life. About that time, God blessed them with a baby boy. Both N and his wife have been baptized and are active in a Bible-believing church, frequently opening their homes for Bible studies. N found a position with a government-entity that says they will sponsor his green card, and he hopes to stay in the United States.

Ethnography #3: A Muslim from South Asia

F was born in Japan even though her family is from South Asia. Her dad, who is not religious, had moved the family to Japan to attend medical school. F is a twin and has two other younger sisters. Her twin sister was born paralyzed and remained bedridden her entire life. When F was three years old, her family decided to move back to their homeland. Because F's father was not very religious, their family would not celebrate Muslim rituals, such as animal sacrifice during Eid-al-Adha.

However, when F was 14 years old, her parents separated, and her mom, who is very religious, moved the four girls 120 miles away to a large city with a population of 18 million. They moved into a home owned by F's maternal grandfather which is next to the mosque he had helped build. F's mom taught Arabic so that people in the community might better understand the Qur'an, and instructed the girls to start wearing hijabs, something they had never done before. F was sent to a highly-regarded Catholic high school, yet she learned only a little about the Bible there. Her Catholic high school had a religion class, yet during that hour, all the Muslim students would go to a classroom to study the Qur'an. Although she had read some of the Bible, she didn't own one, had never visited a church, and did not know any Christians.

When she was 18 years old, F moved to New York City to begin an undergraduate degree in Biology. F's family is upper middle class, but they still had little savings to pay for her tuition. Approximately 85% of her college tuition was covered by scholarship, and she needed to work about 20 hours per week to cover the remainder of her expenses.
I met F briefly during orientation; she received one of our flyers, but never came to join our international student activities. Three months later, she discovered our international student ministry through social media and was invited to come to our home for an international student dinner. She came, along with her mentor, an American from the northeast in his junior year.

The two of them continued to come together to our events and joined a small group Bible study. On Easter Sunday, they decided to visit a church together. After four months, the mentor decided to become a Christian. They both continued in Bible study, attending church regularly until one Sunday a 15-year-old boy from an immigrant family from a Muslim country was being baptized and shared his testimony. He shared how his family had suffered persecution overseas and how he was going to show all his Muslim friends how wrong they are. This was F's last time to attend church. She continued to study the Bible with us for a few more weeks, though when school began in the fall semester she dropped out.

A few months later, F decided to transfer to another university three hours away. We helped her move and continued to follow up with her through social media. During the year, she came back to the city four times – for Thanksgiving, Christmas, Spring Break, and a Summer Break. Each time she came, she lived with us for 5 to 12 days, and during her visits, we shared the gospel and passages of Scripture with her. She read an autobiography of Tim Tebow, watched a Francis Chan Bible study video, and engaged in Bible study. We also had the opportunity to visit her home and meet her family overseas. F recently told us that this Christmas she wants to come back to New York so she can travel with us to spend Christmas with me and my family in Kentucky.

F tells us discrimination is the biggest problem she's faced in the United States. She has had people pull off her hijab and scream at her. A couple months ago, when walking down a street in Philadelphia, a man threw dog food at her until she was out of his range. She wishes the discrimination would stop, but says she really enjoys the diversity of the United States as she's had the opportunity to make friends of different faiths. Before coming to America her view of Christianity was not positive, and now she says she sees Christianity as somewhat positive. Please pray God will reveal Himself to our friend F.

Ethnography #4: An atheist from China

E grew up in a wealthy family in a city of 10 million about 500 miles west of Shanghai. E had visited a Buddhist temple once, but she along with all her friends and family were atheist. Growing up, she never met a Christian, visited a church, or saw a Bible, although she had read a children's story book with stories about Adam and Eve, Noah, and David and Goliath. While she didn't believe in God, E had a positive view towards Buddhists and Christians.

After completing her undergraduate studies in China, E moved to New York City to pursue a master's in East Asian Studies. A scholarship covered about a tenth of her tuition expenses, and her parents covered the rest of her tuition and living expenses. During her first semester in

America, she said her biggest problems were making American friends, feeling homesick, and understanding English idioms. After three weeks in America, one of E's housemates, who had come to a picnic in the park for international students the previous week, invited E and her other housemates to go apple picking with our international student group. She and her roommates decided to form a small group Bible study and began studying the Bible weekly. After about ten weeks of Bible study, she told me, "I still don't believe God exists, but for the first time, I want Him to exist."

E and her roommates continued in weekly Bible study for about one year. Around that time, her friends invited her to a Campus Crusade fall retreat, and she was touched by a skit she saw. A couple of months later, we were taking students to Kentucky for a Christmas homestay program, and she came with us. On Christmas Day, she was sharing with her host family that she didn't want to become a Christian and go to heaven if that meant she would be eternally separated from her family. Her host mom told her that perhaps she is the way God will use to reach her parents. E decided to follow Christ that day and was baptized one month later in New York.

Two of E's close friends who had been in the Bible study group were upset that she had become a Christian. Her decision put pressure on them, and while they enjoyed reading the Bible, both refused to recognize that they are sinners in need of a Savior. E was very hurt when she learned they were disappointed with her decision and that they assumed she thought she was better than they. When E told her parents of her desire to be a Christian, their initial response surprised her. They told her that her decision was fine so long as she didn't spend too much time at church, and they warned her to never give any of her money. Over time, her parents started to notice differences in her life, and her father began to discourage her from following Christ.

E has been growing in her faith, attending church regularly, joining small groups, and has led multiple Bible study groups for non-believing Chinese students. She recently helped her church in Manhattan launch a ministry to international students, which she helps lead.

Ethnography #5: A Muslim from South Asia

J was born into a wealthy and culturally Muslim family and grew up in a city of 750,000 people in South Asia. J's grandfather's job was to take care of the local mosque. His father also had a position of authority at the mosque. To support their family, J's father buys old models of televisions, washing machines, and other appliances from China and sells them at a couple of shops in their city.

J was taught to pray five times a day and that God wouldn't hear his prayer unless he first washed; he started to question why he should do these things. His parents were not strict in forcing him to keep these traditions. His grandfather, however, was very unhappy with J for not praying regularly. He said J was a sinner and tried to send him to a mental hospital though J's father stopped him. His father invited an imam to their house to pray for J so that he would turn back to following Allah. As a boy, J was very shy, and only had two close friends, yet they too started questioning his confusion with Islam. As a result, J's best friend became his mother, as he would often stay inside the home and help her in the kitchen. Growing up J had never visited a church or seen a Bible. Almost everyone he knew was Muslim, though he did know a few Hindus.

After high school, J moved to Kansas for college where he made some good and strange friends. During his second semester, he was in a bad car accident. The police were amazed he wasn't hurt, and friends told him perhaps a guardian angel had saved him. Seeking answers, J visited a Navigator's Bible study but felt lost as they were all Americans and he had trouble understanding them. Around Easter, he was invited to an American family's home and this family became his American family. They loved him and shared what they believed about God. At their house, J could learn about Jesus without the fear of other Muslim students learning about it. J had heard about Christianity before, but this was the first time to learn about it from Christians. They answered some of J's questions, and some other questions remained, especially regarding the Trinity. J had been taught that Christians worship three gods, and what he learned confused him as he was taught Christians only believe in one God.

In the summer of 2015, J made a quick decision to move to New York City to continue his studies. He went to school in Manhattan and lived in Long Island. At first, he felt disconnected from God, then his American friend in Kansas connected J with us. We did Bible study with J and connected him with three others who are in full-time ministry to J's ethnic group. One of these new friends sufficiently answered J's questions about the Trinity in his language, and a few weeks later J announced he wanted to follow Jesus and turn from his sin. A few months later, J was baptized.

In South Asia, some families cutoff or use violence against their children if they rebel against their parents by turning away from Islam. J still has not told his family of his decision, partially due to fear of their reaction. He believes, however, that God gave him a beautiful family and they will be accepting once he tells them.

Our Learning

From these five stories, we will focus our analysis on issues related to their contexts, their encounter with Christianity, and the impact after their graduation. For contexts, we will review their background before coming to the USA campuses and the environments they encounter in the US. Concerning their interaction with Christianity, we will review the most effective methods of interaction and exposure to the gospel. We will finally discuss their whereabouts and contributions today.

Contexts

The students were mainly from countries in Asia with different religious backgrounds. Those from China usually grew up with Buddhist or atheist backgrounds. Although Buddhism is widespread in China, these Buddhist families in our interviews tended to be nominal and traditional in their practices. In these cases, the students usually do not come with a strong commitment to the religion. On the contrary they often show a rather weaker identification and treat Buddhism as merely a family tradition. Parents might not be happy for their conversion to Christianity, but the resistance and rejection do not constitute formal persecution. The general attitude of the Chinese population towards Christianity is relatively neutral. Students converting to Christianity are seldom subject to severe levels of persecution by their parents or other family members. A similar attitude is also experienced by students with atheist backgrounds. Historically China seldom had a "state religion," there is a general popular distrust against government sponsored communist ideology, thus religious conversions are commonly accepted with less resistance. This is contrasted with students of Muslim background from South Asia. Families with Muslim backgrounds are usually much more committed to their religious identity and religious practices. The decision to convert to Christianity is a much more serious decision with significant impact in all areas of a student's life. This also explains why we see a stronger conversion movement among Chinese students as compared to Muslim background students in the USA.

New York, like most of the gateway cities in the US, attracts students from all over the world like a magnet because it offers two important incentives: cultural diversity and employment opportunities. New York is one of the most culturally diverse cities in the USA and attracts visitors world-wide; students being no exception. As our world becomes increasingly urban, postmodern, and globalized, young people are naturally attracted by the multicultural diversity of these gateway cities. Being exposed to a multicultural environment, and even claiming to be multicultural, have become much esteemed labels and experience.

University campuses in cities like New York offer an even higher level of diversity. In addition, New York is a city with strong economic activities and high concentration of immigrant groups. A sanctuary city, it is also an ideal place for international students who need to find employment. As we see from the five stories, most students receive limited financial support from their schools, and many of them need income from outside employment to support their studies. In a gateway city like New York, the immigrant community offers the much-needed ethnic network to find suitable employment within the student's ethnic group. Although foreign students are not legally allowed to work off campus, the fact that New York is declared a sanctuary city offers hope for potential employment and income.

One of the most conflicting areas of the students' context is in their social interaction in the United States. On the one hand students found difficulties integrating into the American society. The major issue for students from China was language. It is imperative to increase English language proficiency for their own studies. However, it is never an easy task to learn a new language and remedial courses on campus may require additional costs. Campus ministry with Bible studies and fellowship events conducted in English become opportunities to learn English which are welcomed by the students. Through the interaction at these activities, foreign students and campus ministers build relationships thus creating an opportunity for sharing the gospel. On the other hand, the students, especially from Muslim background, encounter discrimination in their social interaction. This has a lot to do with the images of Islamic terrorism populated in current American media. Expressions of Islamic religious practices were challenged publicly. Students live under constant tension between their traditional and family identity with Islam in their home countries, and the social challenges against Islam in the United States. Unfortunately, even with the patient support of campus ministers, many students are still facing difficulties embracing Christian faith. For the Chinese students, peer pressure from other Chinese foreign students is also a factor to their conversion. As the foreign students usually have few friends due to being new in the country, they care deeply about how other foreign friends from the same country see their conversion to Christianity. Sometimes it could be a challenge for an individual to decide to follow Jesus Christ. However, it could also be an opportunity for a chain of conversions to occur among the foreign students.

Interaction with Christianity

Through analysis of the five stories, we discovered that international student social events on campus and Bible studies conducted by campus ministers were commonly used for outreach to the international students. As international students first arrive in New York, social events on campus are important opportunities for recreation and connection. It is true that many immigrant communities provide cultural environments similar to their homeland. They speak the same language, eat the same food, follow the same traditions, and even celebrate their traditional holiday events. Yet, because of the status differences with members of the immigrant communities and the urge to learn English in any English-speaking activities, student social events like picnics, barbecue gatherings, or cultural exchange programs specifically designed for international students are more desirable. It's the initial point of contact for many students to be exposed to Christians and the Christian faith. It is also considered as one of the best tools student workers use to reach the international students. Once exposed to Christian friendship, the logical next step for a college student is inviting him/her for a series of Bible studies. As college students are now entering into the age of intellectual exploration and the Bible is considered by many foreigners as the symbol of American culture, many of them are happy to join the Bible studies which are not available in their home countries. Religious curiosity and cultural interests are usually the most common motives to join these Bible studies!

The off-campus support in reaching out to international students takes different forms. As mentioned before, local immigrant churches have been active partners in student ministry. Due to the large number of colleges in cities like New York, an immigrant church is often preoccupied in reaching out to its own second generation who are attending college locally. Some partner with campus ministries like CRU or Intervarsity. Others develop their own college fellowships near campus or within their own churches. Depending on the resources and the priorities of local immigrant churches, only some of them would be involved in reaching out to international students, perhaps only targeting students coming from the local immigrant church's homeland. They seldom reach out cross-culturally. However, among students from their own country, these immigrant churches may be the most successful agents in outreach. Beyond the immigrant churches, mainstream evangelical churches tend to be more successful in partnering with the campus ministers in reaching out to international students as a whole. Because of the ease in communicating in English, there tends to be stronger partnering with campus ministers with the offer of manpower and host families. However, depending on the ties a campus minister has with churches outside of the metropolitan area, a modified host family program is developed. In some of the stories, there is mention of a "Homestay Program" which has been successful in reaching out to international students. It consists of an out-of-state host family experience where a group of students is organized to travel to another state to experience American life outside of Metro New York. International students are offered the opportunity to see other parts of the country and interact with Christians families who live in less populated and more religious environments, many of them located in the traditional Bible Belt of the South. Oftentimes during these trips, students are challenged to examine the authenticity of Christian faith and many of them make a decision to follow Jesus Christ. Even if the student could not take the step of faith, the opportunity of stepping out from their traditional religious circle gives a fresh opportunity to evaluate Christianity and their own faith. The experience of such religious exposure has mostly been positive for all participants.

Future Impact

Students go to college only for a limited time. Eventually, they will all conclude their studies, graduate, and move on. A large number of international students decide to stay in the United States while others return to their home countries. Without getting into discussions on federal immigration policies related to international students, the experience of applying for residence in the US is often itself viewed as a spiritual journey. Graduates face the challenge of finding a job and applying for a working visa. Because of the limited quota for such visa and its random selection process, this is a time of intense prayer and a test of faith for many students who became Christians while on campus. In addition, many employers take advantage of the situations by offering a lower-than-usual salary to these students seeking sponsorship of a work visa. This may prove to be a time of endurance and bearing economic injustice. During this time of uncertainty and injustice, many have found comfort from their Christian faith and their Christian friends. Some rely on their campus ministers and friends. Others who are involved in local immigrant churches receive support from the pastor and church members. However, for those who successfully receive permanent residence in the US, many become active in local churches in New York or in other cities in the country. With their college degrees, professional employment, bilingual abilities, and genuine first-generation conversion experience, those who stay at local immigrant churches may eventually become effective Christian leaders in their communities. There are still others who decide to move to the suburbs and join American churches. With their professional background and transnational life experience, they not only contribute to the life of local churches but also enrich the diversity of these churches and communities.

Our stories do not include many successful and prosperous cases when students return to their countries. However, it is well known that many international students return to their countries and occupy high ranking positions in their national government or become influential members of the society in business, academia, politics, technology, education, etc. It is our desire to see that Christians permeate all sectors of society when returning to their home country, giving testimony of the Christian faith. The successful testimony of an authentic Christian life in the home country often starts from a small chat about faith in one of these Bible studies while studying in the US. This has been a constant reminder and encouragement to the campus workers and those Christians in local churches who are involved in reaching out to international students. Whatever they are doing now is a great investment in the kingdom.

Conclusions

Gateway cities with many colleges and immigrant churches stand at a unique position in diaspora missiology. On the one hand cities attract many students. And on the other hand, there are many distractions to international students in these cities. The gospel still faces the challenge of other cultural and ethnic competitions. Yet the existence of immigrant churches constitutes a natural and stable force of support that draws the international students to attend as their home away from home. The campus workers play an important role of personally engaging the lives of these students and at the same time connecting them to the partner churches in order to develop long-term ministry that goes beyond their graduation. Traditionally experts see two approaches to international student ministries: local church model and campus model. Yet in gateway cities like New York, with a large number of both immigrant churches and multicultural churches, partnership between local churches and campus ministry proves to be effective in reaching out to international students. International student ministries are an important segment of diaspora missiology. It stands at the intersection among student ministry, diaspora missiology, and urban mission. As we are increasingly concerned with the faith of our future generation, the unprecedented level of diversity of our cities, and the rapidly intensified transnational ties through globalization, international student ministry may play an important role in responding to these challenges.

CHAPTER 4
THEOLOGICAL FOUNDATION FOR THE PRACTICE OF DIASPORA MISSIONS AMONG INTERNATIONAL STUDENTS

Christopher D. Sneller

In 2007 I sat down for a burger and fries with a new friend from sub-Saharan Africa. Akiki had moved to Houston recently and began volunteering with our international student ministry at the University of Houston. I asked what his dad did for a living. "He's a minister," replied Akiki over a handful of fries. I thought to myself: I wonder if he's Presbyterian, Anglican, Baptist, or Methodist. He read the look on my face and laughed. "Not that kind of minster," Akiki said. "He's the Minister of the Interior. In fact, he's the longest serving cabinet member." The ensuing story included his dad fleeing from a dictator, obtaining an M.A. from the University of California at Berkeley, and returning home to serve in the government. Outreach to Akiki, his dad, and millions of other international students represents a unique and strategic missions opportunity in world history. Thus, the purpose of this book. In this chapter, I will lay a theological foundation for the practice of diaspora missions among international students. This missiology of international student ministry (ISM) begins with the missio dei (mission of God). After exploring God's unique Trinitarian love, I move to examples of scatterings and of international students throughout the Bible. The final half includes global migration trends (including internationally mobile students) and a response to those trends.

Missio Dei

Our theology of missions must be grounded in the very nature of God. God creates the world to delight in the love that already exists within His Triune nature. What God does in human history flows from Who He is in eternity. To understand missiology, we must go back in time before the creation of the world, before even time existed. God has always been. He is, in Aristotle's words, the Unmoved Mover. He is the primary cause of all things. As God told Moses from a flaming yet unconsumed bush, "I Am that I Am" (Exodus 3:14). In the great Shema God's people are to declare that the "Lord our God, the Lord is One" (Deuteronomy 6:4). God is great; He is "God in heaven above and on earth beneath; there is no other" (Deuteronomy 4:39). So how should God's people respond? By loving Him with all their heart, soul, and energy (Deuteronomy 6:5-7, Matthew 22:36-40). God created humanity to love, delight in, and worship Him. Yet God's love precedes His creation. It flows from His Triune nature.

God manifests love in His very nature, apart from any action He performs. He is the Tri-Unity Who is love. Given the broad semantic range for the word "love" in English, the concept begs definition. Even the Greeks distinguished various kinds of love: sexual desire (eros), friendship (phileo), and charity (agape). The Stanford Encyclopedia of Philosophy summarizes love as: union, robust concern, and valuing. Love is an inner force compelling oneness, selfless concern, and honor. Intrinsically each person of the Trinity is unified with, concerned for, and honoring of the others. As Three-in-one and One-in-three, God the Father, God the Son, and God the Spirit mutually delight in each other. God is, in the words of John Gill, an "inexhaustible fountain of goodness" because of this inner-trinitarian love. Jonathan Edwards, the eighteenth-century pastor and theologian, explained that "happiness of the Deity, as all other true happiness, consists in love and society." God creates the world from an intention to share this love, this delight, with others.

He created this world for Adam and Eve to live in and to delight in His own goodness. Even after they sinned, God extended grace to them. He asked Adam "Where are you?" though He knew (Genesis 3:9). He clothed Adam and Eve and made a covenant with them (Genesis 3:14-19). Included in this covenant was a curse against the serpent and a promise to Eve that a redeemer would come to crush Satan (Genesis 3:15). In this proto evangelium, God expressed His desire to redeem the now-broken world. He would restore what was broken and marred by sin. Soon after evil entered the world, a Messiah was promised. God is one – a Triune being Who delights in Himself and Who creates and redeems in order that His creation may delight in Him. In the Incarnation, the Father sent the Son to redeem the broken world (John 3:17, 12:44-50). The Triune God created the world and is redeeming the world in Christ that all creation might share in His love. This is God's mission.

God delights in being marveled at, in being honored and worshiped, He wants the earth to be filled with knowledge of Him and His glory. The Psalmist proclaims: "Declare His glory among the nations, His marvelous works among all the peoples. For great is the Lord, and greatly to be praised" (96:3, 4) and "All the nations You have made shall come and worship before You, O LORD, and shall glory Your name. For You are great and do wondrous things; You alone are God" (86:9, 10). Redemptive history climaxes around a throne. A great multitude from every nation, tribe, people, and language—that is, every ethne—clothed in white robes crying with a loud voice "Salvation belongs to our God Who sits on the throne, and to the Lamb!" Revelation 7:9-12 depicts this glorious scene when, finally, the Lamb of God, the Suffering Servant, is recognized as the Lion of Judah and worshipped as the King of the Universe. Immigrants, refugees, and international students — once members of a great diaspora community — will play a role in this glorious expression of transcultural worship.

When we understand God's character, we understand His mission. Yet this cannot happen apart from the Cross. God the Son must redeem the world that He created. Athanasius made this point well in the fourth century:

The renewal of creation has been wrought by the Self-same Word Who made it in the beginning. There is thus no inconsistency between creation and salvation; for the One Father has employed the same Agent for both works, effecting the salvation of the world through the same Word Who made it in the beginning.

To summarize: missiology is grounded in theology proper. What God does in our world begins with Who He is. The Iguassu Affirmation — created by a gathering of 160 missions' leaders from 53 countries in Foz do Iguassa, Brazil, in 1999 — did well to begin their theological commitments with this Trinitarian foundation of mission. Any doctrine of God is incomplete without a robust understanding of missiology. When we grasp God's Triune nature, we see that missiology and theology proper cannot be understood apart from each other. Tereso Casino frames it well: "missiology is inherently theological as theology is indispensably missions-oriented." A theology of international student ministry rightly belongs under diaspora missiology, to which we now turn.

Diaspora Missiology

The word διασπορά

Diaspora missiology is built on Biblical stories of scatterings. God created people groups (Genesis 25, Psalm 86) and cultures (Genesis 11) and He sovereignly employs scatterings of peoples for His purposes. Tira and Yammori argue this point then conclude "Every dispersed person and people group has a place and role in God's redemptive history." Diasopora (Gk., διασπορά) is a Greek noun meaning a "sowing" or "scattering." In the Septuagint it usually means "exile" to foreign lands (Jeremiah 25:34, Isaiah 11:12, Ezekiel 20:23, Zephaniah 3:10). Major Jewish diasporas occurred from the end of the eighth century BC onward including the exile of the Northern Kingdom by Assyria in 722 BC and of the Southern Kingdom to Babylon in 605 BC and 586 BC. By the time of Jesus's birth there were probably four to six million Jews in Palestine and several times that number in the diaspora, including communities of more than a million Jews in Asia Minor, Mesopotamia, and Alexandria. In the New Testament diaspora is usually translated as "scattered" or "dispersed." The noun διασπορά is used in John 7:35, James 1:1, and I Peter 1:1 and the verb διασπείρω in Acts 8:1, 4 and 11:19. Diaspora can mean both the "state or condition of being scattered" and the place in which those scattered are found. In his address to the Areopagus, Paul told the Athenians that God "made from one man every nation of mankind to live on all the face of the earth, having determined allotted periods and the boundaries of their dwelling place" (Acts 17:26). Paul framed God's sovereign role in the scattering of peoples.

Diaspora in the Old Testament

Diaspora stories fill the Pentateuch. After violating God's command against eating of the tree, Adam and Eve were sent out of the Garden of Eden (Genesis 3). God flooded the earth in judgment; Noah and his family rode a giant boat, filled with animals, to safety (Genesis 7). The technology of brick and bitumen allowed humanity to begin building. However, in their arrogant, tower-building pride, they sought greatness for themselves at Babel (Genesis 11:1-9). Yahweh judged humanity by confusing their languages and dispersing them across the face of the earth (Genesis 11:9). In these first chapters of the Bible, human sin caused the scattering. Nevertheless, Genesis includes other causes for the movement of people.

God forced Adam, Noah, and the post-Babel crowd to scatter; Abram moved willingly. He left Ur of the Chaldees (southern Iraq) and settled in Haran (Turkey). When his father Terah died, Abram moved to the land of Canaan at the call of God (Genesis 12). The earliest instances of diaspora stem from disobedience and judgment yet, in Abram's case, the motivation was obedience. And the result was blessing. God promised to bless the nations of the earth through Abram/Abraham (Genesis 12:1-9, 15:1–21, 17:1-14). For Abraham's descendants God's judgment and blessing were on the move. Jacob fled his angry brother Esau then returned to his father Isaac at Hebron (Palestine) with wives and children (Genesis 28-33). One of those children, Joseph, was sold by his brothers and ended up as a slave in Egypt. But what his brothers meant for evil, "God meant it for good" (Genesis 50:20). Dispersed by force to the land of Pharaoh, Joseph ended up as the second most powerful man in that kingdom. God used Joseph to enrich Pharaoh Ahmose I (1550-1525 BC) and to spare the lives of his whole family in seven years of severe famine. Ironically, eventually Israel's sons go from being shepherds to slaves. This experience in Egypt provided the existential basis for the ethical concern of God's people caring for the foreigners in their midst.

God layered Mosaic law with commands to care for the sojourners.

Why? Because He Himself loves the sojourner, fatherless, and widows (Deuteronomy 10:17-22). God expects His people to treat them accordingly: "Love the sojourners, therefore, for you were sojourners in the land of Egypt" (10:19). These three categories of landless, and often oppressed, peoples—orphans, widows, and foreigners—were to be treated with special care. This command recurs in Deuteronomy (14:29, 16:11, 14, 24:17-21, 27:19) and is grounded in Israel's experience in Egypt (15:15, 24:18, 22). The experience of being scattered gave Abraham's children unique empathy to love the diaspora community in their midst. That love culminated in allowing sojourners to assemble with the native-born community to have the law read before them that they may "hear and learn to fear the Lord your God, and be careful to do all the words of this law" (Deuteronomy 31:12, 13). Israel experienced God's love and provision and they were to bestow the same for the internationals in their midst. In so doing, the diaspora community would encounter Israel's God.

After God established the Davidic dynasty, Israel's role among the nations changed. Before Solomon, the aliens came to Israel as the result of war, famine, or other "involuntary" factors. They were pushed to Israel because of something in their homeland. As Solomon consolidated his power and deepened his wealth, the nations were drawn to Israel to come learn why. The Queen of Sheba (Yemen) embodied this voluntary pull of foreigners to Jerusalem (I Kings 10:1-13). She had heard of Solomon's fame, of his "words and wisdom," and wanted to learn more. "I did not believe the report until I came and my own eyes had seen it," said the Queen, "Your wisdom and prosperity surpass the report that I heard" (verse 7). She blessed Solomon's God and acknowledged that God delighted in Solomon and established his throne (verse 9). In the Old Testament some sojourners are pushed yet others are pulled. The former usually flee hardship, have limited access to resources, and stay indefinitely. But, like the Queen of Sheba, the reverse is true of the latter: they came to learn something, had considerable access to power, and returned home after a definite period of time. Four Biblical characters defy this general trend.

Daniel, Hananiah, Mishael, and Azariah were refugees and international students, neither by their choice, rather both by God's sovereign design. In 605 BC Nebuchadnezzar besieged Jerusalem. He conquered the city then took King Jehoiakim and Judah's riches back to Babylon. This spoil included members of the royal family and nobility. These youths, who were "without blemish, of good appearance and skillful in all wisdom, endowed with knowledge, understanding learning, and competent to stand in the king's palace," would learn the literature and language of the Chaldeans (Daniel 1:4). Daniel and his friends excelled in their training. To all four God gave exceptional wisdom and skill in learning. To Daniel, in particular, He granted unique insight into visions and dreams (Daniel 1:17). At the end of their Babylonian education, Daniel, Hananiah, Mishael, and Azariah exceeded everyone else in their training course. They were promoted as advisors to King Nebuchadnezzar. In fact, in "every matter of wisdom and understanding about which the king inquired of them, he found them ten times better than all the magicians and enchanters that were in all his kingdom" (Daniel 1:20). As we will see in the final section of this chapter, diaspora missiology includes those who scatter by force and by choice. Some immigrants are pushed to a foreign land, others are pulled. International students are in the latter category. But Daniel and his friends serve as an exception to that rule. They go to Babylon as refugees from war and become international students. We see this push/pull diaspora pattern in the New Testament as well.

Diaspora in the New Testament

Jesus Himself lived in a diaspora community. An angel appeared to Joseph and told him about King Herod's Pharaoh-like blood-lust against young Jesus. Forced to flee at night, Joseph took his family to Egypt. Jesus lived in a diaspora community for part of his childhood. That Jewish diaspora community in the Roman empire often returned to Jerusalem to celebrate Passover. In Acts 2 the Holy Spirit fell on the disciples and they began proclaiming the good news about Jesus in the native languages of "Parthians and Medes and Elamites and residents of Mesopotamia, Judea and Cappadocia, Pontus and Asia, Phyrgia and Pamphylia, Egypt and parts of Libya belonging to Cyrene, and visitors from Rome" (Acts 2:9, 10). Luke spared no geographic detail to emphasize that Pentecost provided a reversal to Babel's curse. Through God the Spirit, languages and cultures of the Jewish diaspora were united in hearing God the Son exalted. Later in Acts, we see the push of the early church out of Jerusalem. After Stephen's execution, a great persecution scattered the Christians who resided in Jerusalem (Acts 8:1). Christians are pushed from their home, forced to settle in new cities. Sometime in the mid-40s AD James, Jesus's brother, wrote to the "twelve tribes in the Dispersion" (James 1:1). Was James's audience part of an earlier Jewish diaspora who became Christians or Christians recently scattered from persecution in Jerusalem? He did not clarify. We can be certain, however, that the young church is dispersed and oppressed. The apostle Peter writes his first letter to "elect exiles of the dispersion in Pontus, Galatia, Cappadocia, Asia, and Bithynia" (I Peter 1:1). These instances represent people pushed from their homeland by persecution.

Acts 8 displays the other type of diaspora movement as well. An Ethiopian court official journeyed to Jerusalem to worship God and learn more about Him. Like visiting scholars today, this treasurer in Candace's court remained in Israel a finite period of time. On his journey home he encountered an apostle. Philip explained Isaiah 53 and God opened the eunuch's heart. He believed and was baptized. Acts 8 opens with the person who will be the key figure in the rest of this book: Saul. The brilliant Jewish scholar ravaged the church, dragging Christians to prison (Acts 8:3). On his way to Damascus Saul encountered the resurrected Christ in his blinding glory (Acts 9:1-19). Paul would become the greatest missionary in the history of Christianity. Like the Ethiopian eunuch, Paul journeyed from a different country to study in Jerusalem. Both the Ethiopian eunuch and the apostle Paul were international students. They were not forced to flee their homelands rather pulled to Jerusalem to study.

The apostle Paul's own life provides the best example of why a unique theology of international student ministry is possible and even necessary. Born in Tarsus (Turkey), Paul went to Jerusalem to learn at the feet of Gamaliel, the leading Pharisee of his day. In Acts 22 a Roman military tribune in Jerusalem was shocked to learn that Paul was a Roman citizen. The tribune explained that he bought his Roman citizen for a large sum of money. "But I," countered Paul, "was born a citizen" (verse 28). How could a first century Jew acquire this powerful status? For most, it was by assimilation and compromise to the Roman way. But Paul clarified he was a "Hebrew of Hebrews" and a Pharisee (Philippians 3:5). F. F. Bruce suggests: "Presumably Paul's father, grandfather, or even great-grandfather had rendered some outstanding service to the Roman cause." Paul's legal status, social standing, and financial situation made a foreign education possible. Paul's parents, Bruce explains, "made sure of an orthodox upbringing" for their teen-aged son by sending him to the "wholesome influences of Jerusalem" in his formative years. In the first century the two schools within Pharisaism were founded by Hillel (110 BC – 10 AD) and Shammai (50 BC – 30 AD). Gamaliel succeeded Hillel as head of his school in Jerusalem. In Acts 5 Gamaliel, "a teacher of the law held in honor by all people" (verse 34), urged the Sanhedrin to not condemn the apostles (verses 27-42). Bruce contrasts Gamaliel and his student from Tarsus: "as against Gamaliel's statesmanlike patience and tolerance, Paul was characterized by a superabundance of zeal." Paul provides the prime example of why a missiology of ISM deserves attention.

A Missiology of ISM

These considerations fall under diaspora missiology, which Wan and Tira define as a "specialized study of missiology and migration theory." David J. Bosch rightly suggests that "mission should be the 'theme of all theology'" so missiology itself may be "termed the 'synoptic discipline' within the wider encyclopedia of theology." Missiology explores the missio Dei in an interdisciplinary fashion that engages theology, biblical studies, and the social sciences. Migration studies touch the various fields of the social sciences, from sociology to demographics, and economics. A theology of international student ministry (ISM), therefore, explores what the Bible and world say about international students and how the two intersect.

Global Migration Trends

We have explored what the Bible says about the sojourner and explored instances of international students in both testaments, now we explore briefly the demographics around global migration trends. "Migration seems to be basic to the human condition," writes Andrew Walls, "for it has been repeated endlessly in human history, and has often been determinative in its effects on the life of peoples." The number of international migrants grew from 173 million in 2000 to 220 million in 2010 and 258 million in 2017. In 2017 the immigration population in the United States reached an historic high of 49.8 million people (up from 34.8 million in 2000). This means over 15 percent of people in the United States are diaspora peoples. First- and second-generation Americans accounted for 24.5 percent of the population in 2013; this number is projected to rise to 36.9 percent by 2025. In the 2017/18 school year International students in the United States totaled 1.09 million. In the same year there were 572,415 international students in Canada and 458,490 in the UK. Australia has experienced rapid growth with 554,188 international students in February 2019. In total in 2016 there were 4,854,346 international students world-wide. International students represent less than 5 million out of 258 million people in the global diaspora, nevertheless they represent a significant and strategic component of the global diaspora.

Figure 1– UNESCO's 2018 Numbers of International Students Globally

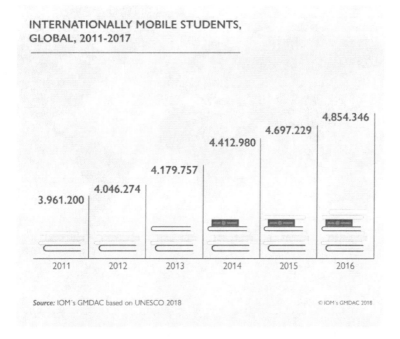

INTERNATIONALLY MOBILE STUDENTS,
GLOBAL, 2011-2017

Source: IOM's GMDAC based on UNESCO 2018   © IOM's GMDAC 2018

A theology of ISM deserves consideration because Biblical precedent establishes a case for it and global migration trends make it all the more urgent. Peoples in the diaspora are either pushed or pulled from their home countries. Mazzrol and Soutar argue that "economic and social forces within the home country 'push' students abroad" and "pull" factors "operate within a host country to make that country relatively attractive to international students." They are pushed to a new land by war, persecution, natural disaster, or extreme poverty. The pull, on the other hand, tends to be voluntary. Families and individuals are pulled to new countries for education, a better quality of life, greater political freedom, or at the invitation from family abroad. There are both push and pull factors for every migrant: elements pushing them from their home country and pulling them to new ones. However, for the sake of this chapter, I identify refugees in the "pushed" category and international students in the "pulled." In Figure 2, Enoch Wan has summarized global movement in three areas: two kinds of force (voluntary or involuntary), three kinds of choice (more, less, and least), and five types of orientations (outward, inward, return, onward, stay-put). Diaspora peoples are compelled to migrate for various reasons. We do well to reflect on the similarities and differences of migrants who are "pushed" and those who are "pulled."

Figure 2– Forces, Choices, and Orientations of Migrants

Migrant / Orientation	Voluntary More choice/option.. **Proactive Migrants**	Involuntary ... less choice / fewer options... ←············→	... little choice/few options **Reactive Migrants**
Out-ward	• tourists • visitors • students • professional transients • business travelers	• economic / labor migrants • rural-urban migrants • anticipatory refugees • people induced to move	• refugees • expellees • internally displaced people • development displacement • disaster displacement
In-ward	• primary migrant newcomers • family reunion / formation	• visitors, students or tourists who seek asylum	• asylum seekers • refugee seekers
Re-turn	• returning migrants & refugees • voluntary repatriates • voluntary returnees • repatriates long-settled abroad	• returning migrants & refugees • mixture of compulsion • inducement & choice	• deported / expelled migrants • refugees subject to repatriation • forced returnees • repatriates long-settled abroad
On-ward	• resettlement • dispersal by strategy	• third country resettlement of refugees	• scattering • forced dispersal
Stay-put	• staying by choices • household dispersal strategy	• people confined to safe havens / countries / areas	• staying of necessity • containment

Similarities: Call to love all foreigners in our midst

God commands His people to love all foreigners, regardless of their reasons for migrating. We already explored how God grounded Israel's call to love sojourners in their experience in Egypt. Jesus deepened this command. When a lawyer asked Him the greatest commandment, He reiterated the call to love God with your whole person and to love one's neighbor (Deuteronomy 6:5, Leviticus 19:18, 34). In Luke 10:25-37 Jesus told a parable of a despised Samaritan who becomes the hero of the story by sacrificially caring for a person in need. He expanded the definition of neighbor beyond ethnic boundaries. Your neighbor is anyone in need. Jesus amplified the command to love the oppressed and stranger in Matthew 25. He described the final judgment when the King will separate those who inherit God's kingdom and those who do not. Those in the kingdom served the marginalized: giving food to the hungry, drink to the thirsty, clothes to the naked, presence to the sick and imprisoned, and a welcome to the stranger. Jesus concluded: "Truly, I say to you, as you did it to one of the least of these My brothers, you did it to Me" (Matthew 25:40). Paul tells the church in Rome to put love in action by sharing with those in need and showing hospitality (Romans 12:13). The author of Hebrews echoes this call to brotherly love, "Do not neglect to show hospitality to strangers," then adds an intriguing aside, "for thereby some have entertained angels unawares" (Hebrews 13:1, 2). Followers of Jesus are commanded to love their neighbor and to show hospitality. Christians must show a Trinitarian-like love to the 258 million people in the global diaspora. God compels us to union, to robust concern, and to value migrants, whether they are pushed or pulled to new lands.

Differences: Unique issues with international students

In I Corinthians 9:19-23 Paul established an important principle of contextualization. He explains that his evangelistic strategy varies regarding those under the law and those outside the law. He adapts his approach to a Jewish or Gentile audience. The message of the gospel remains the same yet how it is communicated varies. Paul became "all things to all people, that by all means I might save some" (I Corinthians 9:22). Likewise, our strategies need to be adjusted to a Filipino construction worker in Saudi Arabia or a Saudi international student in Philadelphia. Many refugees are unable to return to their country of origin. They will migrate until they find stability. International students are different. They graduate with advanced degrees with an abundance of opportunities before them. Many return home to their places of influence. Some remain in their countries of study (depending on work visa situations). And some become global nomads, moving to a new country in search of the best employment. This present volume seeks to reflect on the theology and practice of diaspora missions to international students then provide case studies to illustrate these ideas.

The Ethiopian eunuch and the apostle Paul demonstrate from Scripture that international students are strategic. They often come from places of influence and return to places of power: socially, economically, and politically. They represent the crème de la crème with unique access to power. "International students who return to their home countries have an impact disproportionate to their numbers," writes Michael Pocock. "They return to head up government departments and major businesses, spearhead research and development in the sciences . . . Some become the presidents, kings, and premiers of their nations." Shinzo Abe, the Prime Minister of Japan, studied at the University of South California. Juan

Manuel Santos, a recent President of Colombia, earned a BA at the University of Kansas, MSc. from the London School of Economics and Political Science, and MPA from Harvard University. King Abdullah II of Jordan did primary and secondary school in England and the United States before enrolling in Oxford University. One website identifies recent leaders of 28 countries who were international students. The apostle Paul serves as the prime Biblical example. In his recent book Paradigm Shift, Jack Burke makes this important connection:

Like Paul, the Christian international students who return to their homelands today as well-trained missionaries, are better qualified and therefore more effective in carrying out the Great Commission to their own people than their non-citizen missionary counterparts. Also, being self-supporting is the most economical means for missionary work.

Establishing a biblical theology of ISM and examining current trends in global migration leads me to conclude with topics for further reflection.

1.   Organizations working with international students need to reflect on how to best equip students for a lifetime of following Jesus. Students devote tremendous time, energy, and money into preparing for their future professions. And what spiritual and theological investments are made preparing them to return home? Academically, it would be interesting to explore how the diaspora experience of international students effects them in comparison to their peers who do not migrate for education.

2.   ISM practitioners need to pay close attention to broader trends in globalization. We need to be aware of the latest global demographic trends and of developments in migration studies. International students develop a unique—and sometimes confusing—transcultural identity. They become a distinct class of global citizens. We need to help them understand and articulate that identity.

3.   Lastly, far more research is needed in exploring the specific influence of former international students on various segments of society. Earlier I mentioned a few former international students who now serve in top government roles. But how have former international students impacted the church, the academy, and industry? Burke sets a good example in Paradigm Shift by telling stories of Patrick So and Hing Sin in Hong Kong, Bakht Singh in India, Michael Cassidy in South Africa, and others. We need to research and document more stories like these.

Conclusion

Akiki returned home to sub-Saharan Africa after obtaining his MBA. His father now serves as Prime Minister. International students represent a unique missions opportunity, worthy of sustained theological reflection and loving engagement. Alexander Best expressed the opportunity well: "God is re-gathering nations, drawing their brightest hopes for the future, to a global campus near you."

Bibliography

Athansisus. *On the Incarnation*. Crestwood, NY: St Vladimir's Seminary Press, 1996.

Australian Government, Department of Education and Training. "International Student Data Monthly Summary: February 2019." Accessed 21 May 2019. https://internationaleducation.gov.au/research/international-student-data/pages/default.aspx

Bauer, Walter. *A Greek-English Lexicon of the New Testament and Other Early Christian Literature*. Revised and Ed. Frederick W. Danker, 3rd ed. Chicago: University of Chicago Press, 2000.

Best, Alexander. "Ten Reasons Why the Global Campus is the Future of Mission." *Evangelical Missions Quarterly*, Volume 55, Issue 2, April-June 2019, 21-25.

Bieler, Stacey. *Patriots or Traitors? A History of American-Educated Chinese Students*. New York, NY: Routledge, 2004.

Bosch, David J. *Transforming Mission: Paradigm Shifts in Theology of Mission*. Maryknoll, NY: Orbis Books, 1991.

Brettell, Caroline B. and James F. Hollifield Eds. "Introduction." In *Migration Theory: Talking Across Disciplines*. New York: Routledge, 2015.

Bruce, F.F. *Paul: Apostle of the Heart Set Free*. Grand Rapids, MI: William B. Eerdmans Publishing Company, 1977.

Burke, Jack. *Paradigm Shift: Why International Students are so Strategic to Global Missions*. Bloomington, IN: WestBow Press, 2019.

Canadian Bureau for International Education. "International Students in Canada." Accessed 21 May 2019. https://cbie.ca/infographic/

Chinn, Lisa Espinelli. *Think Home: A Reentry Guide for Christian International Students*. Downers Grove, IL: Intervarsity, 2011.

Edwards, Jonathan. "Writings on the Trinity, Grace, and Faith." In *The Works of Jonathan Edwards*. Ed. Sang Hyun Lee. New Haven: Yale

University Press, 1957-2008.

Elwell, Walter A. and Philip W. Comfort, Eds. Tyndale Bible Dictionary. Carol Stream, IL: Tyndale House Publishers, 2001.

Gill, John. *Gill's Complete Body of Practical and Doctrinal Divinity: Being a System of Evangelical Truths, Deduced from the Sacred Scriptures*. Ed. William Staughton. Philadelphia: Delaplaine and Hellings, 1810.

Helm, Bennet. "Love." In *The Stanford Encyclopedia of Philosophy* (Fall 2017 ed.). Ed. Edward N. Zalta. Accessed 16 May 2019. https://plato.stanford.edu/archives/fall2017/entries/love/.

HESA. "Where do HE students come from?" Accessed 21 May 2019. https://www.hesa.ac.uk/data-and-analysis/students/where-from

Institute of International Education (IIE). "2018 Open Doors Report." Accessed 21 May 2019. https://www.iie.org/Research-and-Insights/Open-Doors

Mazzarol, Tim and Geoffrey N. Soutar. "Push-Pull Factors Influencing International Student Destination Choice." *CEMI Discussion Paper Series*, DP 0105, 2001, Centre of Entrepreneurial management and Innovation. www.cemi.com.au.

Mirza, Nate. *Home Again: Preparing International Students to Serve Christ in Their Home Countries*. Colorado Springs, CO: Navpress, 2000.

Pocock, Michael. "Global Migration: Where Do We Stand?" in Diaspora Missiology: *Reflections on Reach the Scattered Peoples of the World*. Eds. Michael Pocock and Enoch Wan. Pasadena, CA: William Carey Library, 2015.

Taylor, William D, Ed. *Global Missiology for the 21st Century: The Iguassu Dialogue*. Grand Rapids, MI: Baker Academic, 2000.

Tira, Sadiri Joy. *Scattered to Gather: Embracing the Global Trend of Diaspora*. Manila: LifeChange Publishing, 2010.

Unesco 2018. "Migration Data Portal." Accessed 21 May 2019. https://migrationdataportal.org/themes/international-students

United Nations Department of Economic and Social Affairs. "International Migration Report 2017." Accessed 21 May 2019. https://www.un.org/en/development/desa/population/migration/publications/migrationreport/docs/MigrationReport2017_Highlights.pdf

USA Study Guide. "Famous International Students." Accessed 21 May 2019. http://www.usastudyguide.com/famousstudents.htm

Walls, Andrew. "Mission and Migration: The Diaspora Factor in Christian History." In *Global Diasporas and Mission*. Eds. Chandler H. Im and Amos Yong. Oxford: Regnum Books International, 2014.

Wan, Enoch. "Diaspora Missiology." In *Occasional Bulletin*, Spring 2007, 1-10. www.emsweb.org.

Wan, Enoch and Sadiri Joy Tira. "Diaspora Missiology." In *Missions Practice in the 21st Century*. Eds. Enoch Wan and Sadiri Joy Tira. Pasadena, CA: William Carey International University Press, 2009.

CHAPTER 5
REFLECTIONS ON THE INTERNATIONAL STUDENT MINISTRY

Florence Tan

All Scripture is taken from the New King James Version (NKJV)

Synopsis

God loves the world including the foreigners. As His beloved children, we are instructed to show love to them. Among them are the international students who have criss-crossed the globe to better their education with the hope of improving their career choices. They form an ever-growing sizeable population in many developing cities and tertiary institutions of developed countries. Christ's disciples can stretch their helping hands to them when needed, offer words of comfort and confidence from an honest heart and welcome with warm hospitality to their homes. Surely the away-from-home learners will witness and be confronted with opportunities to accept God's love, salvation through Christ the only way and be sanctified in the Holy Spirit as prompted.

Creator God loves all the sojourners of this world: nationals, citizens, migrants, refugees, transient student/trainee population, etc. Salvation is for all so concerned believers are alert to the Father's working in all people groups, in this our particular consideration, the people studying in foreign lands.

Focus On Father's Wind - John 3:8

"The wind blows where it wishes, and you hear the sound of it, but cannot tell where it comes from and where it goes. So is everyone who is born of the Spirit."

The omnipotent God zeroes in where He wills (Ephesians 1:3-6), on those willing and open as keen disciples learn to sensitively pick up the cues for moments/processes of conversion. Salvific work has been completed through His Son's atoning death on the cross and witnessed resurrection (1 Corinthians 15:3, 4) illustrating His ability to give new eternal life, and the sealing of heaven citizenry through the responsibility of His Holy Spirit. Bible-believing Christians concur that the power of the Spirit is the essential and only part in anyone's conviction to pray to receive Christ as Saviour, by faith claiming on the hope of eternal existence with the beloved Lord Jesus (John 16:9).

A Chinese lady from a Communist background and pursing her doctorate was won over by the love extended to her in terms of friendship and consistent caring connection. Hers had not been a once-and-for-all decision for Christ, but rather spread over several years, initially in a western country and subsequently in the East.

The lady managing the host programme of a tertiary institution has been bringing a small band of ardent Christian labourers for the harvest field to annually and intentionally attend to incoming international students through small group discussions. This kind of connection allows the hosts to facilitate the school's planned workshops, be tourist guides and invite newcomers to the home for meals with the local flavour. All these are done, by all means to save some!

To get active minds to the level of acknowledging spiritual interests, focus begins with touching on mental alertness and agility, and kindly concern for general physical body health and well-being. Sessions to teach and help improve thinking are organised so that the less exposed mind is satisfactorily and progressively engaged together with activities that engender laughter and stimulate wellness. Additionally, developing awareness and appreciation of the varied cultural and different social surroundings may encourage the inclination towards divine attentiveness resulting in lasting fruit. It must be recognised though that God is the One who causes seed to germinate, gives growth and blesses with increase (1 Corinthians 3:7).

The channels of blessings can ready themselves with good and proper answers to queries when the Lord springs the door open (1 Peter 3:15). He enables with grace and gives glory (Psalm 84:11).

Find Fields For Witnessing - Mk 16:15

And He said to them, "Go into all the world and preach the gospel to every creature."

The obedient follower of Christ seeks to tell the good news within the irregular boundaries of one's area of influence be it home, neighbourhood, district, state or country, further afield and abroad (John 4:35-38; Romans 10:15-18). Since there are many areas of concentration the dissemination of the gospel can be done effectively from "home" base.

Many international students welcome the idea of dropping by a place where they can find comfort when being in a "home" away from home. Here is the case of warm Christian hospitality never failing to cheer during times of study fatigue, part-time work tiredness, weariness from the bombardments of unfamiliar cultural activities, and homesickness.

Singaporeans Charles and Molly are super examples of being the providers of great delicious food and relaxing family atmosphere in their modest house in Swansea. Literally hundreds have tasted their complete meal offerings resulting in many touched hearts turning to Christ.

The author remembers from Day One upon arrival at the American city for graduate studies, there was a stirring within to jump-start an international adult Sunday School class. The gospel was shared and two nursing scholars from the Far East had accepted Christ as Saviour after two days in the country. So began a small group each Sunday with simple discipleship lessons. The group soon doubled and then tripled to include drop-ins from different lands. Mostly Asians, the academic ones brought their relatives and friends, non-academic and working people. The student population spilled over with transient guests and invitees from the ASEAN block. The veritable vehicle had expanded with those who rolled in and rolled out, now morphing into a more heterogeneous cluster.

The author had been the recipient of a one-dollar car, a nineteen year old Lincoln Mercury. What fun to be able to drive around folks (seven/eight at a time) all over the city and into the counties enveloped in the expansive American city. The jolly rides brought the foreign students busy with piling homework and tight campus working schedules to garage/ car boot sales and jaunts to nearby little towns for a looksee or walk-around. Exclusive private dinner parties on a modest budget organised by bigger tertiary better established institutions gather for a mini-concert or small group chat or even a tete-a-tete. These activities surely lay groundwork for deeper friendships making it easier to enter into spiritual conversations when the timing is right. The work of "Andrews" and "Philips" cannot be overstated as the Lord opens wide the doors ending with commitments from "Peters", "Ethiopian eunuchs", "Corneliuses" and the like.

Familiarise Foreign Ways - 1 Corinthians 9:19, 22

For though I am free from all men, I have made myself a servant to all, that I might win the more; ....to the weak I became as weak. I have become all things to all men, that I might by all means save some.

Each person comes into existence through first birth (John 3:3-6). The individual typically grows in an environment exposed through parental influence for better or for worse taking on their cultural habits and values. Ethnic and traditional mores may morph into many different attitudes and patterns of behaviour soon or eventually during growing up years greatly accelerated by the impact of social media.

Nevertheless the message of God's covenant with man remains the same. He promises meaningful life on earth during present-day uncertainties and in the midst of throes of political instability and major power trade wars.

The honest and seeking for the Truth person, a temporary resident with a student visa, is confronted by spiritual and psychological demands. As such the thought of a second birth is real and requires response. The serious possibility of an overhaul in one's way of thinking and different choice of point of reference in one's life can be overwhelming and heart-wrenching, even at any age.

For the very young adult, when everything moves at breakneck speed, such a challenge can be muted by a slow-down (if at all possible!) frequent interactive exchanges, verbal and/or textual. The older seasoned adult, given to more meditative inclination (perhaps fewer such less other-distracted models these days?) may realise the need for a second birth, of the spiritual kind (John 1:12).

Sincere friendships can help tip the scale in the context of helping the foreign learner/scholar to be assisted in the familiarising of manner of living for the newly arrived (John 15:13). If only he/she can experience the best friendship in Jesus (Proverbs 18:24). It can never be over-emphasised that there is the need to show the Way that is the Lord Jesus. Earthly friends for life but be sure that the international student gets to see and hear in one way or another the true meaning of life which can be lived out abundantly through the Life found only in Jesus.

The exceptionally bright and independent North Indian goes with rich-in-love high level religious status to advance her educational standards in another Asian country. This youngster with impressive emotional intelligence sees the light and walks nearer to it, but not there yet. In her case, it takes two years and even more to walk into the Light. She is exposed and living in a home environment that is lighted up all the while, will eventually soon be drawn to His Light and only by God's grace. There is the hard tussle for spiritual liberty to enter into the second birth when the first birth circumstances are so near and dear in heart intrinsically attached to the beloved earthly parents. She understands and does not want to break their hearts!

Follow Fellowship Walk – Matthew 28:19, 20

"Go therefore and make disciples of all nations…teaching them to observe all things that I have commanded you; and lo, I am with you always, even to the end of the age." Amen.

She is approaching adulthood. Born to a Korean missionary couple she is more accustomed to the adoptive country (the mission field). This third culture kid has been nurtured in a Christian family surrounding having made a clear-cut decision to follow Christ. Still there are lots for her to learn. Continuing in this country for her tertiary education, she is further exposed to deeper Christian discipleship in yet another Asian nation for personal training.

Here is an alternative to more self-development making discoveries in the four areas of the mental, physical, spiritual and social (Luke 2:52). A four-week stint is added to her (personal/internal) resume.

What did she achieve? She picked up tips to improve her thinking: to ponder deeper from a shallow base and gained a wider perspective. Over two weeks, she accumulated swimming skills and had been prompted to move physically faster in personal and household undertakings. She went into discussions on spiritual issues at length and greater depth in comparison to her normal experience. Plus she had been able to cover numerous tourist and cultural sites and activities all tailor-made for this her cross-cultural journey. She had been fortunate to attend three different kinds of concert – all for free: outdoor musical concert by the park, orchestral performance in the Grand Old Dame that is the Victoria Memorial Concert Hall and a high school charity event of a high standard at the slick University Cultural Centre.

Beyond the feeding of milk, she was slowly introduced to meatier stuff (1 Peter 2:2, 3; Hebrews 5:13, 14). From basic follow-up she graduated to intermingle face-to-face with fellow Christians who came alongside to befriend and/or minister and showered blessings on her.

During the month-stay she, being a modest linguist of sorts, had opportunities to function as an interpreter (English to Thai) in the sharing of the gospel with a pre-believer. She witnessed the concerted evangelistic effort bringing the message to tens of thousands at the Sports Hub. These initial steps prepared her for fuller participation in edifying and equipping aspects of fulfilling the Great Commission.

The above vignette emphasises the benefits of cross-border coaching of young people of the intensive kind in true millennial discipleship.

Fly On His Wings – Malachi 4:2

But to you who fear My name the Sun of Righteousness shall arise with healing in His wings; and you shall go out and grow fat like stall-fed calves.

Festive seasons and joy rides are the favourite times and happenings for those new to the town and country. Bright lights and inviting goings-on bring locals and outsiders together. Christmas and Easter are celebrated with commercial enthusiasm and religious fervour. Now is the right time to share God's love and the good news at personal, family and church level, the real meaning of the calendar events as they are noted nationally at places like The Lion City that is Singapore.

The family feasts of united body life in any believer's household or assembly or congregation reflect the good and preferred order of Christian worship activity, a testimony to outsiders of the faith or city-state or country. The Lord's Supper or the Breaking of the Bread or the Holy Communion marks the outstanding Christian practice for the united participation of all baptised (including international visitors) believers (1 Corinthians 11:23-28). It serves as a platform for joint exposure and experience for the newly initiated as well as the mature Spirit-filled follower welcoming the curious seekers of the Truth.

These celebrative occasions are excellent to draw multi-nationals, be they young or older, to focus on the worship of the one true God. The more mature interact to educate, edify, exhort and equip the fresh interns and babes. Upon returning to homeland after their respective educational schedules and training, few there may be who would rise up to take leadership, render deeper spiritual guidance and join or even commence a ministry in their relevant ubiquitous work places.

Beyond the four walls of the church building and Sunday activities, daily grind of life continues into the week for all. In the home or the marketplace, the abundant life can be relevantly lived out. The foreign student can catch a glimpse in many a good example in the salaried education officer, administrator, the part-time tutor or the tenured professor or even the avid fellow student. He or she can take advantage of or encounter positively the numerous offers of volunteers to spontaneously do a cursory trip to the city's Chinatown or Little India, the delectable taste of mum's cooking, historical anecdotes or a mere helping hand to cart personal belongings across town or campus or city to the suburbs or another state.

The most natural and effective form of witnessing is the example of the genuine believer exuding the blessed life (John 10:10). He demonstrates his denial of right for the Accuser of the Brethren or the Father of Lies to prompt and take over through spiritual suggestions. He is free to happily serve, a definite show of love (Job 31:32). Where there is love, fear of any kind is ward off (1 John 4:18). The needy and unsteady recently arrived or sensitive seeker can usually note and respond naturally.

Like the eagle flying with dedicated strength, the evangelistic overcomer can carry on knowing Christ, becoming like Him and making Him known. Before reaching the finishing line and having fought the good fight with grief, anger and fear, each authentic Christian would have had his nemesis to deal with during his earthly journey. Christ who heals the broken hearted and sets them free from internal and external stresses and bondage often the causes for many diseases, guards and flies with him who has to be constantly depending on the Wind beneath his wings. He soldiers on to be a humble witness.

Only the omniscient God opens hearts of the many from other lands pursuing spiritual answers. Believers simply trust that He will show the Way of salvation and sanctification to Life eternal with the heavenly Father God, supreme over all mankind. He is kind and caring, certainly to the foreigners, the students and scholars here being given special mention and attention in this write-up.

NOTE: all unidentified individuals and unspecified places in this write-up are true living examples and actual geographical locations.

Recommended books to read:

Lau, Lawson: *The World At Your Doorstep* USA: Intervarsity Pr, 1984

Phillips, Tom with W. Terry Whalin: *The World At Your Door* USA; Bethany House Pub, 1997

Tan, Florence Poh-Lian (author/editor): *Connecting For Christ – Overcoming Challenges across Cultures* Singapore: FPLTan, 2009

CHAPTER 6
HISTORY OF INTERNATIONAL STUDENT MINISTRY IN INTERVARSITY/USA

Stacey Bieler and Lisa Espineli Chinn

InterVarsity/USA traces its roots to the Christian students at the University of Cambridge, England in 1877, who, in spite of disapproval from university officials, met together to pray, study the Bible, and share the Gospel with other students. These students formed the British Inter-Varsity (*inter* means between and *varsity* was the British term for college level students) as similar groups began on other campuses.

The student movement spread to Canada in 1928 in response to pleas for assistance from the British InterVarsity. In 1937 independent student groups were springing up in the United States. The following year, Stacey Woods, the Canadian InterVarsity Director met with students from the University of Michigan campus in Ann Arbor, Michigan. As a direct result of that visit, the first InterVarsity group in the United States was formed. Other groups at Wayne State University in Detroit, a teachers' college in Ypsilanti, and Michigan State University in East Lansing were also birthed.[51]

However, it was four years later that InterVarsity/USA (IVCF) was officially incorporated on November 14, 1941. The Canadian movement loaned three staff, and Stacey Woods served as director of both the US and Canadian movements.

Critical Role of a Former International Student

Such a decision, to take on the growing interest in the United States by the Canadian movement, did not come without toll or cost. In the words of Stacey Woods,

> It was in April 1938 that after much heart searching and prayer by the Canadian Inter-Varsity board, they hesitatingly gave approval to commence evangelical student work under its auspices in the United States of America...They only partially realized what the cost to the Canadian movement would be and the degree that such undertaking would lead to the weakening of the Canadian student work. Suffer it did! For the next 15-30 years. There was first-of-all World War II,

---

[51] C. Stacey Woods, *The Growth of a Work of God: The Story of the Early Days of InterVarsity Christian Fellowship,* (Downers Grove, IL: InterVarsity Press, 1978),19.

which left not a single male staff worker in Canada. Then there [was] the divided leadership of a general secretary of two national movements...[52]

The cost of leadership for InterVarsity/USA and InterVarsity Canada was **borne by a former international student from Australia**! C. Stacey Woods studied at Wheaton College and the Evangelical Theological Seminary (now known as Dallas Theological Seminary). He was one of nine international students from seven countries at the seminary in 1931.[53] He had no intention of serving in Canada nor the United States. His plans were, after his American education, to work in India with Howard Guinness, then Australia, and pursue ordination in the Church of England in the diocese of Sydney. God had other plans.

First Vision for International Student Work

World War II changed the campus scene dramatically. Constant news of wounding and death among InterVarsity student leaders from 1938 to 1941 had a sad and sobering effect. On campus students, both men and women, became serious and intent as Christians. Daily prayer meetings were crowded, and prayer became urgent. The gospel seemed to have become less of an option and more of a necessity. The meager Bible study guides we had were snapped up. Apart from our thinly spread staff, new groups of students were springing up spontaneously. There was no time for form or structure, let alone standard operational procedure.[54]

Though both InterVarsity Canada and InterVarsity/USA faced a rapidly changing world, challenges of a pioneering movement, short-staffed with exploration of student work in other countries, they already had a vision for international student work. Both of their boards authorized the work, so Woods took the initiative in the spring of 1944.

Educational Mecca of the World

Christy Wilson, son of missionaries in Iran, became IVCF's missions secretary after the Student Foreign Missions Fellowship (SFMF), an organization on Christian colleges that encouraged missions, merged with IVCF in January 1945. He served as traveling staff while an undergraduate student at Princeton and as secretary of SFMF while a student at Princeton Seminary.

In Wilson's article, "Entertaining Angels," in the June 1945 issue of

---

[52] Woods, 21.
[53] A. Donald MacLeod, *C. Stacey Woods and the Evangelical Rediscovery of the University*, (Downers Grove, IL: InterVarsity Press, 2007), 52.
[54] Woods, 26.

HIS, IVCF's magazine for students, he mentioned that the US was becoming *the educational mecca of the world.* His deep interest in international students grew out of his own experience as an American missionary son in Persia (present day Iran) and a member of an alien minority. The editor's note mentioned plans to reach internationals students on three campuses through the distribution of the New Testament to all foreign students in their own languages, a Bible study class that had started at the International House in New York City, and a conference for internationals soon to be held in the Chicago area.

In 1946, Wilson wrote another article, "The Students are Coming," where he stated, "Let every Christian in America realize that this is the most strategic opportunity there has ever been for reaching leaders of foreign lands for Jesus Christ."[55]

It seemed natural at that time that the work among international students would fall under the larger focus on missions in InterVarsity. At the first Urbana[56] missionary conference held at the University of Toronto at the end of 1946, Bakht Singh, a former international student from India who studied mechanical and agricultural engineering at the University of Manitoba in Canada, was one of the plenary speakers. Reaching Chinese students in 1947-49 was assigned to Hong Sit, a graduate student in the US who had been a staff member of the China InterVarsity Christian Fellowship.

The international student population in the U.S. in 1945 was 7,772 and it nearly doubled, to 14,956 in 1947.

David Adeney: The First Director of International Student Ministry, 1952-1955

David Adeney, an Englishman of missionary parents, went to China in 1934 as a single missionary with China Inland Mission (CIM), now Overseas Missionary Fellowship (OMF). He married Ruth Temple, an American CIM missionary from Minnesota, while in China.[57] They served together until 1941. World War II kept them from returning to China, until January 1946, when David returned to assist a new evangelical movement, the China InterVarsity Fellowship.

---

[55] Stacey Bieler, *The History of International Student Ministry in InterVarsity Christian Fellowship-USA 1944-1980,* (Unpublished, 2009).

[56] *Urbana* is InterVarsity's triennial student missions conference, co-hosted by InterVarsity/USA, Inter-Varsity Christian Fellowship of Canada and Groupes Bibliques Universitaires et Collégiaux du Canada. After the first conference in Toronto, the subsequent conferences were held in the United States. From 1948 until 2003, it was held at the University of Illinois in Urbana, Illinois.

[57] Carolyn Armitage, *Reaching for the Goal: The Life Story of David Adeney,* (Wheaton, IL: Harold Shaw Publishers, 1993), 67.

When the People's Republic of China was established in 1949, western missionaries were forced to leave the country. In 1950, *China Inland Mission* loaned Adeney to IVCF to become the Midwest Regional Director. He assumed that post with memories of the rapid growth of student work in China and the fresh recollection of the commitment and sacrifice of the Chinese students making a stand for Christ under the new communist government.[58]

His Midwest Directorship lasted for two years. In January 1952, the Senior Staff Council recommended that Adeney be assigned to focus on foreign student work and be slowly released from his other responsibilities. From the executive minutes of the meeting, the council noted, "Recognizing that God is calling us to reach foreign students to the limit of our ability in a new way without prejudicing that work to which God has already called us, we consider this as an integral part of our campus work."[59]

The Council also recommended the appointment of two additional staff members focusing on international students in New York and Chicago, and that a foreign student center in New York City be established.

3,900 Names of Chinese Students

Adeney was known for his address booklet filled with names of some 3,900 Chinese students stranded across the United States after 1949. Numerous Chinese students who became pastors tell of his influence in their lives.

Some of the highlights during Adeney's time as International Student Ministires (ISM) Director include:

1. Links and goodwill with the Committee on Friendly Relations Among Foreign Students (CFR), a group that grew out of the vision of John R. Mott.[60] In 1944, CFR convened a consultation to answer how they could better serve international students which was projected to grow to over 10,000 in 1946.[61]

    He met with the CFR General Secretary John Benjamin Schmoker in the summer of 1952 and maintained regular correspondence. Adeney attended the NAFSA (National Association of Foreign

[58] David Adeney *China: Christian Students Face the Revolution,* (Downers Grove, IL: InterVarsity Press, 1973), 15.

[59] Bieler, 4.

[60] Leiton Edward Chinn, "Diaspora Missions on Campuses: John R. Mott and a Centennial Overview of the International Student Ministry Movement in North America," in *Global Diasporas in Mission,* Regnum Edinburgh Centenary Series, Vol. 23, 2014.

[61] Mary A. Thompson, Ed, *Unofficial Ambassadors,* (New York, NY: International Student Service, 1982).

Students Affairs)[62] in San Francisco where he spoke to over thirty foreign student advisers, State Department officials, and foreign embassy attaches. In February 1954, Schmoker responded that in his visits to various schools, foreign student advisors had changed their attitudes toward IVCF and that he would further explore cooperating with IVCF on the VISIT (a welcoming program).

2. The vision of ISM spread through Adeney's journeys across the United States, speaking at IVCF groups, churches, conferences, and "religious emphasis" weeks on campuses. Adeney urged staff workers to encourage their students to have a friend from abroad, to have one or two key students to lead the work on each campus, and for alumni and friends to open their homes to internationals.

3. Growth of ISM activities in New York and Chicago. Through the work of Marie Huttenlock, an international student specialist in New York City, the outreach to international students flourished. She lived near Columbia University, one block from the International House, where she started Bible studies and wrote, "Organized, consecutive Bible studies are one of the most natural ways to reach foreign students for Christ and penetrate the thick barriers of culture and prejudice with the Gospel message."[63] Huttenlock helped plan a conference in the Fall of 1953 that brought sixty-five internationals from fourteen countries. IVCF alumni also caught the vision and hosted over one hundred students on an outing.

   In the 1950s internationals from twenty countries in Chicago attended a Thanksgiving conference that included dinner in American homes, sightseeing tours, evening films, talks, and discussions. One of the students attending the Bible study at the International house in Chicago was Miyai-san who became a Christian on the eve before his return to Japan through a conversation with Adeney and Feng Xi-Zhang, a Chinese Christian. Miyai-san returned home and became vice-president of Shell Oil in Japan, a leader in his church, and a member of the board of Kirisutosha Gakusei Kai (KGK), the Japanese equivalent of InterVarsity/USA.

4. Dedicated follow up with key students, graduates, and friends to encourage them and give suggestions about the work. Adeney also collected training materials for students and volunteers for specific

---

[62] Today it is called *NAFSA: Association of International Educators* which is the leading organization committed to international education and exchange with more than 10,000 members worldwide.

[63] Bieler, 7.

groups e.g. Indian, Muslim, and German students.

A Critical Need

In his December 1953 report, Adeney addressed the critical need for more staff dedicated to international student work. He wrote to Woods,

> While we are encouraged by signs of an active witness to international students in some universities, I think that we must admit that we are only just touching the fringe of the work. Unless, in each place, there is someone who has a real vision for the work and is prepared to push ahead in faith, the tendency is for the Christian students to neglect entirely this important form of witness. I personally feel that, ideally, we should have several staff workers who would give their time entirely to work among foreign students...I realize that we cannot expect to run a full program, integrated with local churches and Christian homes, unless we have considerably more help...but, if we are to do even a minimum and adequately fulfill our responsibilities in the witness on campus, I feel that we really need three full-time foreign student workers.[64]

To this report Woods responded, "Certain staff members have mentioned to me their concern lest the Foreign Student work proves so demanding that this, if properly attended to, leads to a neglect of our first call, the American student."[65] He further reminded Adeney that the initial plan was to have ISM integrated to the total campus work, not to have a specialized department with specialized workers. Woods suggested that organizing InterVarsity alumni might be the best way to address this need because of their maturity and ability to provide Christian homes. By doing it this way, it would not divert energy from the campus picture.

Bob Finley, who worked simultaneously with Youth for Christ and InterVarsity Christian Fellowship as an evangelist among high school and college students, returned from an evangelistic trip in Asia in 1951. When he saw that IVCF was not going to have more focused staff for international students, he founded International Students, Inc (ISI) in 1953. He advocated friendship partners through a church-based rather than a student-based ministry patterned after the Tenth Presbyterian Church model in Philadelphia.[66] Although there were merger talks, it never

---

[64] Bieler, 6.
[65] Bieler, 6.
[66] Bob Finley, *Reformation in Foreign Missions,* (Charlottesville, VA: Christian Aid Mission, 2010), 32.

happened.[67]

Role of Camps

In the 50s InterVarsity transitioned from renting camps to acquiring them in remote places where students could be near God's creation while learning His word. Bear Trap Ranch in Colorado, Cedar Campus in Upper Michigan, and Hudson House in Nyack New York, became the sites for houseparties, i.e. events especially designed for International students, that included outdoor activities, Bible discussions, and opportunities to make new friends. Such relaxed atmosphere in a Christian community setting helped break down barriers. Gene Thomas, director of Bear Trap Ranch wrote on the brochure of the 1956 Christmas houseparty, "Many students say, 'We hear Christianity argued, debated, defended and attacked, but we never hear it explained.'"[68]

During the three years that Adeney served as director of ISM, he was also asked to serve as missions secretary (1953) and directed the 1954 Urbana Missionary Conference with the theme: *Changing World: Changeless Christ*. One hundred twenty international students from forty countries were hosted at a tea in their honor. In 1956, Adeney moved to Hong Kong to serve as Associate General Secretary for the Far East for the International Fellowship of Evangelical Students (IFES).[69]

Paul Little: The Second ISM Director, 1956-65

Paul Little grew up in the Plymouth Brethren tradition in Philadelphia. He attended the University of Pennsylvania Wharton School of Finance and Wheaton College (M.A. Biblical Literature). He married Marie Huttenlock, the international student specialist in New York City.

In the late 50s, IVCF had several leadership changes. In 1958 Woods, after being asked to choose one area of leadership by the IVCF Board, chose to serve as IFES general secretary and moved the headquarters to Lausanne, Switzerland. In his absence, Charles Hummel became the interim general secretary until Charles Troutman was appointed to the position in 1959. Paul stepped in as interim supervisor of the regional directors and later assumed the full-time directorship of the new ISM department.

---

[67] Keith and Gladys Hunt, *For Christ and the University*, (Downers Grove, IL: InterVarsity Press, 1991), 170.

[68] Bieler, 8.

[69] IFES was established in 1947 at a planning conference at Harvard University with InterVarsity/USA as one of the 10 founding members. Stacey Woods collected a third role as General Secretary of IFES. Today, it is a world-wide fellowship of student movements in more than 150 countries. See *C Stacey Wood and the Evangelical Rediscovery of the University* by A. Donald MacLeod, p. 103

During Little's tenure there were numerous publications and information on international student ministry and for international students. These include:

1. Publication of *Christian International Students* from 1956-60. In ten issues, Little had four to five articles or testimonies with a list of upcoming summer training and houseparties. Authors included former international students like John Mbiti from Kenya who studied at Providence Bible College (now Barrington College in Rhode Island) and P.T. Chandapilla who studied at Columbia Bible College in South Carolina before returning to India, then served as the General-Secretary of the *Union of Evangelical Students of India.*

2. In 1959, Little also wrote a seminal booklet, *Guide to International Friendship* which was reprinted many times and used as late as the 1990s.

3. In the 50s, *HIS* magazine published twelve articles about internationals that addressed various topics like practical suggestions on hosting international parties, friendships, and hospitality. One article, written by a South American, stressed the importance of treating foreign students as equals and to help for the sake of helping, not merely an opportunity to preach, respect other cultures and religions, and read about other cultures.[70]

4. *HIS* magazine in the 60s featured sixteen articles about international student work. Articles were written by internationals from East Africa (about missionaries and a testimony), from Holland (a testimony), from Kenya (preparing for missionary work through friendship with international students), the Middle east (comparison of communism and nationalism), and by staff that included a three-part series entitled *World at Your Doorstep.*

5. *Approach to International Students* was a two-page introduction to reaching international students written by George Ensworth, the Mid-Atlantic Regional Director in 1957. He encouraged finding someone permanent in the campus or a community that would gather graduate students and Christian families to read Little's booklet *A Guide to International Friendship.* In his article Ensworth outlined a year's program with internationals.

6. In 1960, a ten-page bibliography, *Key Books for International Understanding,* was put together by Jennie Wu for graduates in the Bay area to "unlock the doors of ignorance, provincialism, and misunderstanding that are blocking our perception of the

---

[70] Bieler, 13.

enriching horizons of other lands and peoples."[71]

The Role of Christian Faculty, Graduate Students, and Families

Many faculty members were a great source of encouragement and support in InterVarsity's history. The following are two examples as they relate to international student work.

Ed and Gladys Baldwin had been faculty advisor for the IVCF chapter at Penn State and led Bible studies with Chinese students. Following their move to Pittsburgh in 1952 to work for Westinghouse, they intentionally looked for a large home near Carnegie Institute and University of Pittsburgh in order to host monthly dinners for international students with American IVCF graduates assisting. Their ministry spanned many years and other cities. The Baldwin's work served as a model of how to serve, how to have conversations, and how to build relationships.

Another faculty member was Dr. Archie McKinney, professor of medicine at the University of Wisconsin in Madison. He was encouraged to help with International student ministry in 1961 by then InterVarsity president, Dr. John Alexander. McKinney resurrected the *Tour of Madison* which was started by Alexander in the late 40s. By 1965, tours and monthly Saturday night dinners and Bible studies were offered. The inductive Bible study method was used, rather than preaching, to help Muslim students feel free to attend. McKinney refers to the ministry as *seed-planting*. The Tour of Madison was picked up by Terrell Smith, an ISM staff worker, and continues to this day.

Graduate students served as volunteers and volunteer staff on campus. When the Committee for Friendly Relations Among Foreign Students (CFR) asked InterVarsity to officially represent them at *Operation O'Hare* to meet new arriving students, twenty-five volunteers met one hundred ten flights from overseas the first year.

In the late 50s, Bill McElwee Miller, an international student specialist in New York City, started a host family program. He looked for one key family, adaptable culturally, purposeful in ministry, having good judgment in the selection of other participant families ... able to exemplify the love of Christ in family life – at work and play.[72] Over one hundred fifty families from twenty-two churches were befriending over three hundred new students in the fall of 1960.

In 1962, Ned Hale was added to the staff serving internationals in Chicago. Two hundred fifty students had continuing relationships with

---

[71] Bieler, 14.
[72] Bieler, 10.

Christians in various churches and campus groups. Over one hundred students and families were participating in monthly coffee-hour in five locations. Many students also spent Thanksgiving in homes.

City Tours and Collaborative Efforts

Tours were an added feature for students in New York during the Thanksgiving houseparty at InterVarsity's Hudson House. International students visited famous sites, and in the evenings played, sang, saw films, and had serious discussions about God.

In Chicago students toured various sites and had Bible discussions. Students from out of town expressed their preference for staying in American homes over the *Chicago Tour*. The next houseparty offered homes stays for students who were feeling isolated in the large universities.

In February 1964, InterVarsity collaborated with other ministries (Campus Crusade for Christ, Chinese for Christ, First Presbyterian Church of Hollywood, Hospitality International, ISI, International Student Service of Southern Baptists, and Navigators) for the second annual one-day training seminar for American Christians on friendship with international students held at Hollywood Presbyterian Church. A year later, another event for Christian international students was offered by IVCF, ISI, Hospitality International, and the Southern Baptists, that featured speakers from different countries and organizations.

An Easter conference at Lake Geneva Wisconson was sponsored by InterVarsity in cooperation with other organizations and attended by seventy-five Christian international students.

Influential Students

There were outstanding students during these years whose commitment to Jesus influenced other people, institutions, and ministries. For example, Nate Mirza, an Iranian student who became a Christian through IVCF during his first quarter at Cal Poly in San Luis Obispo, California, went on to Lebanon, India, and Iran with the Navigators. In 1977, he became the first director of the Navigator's international student ministry, had a ministry among internationals at the University of Wisconsin in Madison (1977-1988), and wrote *Home Again* in 1993. He continues to serve as an encourager to Navigator ISM staff and to returned international students.

Lamin Sanneh was one of the fifteen international students who spent Christmas together at a houseparty at Hudson House in 1963. He was an undergraduate at a small Christian school and had recently converted from Islam in his home country in Gambia. He went on to do advanced studies in Alabama and London, became a professor at Yale Divinity

School, and authored several books.

Daniel Lam from Hong Kong studied engineering at the University of Illinois, Chicago. God used his leadership and passion for evangelism to grow the InterVarsity chapter and lead his Japanese roommate, Masayuki Kamo to Christ who later returned to Japan and served there.

Urbana Mission Conference and Internationals

Lam and his pastor were instrumental in bringing two hundred seventy Chinese students and graduates to Urbana '64. Through special panel discussions, the students considered their responsibilities as missionaries to the world. After graduation, he went into business, partnering with different organizations.

Twenty-three Korean students formed the Korean Students Christian Fellowship in the USA (KSCF) at Urbana '61. In 1962, there were thirteen chapters across the country. Their newsletters included news and challenges: Korea demands heroes who will stand unbent for the Truth, who will not be swayed by fame and power, who will serve rather than be served.[73] Korean students were also encouraged to support the newly formed IVCF in Korea in 1962.

God used Urbana in other ways in the lives of international students which will be addressed later in this chapter.

ISM in Prominent Place

Under the directorship of Charles Troutman (1961-64), International student ministry was the fourth of four purposes of the InterVarsity movement.[74]

It is the purpose of the InterVarsity Christian fellowship to establish and assist groups of students in the universities, colleges, and nursing schools of the United States whose objectives are:

1. To witness to the Lord Jesus Christ as God incarnate, and to seek to lead others to personal faith in Him as Lord and Savior.

2. To deepen and strengthen the spiritual life of students by the study of the Bible, by prayer, and by Christian fellowship.

3. To present the call of God to the foreign mission field, and so help all students to discover God's role for them, at home or abroad, in world-wide evangelization.

4. To befriend and win to Christ students from abroad, and to

---

[73] Bieler, 13.
[74] From Ned Hale's personal archives.

strengthen them in the Christian faith.

Keeping the ISM Vision Alive Without a National Department 1964-1981

In 1964, Paul Little was asked to specialize nationally in evangelism and had to leave the ISM Director position.

In January 1965, after Urbana '64 and the national staff conference, the international student staff stayed for two extra days to write the qualifications and job description for an ISM staff. The two foremost goals of an ISM staff were to evangelize non-Christian internationals and to build up Christian international students. Other qualities include:

1. Definite sense of call particularly to international student work

2. Have some kind of previous experience with international students on campus, as a returned missionary, or as foreign student advisor

3. Spend three months with staff with ongoing international student work to see what can be done with community resources, get new ideas, and counsel

4. Does not need extensive theological training.

Specific responsibilities were meeting new arrivals, visiting foreign student advisors, training families for coffee hour discussion, arranging home visits over holidays, working on special projects that also involve American students, encouraging graduate and faculty involvement, training American student chapters on friendship evangelism, creating evangelistic literature, reading books and recommending them to others, discovering evangelistic films, and finding others who enjoy entertaining students and have a similar philosophy of evangelism.

Seeking to find a place in the organization for ISM, one of the ISM staff in Boston, William "Butch" Dickerson, wrote to Eric Fife, IVCF missions director, about the pros and cons of having ISM in the mission department. He responded that Paul Little continued to advocate about international student work at national directors' meetings, that the word *missionary* would be problematic for ISM, and wondered if the department should be renamed *International Department*.

William "Butch" Dickerson, ISM Coordinator

Dickerson also wrote to Dr. John Alexander, InterVarsity President, about the need for a department head for international student work. After Alexander's meeting with the senior staff, the creation of a department was rejected, and the role of a coordinator was accepted. Dickerson was asked to consider the position by Alexander. Dickerson's reply was, "As you know, ministering to internationals is one of the specifically stated purposes of the Inter-Varsity movement. It does not seem as though we are giving sufficient attention and emphasis to this ministry as a whole and I want to do whatever I can to help bring this emphasis to this ministry."[75]

After discussions with Alexander and two regional directors, two areas of agreement emerged:

1. All international student staff were to be integral members of the area and regional teams. They were not the only staff reaching internationals. They would be responsible to stimulate international outreach and to serve as resource people.

2. ISM staff were to communicate regularly with each other, work together on regional and national conferences, houseparties, and training programs.

As ISM Coordinator, Dickerson would keep the goals of ISM before the movement, staff and board members; see where new work was needed; recruit and train personnel; create materials; encourage Christian internationals; maintain liaison with IFES; coordinate international students transferring within the US; maintain working relationships with NAFSA, Institute of International Education (IIE), CFR; and coordinate international student activities on the national scale.[76]

Dickerson designed a brochure entitled *International Students* with a quote from then Secretary of State, Dean Rusk, "We must be concerned not only with the academic experience, but with the total personal experience of the foreign students who are currently attending American colleges and universities."[77]

The publication also expressed the values and posture that InterVarsity has towards non-Christians and the university. To the non-Christians, it stated that the primary purpose throughout was to encourage the development of lasting friendships and the honest sharing of ideas and commitments. To the university, IVCF insisted upon honesty in all advertising and invitations so that every student would know the type and content of the meeting to which he is being invited. [78]

Dickerson recognized his need for help to get the job done. He looked to Ned Hale's knowledge, experience, and dedicated help. Hale put together a folder of materials to be used for families and churches. Dickerson encouraged Hale to be a part of NAFSA and be involved in COMSEC (community section). William Carr, former ISM staff in the Bay area, wrote a foreign advisor's brochure.

---

[75] Bieler, 20.
[76] Bieler, 19.
[77] Bieler, 20.
[78] Bieler, 20.

The mid-60s

Different staff around the country busied themselves in reaching international students.

In California, Roger Fung oversaw a team of people who sponsored several activities for students from Cal State College Los Angeles, Cal Tech, Fuller Seminary, and Pasadena City College. They included coffee hours, monthly prayer fellowship, socials with American graduates and families, and an Easter houseparty with ISI.

Each staff in California sent a summary of their ISM goals and strategies:

1. Fung put a high priority to exhorting and encouraging Christian internationals even though it requires much time in prayer, counseling, visitation, and friendship with future leaders. He also expressed the need for Christian families near each of the major colleges and universities.

2. Jim Berney hoped for staff who could mobilize the Christian community and organize the work in the Bay area and Peter Kemery suggested the creation of a Greater Bay Area Graduates Fellowship to encourage IVCF groups, assist with ISM, and support IFES work respectively.

3. Jim Rutz's strategy was to make evangelism central. His idea of growth was through addition (contacting internationals and Christian families) and through division (systematically subdividing and allowing new leaders to emerge).

4. Bob Young's brief summary: Make more effective what is already being done in: prayer, loving concern for individuals, Scripture study, leadership training sessions, houseparties, personal work: If we are faithful in this day, there will be fruit for 2000 A.D.[79] Young went on to start the IFES work in Argentina.

In the Chicago area, a total of eight coffee hours were held in the fall of 1965. They had the usual offering of a stimulating film, a guest speaker or singer, and a discussion. In the spring of 1966, they covered Easter topics, John Stott's *Basic Christianity*, heard testimonies, musical performances, and a special guest speaker.

In Michigan, Frank Currie hosted his third coffee hour in May 1966. The talk about prayer led to a student's testimony on the power of prayer in his life. Christian faculty members spoke at different Christmas houseparties at Camp Barakel two hundred miles north of Detroit.

Peter Northrup, Regional Director for the Great Lakes and Central

---

[79] Bieler, 22.

Region, published the different international student events happening in Illinois, Wisconsin, Colorado, and Michigan during the 1965-66 school year. He encouraged staff to put some of the scheduled events in the staff's calendar to get some ideas for their own contexts. He expressed what perhaps other staff and directors felt, "For a long time many of us have been disturbed about the needs of internationals throughout the regions and yet have felt a certain frustration when even thinking about it since other work demands are so pressing and international student work takes so much time."[80]

To help chapters reach out to internationals, a job description for the International Student Chairman on the leadership team was created in January 1966. The objective of the two-page description was that each student in the chapter should make at least one close friend with an international student.[81] It included guidelines for activities from spring to the next summer.

Other events in the mid-60s included a summer *Seminar on Christian Discipleship and Evangelism* in Boston Massachusetts, that focused on basic Christian doctrine, character development, and the church around the world. To address the need to prepare Christian international students for reentry, Hale sent out a bibliography of books about or by famous Christian nationals to encourage and provide vision for Christian international students. Dickerson also hosted a dinner and discussion on culture shock and Rob Marvin of ISI, who had come from visiting returned students in East and West Africa, shared about some of the readjustment difficulties they faced.

In June 1967, Hale compiled a list of cities/schools with the highest population of internationals and those that had an IVCF or ISI staff. He acknowledged the need for a staff member in places like Chicago and New York where there is an on-going hospitality program, otherwise, the work would *rot on the vine.* Placement of new staff would depend on the presence of ministry and financial supporters. His list had New York City, Chicago, Eastern Michigan, San Francisco Bay Area, University of Minnesota, University of Wisconsin, Honolulu Hawaii, University of Washington, Washington, DC, and Los Angeles.

Partnerships in the 70s

Beginning in 1970, IVCF, Campus Crusade, and ISI co-sponsored at least six Easter conferences for internationals in Philadelphia. Speakers came from sponsoring groups, a mission group, as well as university and seminary professors including Dr. Yamauchi of Miami University and

---

[80] Bieler, 22.
[81] Bieler, 24.

Myron Augsburger of Eastern Mennonite College and Seminary. The sponsorship for the sixth conference expanded to include: Egyptian Evangelical Fellowship, Indo-Pakistani Christian Fellowship, International Missionary Fellowship (Korean), Japanese Evangelical Fellowship, Philadelphia House, and Spanish Baptist Church.

Elective seminars in 1975 included Modern Science and Christianity, The Challenge of World Mission, Prospects for the Future Evangelization of China, Archeology and the Old and New Testament, The Making of a Christian Family, How to Witness, and Spiritual Dimension of Patient Care.

In Philadelphia, IVCF held a variety of international events in 1970-71. There were Bible studies and prayer groups on Tuesdays and Thursdays, and a home party held monthly from October to March. Homes in Lancaster County Pennsylvania, Northern New Jersey, New York City, and the Philadelphia suburbs were available for international students.

The International Christian Training Center, directed by Korean staff worker Young Son, was held from 1973-74 at IVCF's Hudson House in Nyack New York. It was designed to train people in communicating the good news of Jesus Christ to foreign students who would become future world leaders.

Houseparties at Bear Trap Ranch

In 1971, Hale, who served as ISM staff in the 1960s, became the Central Regional Director over fourteen states and Director of Bear Trap Ranch. He set a policy of assigning every staff in the region to serve at an international houseparty once in their first four years on staff. This structure helped many staff learn about reaching international students that they could apply back on campus.

The houseparty followed the format of a tour of the Air Force Academy, Pike's Peak, or Garden of the Gods in Colorado Springs, and a featured speaker. A Swiss staff confirmed what Paul Little had said: the whole world revolves around personal relationships. Another staff shared that the houseparty was one of the most effective on-the-job training tools in evangelism offered by IV… I have never enjoyed being on staff at a conference more![82]

International students had very positive feedback and wanted to come again because it transformed their lives.

International Students in 1970s *HIS* Magazines

HIS, the leading InterVarsity publication at that time, published six articles

---

[82] Bieler, 28.

focusing on international student ministry:

1. *Witness with a Sears Catalog* was about assisting a Japanese spouse learn English and become a Christian

2. *Strategic Ministry* encouraged combining hospitality and Bible study

3. *Where to Go to Buy Boots: A Foreign Student May need Your Advice* regarding a Ghanaian student who encouraged Americans to include internationals in their lives to combat prejudices the student may encounter

4. *Culture Shock in Minnesota or Can a Foreign Student Find Happiness with an American Hamburger?* where an Indian student described how to address culture shock

5. *Am I My (International) Brother's Keeper?* was about the difference hospitality can make for the Gospel

6. *The Chinese are Coming! The Chinese are Coming!* David Adeney, then the vice-president of *IFES*, encouraged developing friendships with the new wave of Chinese students.

References to international students were present in five other *HIS* articles. Interviews of international students and an international panel appeared in *The Missionary My Country Needs, On the Way,* and *Wanted: One Missions Secretary.* Paul Little and Dr. Alexander gave international student examples in the article *Plan for Stalled Conversations* and *A Forum on Campus Impact* respectively.

Recruitment, Training, and Missions

Hale sent those who were interested in starting an international student ministry in the fall of 1975 numerous items from his vast collection of resources which included: data from the IIE, various articles (by staff, from *HIS* magazine, and from *Newsweek*), a Bible study guide, information about NAFSA and ISI, and a motivational article by Paul Little.

In 1977, David Bryant joined InterVarsity as a missions specialist. He developed and introduced *Breakthrough* weekend conferences across the country to explore what *world Christian discipleship* means. The Saturday afternoon schedule suggested a panel of international students to share about their experiences, thoughts about Jesus, and impression of missionaries. As a response, American students were asked to write their answer to the question: *Would you be willing for God to breakthrough to you to reach the ends of the earth through an international friendship? Could this begin for you this week? How?*

Ned Hale: 1981-2000

Ned Hale became the National Director of the *resurrected* International Student Ministry department in 1981under the leadership of Bob Fryling. Fryling, as the National Campus Ministry Director, wanted to bring more diversity and multi-ethnic specialists into the organization due to the rising ethnic diversity on campuses, especially in urban centers.

Hale was the natural choice to be at the helm of this department. He had a prominent voice and involvement in international student ministry in the previous years with a wide influence through various leadership positions in the organization.

When Hale joined InterVarsity staff in 1962, there were four ISM staff, called staff *specialists* or *focused* staff, out of a total of about forty serving the whole nation (10%). His original vision was to enlist a new body of staff workers working within each region and local staff team. In the 80s he succeeded in securing an ISM staff in about half of the area's staff teams.

Growth in the 80s

Houseparties or evangelistic holiday conferences continued to be led by staff, volunteers or faculty at InterVarsity's major training centers, Bear Trap Ranch in Colorado (now owned by Foundation of the Heart Ministry), and Cedar Campus in Michigan. Speakers at these events in the 80s included professors, mission leaders, pastors, former InterVarsity staff, and staff from other campus organizations like ISI and Navigators. Speakers had to have a good combination of strong cross-cultural/relational skills, competence on the subject matter, and ability to present the Gospel in a clear, compelling, and sensitive manner.

A wave of new interest in international students came through the new multi-media show called *Friends* and the release of an InterVarsity Press book, *The World at Your Doorstep* by Dr. Lawson Lau for Urbana '84. As a result, Bear Trap Ranch launched a houseparty during Urbana. Hale wrote, "More students than usual came, and everyone was asking, "why hadn't we thought of doing this before?" Up until then, staff had been seen as the backbone of houseparties. But with increasing numbers of community volunteers getting involved and helping, it had become apparent that staff could attend an Urbana, volunteers could run a houseparty, non-Christians could attend the houseparty, and Christian internationals could choose between the two."[83]

In response to this rise in interest, Bear Trap added a second houseparty over New Year's, and Cedar Campus in Michigan did the same. This became a tradition into the 1990s. Other campus ministries also

---

[83] Ned Hale, "Reflections on Houseparties for International Students," (ism.intervarsity.org).

brought their students from Houston, Oklahoma, and Kansas.

Houseparties were perfect venues for non-Christians. Hale shared about an Iranian student who attended one of the houseparties where he was speaking. It was during the hostage crisis when Iranian students were politically polarized. The student took him aside quietly and said,

"Mr. Hale, I don't know what to do. I want to believe in Jesus, but I can't. Please help me to believe!" He went on to explain, "I grew up in Qom, the home city of Khomeini, and one of the most conservative of Muslim cities. I wanted to be a Mullah when I grew up. Now I am a student in South Dakota and am so disillusioned with Islam I can no longer be a Muslim. Yet I have always had a strong faith in God and cannot live without religion. All my life I have been told that I must not believe in Jesus as Christians do...that it is the sin of blasphemy against God to do so. Can you help me believe in Jesus?[84]

Hale gave him further words from Scripture and at his request, a brief explanation of the Trinity. He said he would let Hale know his decision. In response to Hale's follow-up letter weeks later, he wrote, "Dear Brother Hale: This past weekend I was baptized in the church here in Vermillion. Praise God!"[85] Years later, Hale met someone of the same church who confirmed all that transpired and the student's continuing walk with Jesus and his fellowship with other Christians.

The Birth of the Association of Christian Ministries to Internationals (ACMI)[86]

In May 1981, a special consultation for individuals, churches, campus groups, and mission agencies was held in Colorado Springs Colorado at the ISI headquarters. This consultation was the brainchild of Dr. Jack Burke,[87] an InterVarsity alumnus of the University of Oregon, who was serving as the Director of the International Students and Scholars Services at the University of Houston.

Hale, the man who had always believed and engaged in collaboration

---

[84] Hale, "Reflections."
[85] Hale, "Reflections."
[86] ACMI's name was later changed to Association of Christians Ministering Among Internationals.
[87] As a college student, Burke heard that his staff worker, Rosalyn Rinker, required InterVarsity students to have international friends. Desiring to meet the staff's expectation, he introduced himself to the first international student he saw while crossing the street on campus. The student, from Baghdad, Iraq, even said yes to his invitation to attend a weekend InterVarsity retreat on the Oregon Coast! This friendship and other international connections solidified Burke's vision for outreach among international students. His path led him to be an advisor for international students at a university. From an interview by Lisa Espineli Chinn during an InterVarsity ISM staff gathering at ACMI Conference in the early 2000s.

with other ministries, became one of the founding fathers of ACMI that was birthed after the initial consultation. Among the InterVarsity staff invited to the consultation by Hale were Dr. Katie Rawson, ISM staff in Raleigh North Carolina, Amy Jen, ISM staff in Indiana, and Lisa Espineli, campus staff in the DC area.

Hale served on the ACMI Board in its early years and watched it grow as its annual gatherings were held at different cities in the USA and Canada. This new association showcased the promise and reality of what international student work would look like if we knew, trusted, and learned from each other. It facilitated sharing of strength, gifts, and resources to advance God's work among international students in the United States.

Addressing the conferees at ACMI in 2003, Hale shared,

> One of my greatest delights was being part of the formation of the Association of Christians Ministering to Internationals (ACMI) in 1981, which provided in its annual conferences a resource for training new staff and volunteer workers. It was invaluable to InterVarsity staff and volunteers in reaffirming our ISM vision and calling, and helped keep us all from discouragement or growing "weary in well doing" by relating to the larger body of international workers…Many paid staff of churches and mission groups or volunteer ISM workers who were not attached to an organization found a home in ACMI. Many of us in the larger organizations with an ISM Department were able to join hands speaking and giving training seminars to the benefit of others both within and outside our organizations who came to the annual training conferences. ACMI has gone a long way toward bringing all the Evangelicals together and instilling a new vision for prayer and cooperative ministries at local campus levels.[88]

Hale also participated in the first ACMI consultation in 1987 in Denver Colorado, and a second one a few years later to discuss relevant issues in international student ministry and the future of ACMI. In the early 1990s, more than twenty ISM leaders began meeting together at the ISI national offices in Colorado Springs Colorado.

One of the practical things that came out of these meetings was the invitation from Paul Cedar of Mission America to form an *International Student Track* at their annual meetings attended by hundreds of pastors. As a result, a new partnership was forged to distribute the *Jesus Film* in many languages among international students.

Hale encouraged IVCF ISM specialists to attend and present seminars

---

[88] Ned Hale, "Appreciating Our Past, God's Sovereign Work," (Plenary address, ACMI Conference, Wheaton College, Wheaton Illinois), May 28, 2003.

at the ACMI annual conferences. He also used the event to gather IVCF staff for special meetings. In addition, an evening dessert was organized for InterVarsity friends and alumni for fellowship, and other alumni and friends of InterVarsity for a special evening dessert to acknowledge and affirm their shared vision for international students. He also attached ISM staff meetings to the ACMI conferences.

Resources and Publications

To supplement the work on the campus, resources were needed. As mentioned earlier, *Friends* was a landmark 30-minute slide-tape show developed by the ISM department and 2100, the multi-media arm of InterVarsity. It had an amazing exposure to a total of 75,000 delegates in four Urbana conferences from 1984-1993. Later it was converted to a video format which was widely used in churches and campus groups all over America.

In 1996, 2100 introduced *Bridging the Gap*, an educational and training tool for students and community volunteers.

At two Urbanas (84 and 87), *book-of-the-day* choices were InterVarsity Press (IVP) books, *Internationals at Your Doorstep* by Lawson Lau and *China at Your Doorstep* by Stacey Bieler and Dick Andrews respectively. These advanced the ministry among internationals in InterVarsity and in other groups. The exponential growth of Chinese students in the U.S., and their new interest in Christianity after Tiananmen Square in 1989, often led to an abundance of Chinese students and scholars at ISM gatherings.

In 1999, IVP published *Passport to the Bible*. This was written by a team of seven ISM staff and edited by Fred Wagner. The book featured four basic Biblical themes in twenty-four cross-cultural Bibles studies and offered definition of new and difficult vocabulary. Despite initial doubts by IVP in terms of its marketability, the book sold thousands of copies and is still available today.

Internationals on Campus

The ISM department launched the journal, *Internationals on Campus (IOC)*, in 1984. It contained articles by ISM staff, volunteers, faculty members, testimonies of international student conversions and journeys of faith, calendar of upcoming events (including non-InterVarsity conferences) relevant excerpts from books and articles, and prayer requests.

The journal had extensive reports on the post-Urbana conferences for Christian International Students and served as the department's main communication tool within InterVarsity and the larger Christian community. Some of the topics included in the journal were: *The Social Creation of Identity: Reexamining Myths About Chinese Society; Why I Rejected the Christian Faith; From a Communist to a Christian; The Philosophical and Moral Bases of American Democracy.* On several occasions, the journal also included articles and prayer requests submitted by Canadian ISM staff.

Conference for Christian International Students and Scholars

One of the many benefits of the formation of ACMI was the increased camaraderie and exchange of ministry ideas among its members. On one occasion, Ned Hale and Leiton Chinn, on loan from ISI to Interaction, Inc., were talking when Chinn shared an idea of having an extended three to four-day post-Urbana conference for international students. Liking the idea, Hale held the first *Conference for Christian International Students and Scholars* in 1988. This additional event consistently attracted over 400 Christian internationals from over seventy countries of the world. In 2001, it was attended by 870 delegates from eighty countries. The participants heard from twenty plenary speakers who shared at various panels and individual talks and chose from eighty elective seminars.

Hale reflected, "Many students commented that this gathering of fellow believers was a 'taste of heaven' for them and much needed preparation both for going back to campus and after that going into places of work around the world as ambassadors for Christ and workers in His Kingdom."[89]

God did an astonishing thing in January 1994. Japanese and Korean students demonstrated reconciliation. God had already moved the hearts of the Japanese students during Urbana '93 through Peter Cha's talk about reconciliation and that challenge became stronger during the international student conference. God's Spirit worked in the hearts of a Korean delegate to approach the Japanese delegation to join them in prayer. As the Koreans were interceding for the Japanese, the prayer was changed into a prayer of confession and repentance. Korean brothers and sisters, weeping, began to repent for their hardened hearts for not forgiving Japan.[90] When it was the Japanese turn to pray, they, too, confessed their sins. Setsu Kuroda (now Shimizu) recalled,

> It was then that we knew that we were forgiven by the Lord and by our brothers and sisters in Christ. And we felt bound together in a way we had never known before… Korean brothers and sisters sang a blessing song to us having their hands opened and reached towards us. We, Japanese delegates, knelt down on the floor in front of them

---

[89] Hale, "Appreciating Our Past."
[90] Setsu Kuroda, "The Re-Creation of God's Family Through Reconciliation," (*Internationals on Campus,* Spring, 1994), 4.

with our hands stretched out and open to receive this blessing from them. We then sang, "Shine, Jesus, Shine" together with all our hearts and souls and with prayers of thanksgiving. Tears of joy ran down our cheeks and delightful laughter filled the room. It was as though the transparent wall between us was completely taken away and there was no longer anything to stop us to enjoy and love one another. What a night![91]

What God was already doing between these two groups was revealed to the whole gathering, as the Japanese were led to repent for the sins of their nation and ask forgiveness from the rest of the conference participants. Terrell Smith, an ISM staff reported,

Setsu confessed weeping, as all 40 of the Japanese knelt and bowed their heads to the floor (the most significant and deep way to bow in their culture). "We repent of our sins in front of you, asking for your forgiveness. We are truly sorry." The Korean students then "deep bowed" to the Japanese in order to say "thank you" and to forgive.[92]

This public and powerful display of forgiveness and reconciliation convicted other groups like the Tamils for their hostility and violence against the Singhalese in Sri Lanka.[93]

The presence and sacrifice of Urbana speakers from other countries to stay extra days to be at this gathering added an immeasurable value to the event. At one conference, Lindsay Brown of Wales, David Zac Niringeye of Uganda, Lisa Espineli Chinn of the Philippines, and Ajith Fernando of Sri Lanka were featured speakers.

The immense impact of these special-focused conferences is undeniable. God used them to encourage and challenge international students in their own Christian walk and witness as students, and as they returned to their home countries. These conferences were offered five times, the last one held in January 2001.

Gifted Staff on the Team

Over the decades, God provided gifted and committed ISM staff to InterVarsity. Some notable ones who served under Hale were Terrell Smith, Katie Rawson, and Fred Wagner.

Terrell Smith, a graduate of University of California, Berkeley, joined InterVarsity in 1971. He first served on staff in California and Wisconsin,

---

[91] Kuroda, "The Re-Creation of God's Family."
[92] Terrell Smith, "Conference Brings International Students Together, and to Christ," InterVarsity Conference, Fall, 1994.
[93] A similar reconciliation experience happened at one of the International Students Tracks at an Urbana conference between Chinese from Taiwan, Hong Kong, and China.

then served for eleven years in Germany with *Studenmission en Deutschland* (SMD), a sister movement of InterVarsity/USA. He authored *The World at Your Doorstep* which was published in German. He also co-authored *Passport to the Bible* (IVP), and *Exploring the Bible*, a fourteen-week Bible study guide designed for international students and scholars. As an evangelist among international students, he enjoyed playing ping-pong and hanging out at the student center at University of Wisconsin-Madison, answering their questions, and delighting them with his stories. He also served as a Training Coordinator and later as director of the Urbana '06 International Students Track (IST).

Dr. Katie Rawson, who has two doctorates (French Literature and Missiology), has over thirty years of ministry experience. Her time in France as an international student led her to ISM in InterVarsity. She served for many years as ISM staff at UCLA and North Carolina State University, then as ISM Training Coordinator and as Regional ISM Coordinator for the Blue Ridge Region. She is currently the Senior Resource Developer. Rawson was a co-author of *I-DIG: International Discipleship Groups*, and *Passport to the Bible.* She communicated her heart for cross-cultural evangelism in her book, *Crossing Cultures with Jesus,* an IVP book released in November 2015.

In 1986, Dr. Fred Wagner left his role as IVCF Northwest Regional Director to rebuild InterVarsity's work among international students. He drew from his early experience with the Portland International Fellowship (PIF) which was formed in 1961 by concerned Christians, including InterVarsity alumni, who were reaching international students. Wagner wove together the remaining threads of ISM in Portland. Thus was born the ministry of FOCUS (Friendships of Overseas Citizens and University Students), a multi-organizational approach to ISM in Portland which continues to this day.[94] He directed the ISM work in the Northwest until 2005 and led numerous Global Projects (short-term mission teams) to China.

Parting Words

Hale reviewed God's faithfulness in InterVarsity and recounted the many advances in reaching international students. In 2003 he gave a plenary talk at the ACMI conference and shared his personal satisfaction:

> As I approach the years when I may not be able to accomplish as much physically, I find that the vision for "loving the stranger in our midst " (**Leviticus 19:34**) continues to grow in me. . . in the memories of past

---

[94] Fred Wagner, "History of ISM in Portland," (article in Espineli Chinn archives).

personal ministries with individuals are sustaining to me, especially those who have found flourishing ministries of their own and where the ministry vision has multiplied in their lives. Some international Christians became my lasting friends and went on eventually to become missionaries and Christian leaders.

He concluded with,

My hope is that in coming years, not only InterVarsity, but all of God's people involved in higher education, will find that in "loving the stranger" on campus, they are actually not only obeying Jesus Christ but loving Him in loving the stranger. Perhaps even then it will still be a surprise to us all when we stand before the Master and he says: "I was a stranger and you welcomed me...just as you did it to one of the least of these...you did it to me" (**Matthew 25:35, 40**). May God give us all His grace and wisdom to form loving relationships with internationals and to introduce them into cross-cultural relationships and groups where they can see the love of Christ displayed in all its ethnic diversity and power![95]

Ned Hale is a humble man who was tireless in his pursuit of what would be good for international students. He gathered and shared resources that would equip staff and volunteers. Hale is also a very generous man who has a larger Kingdom view in mind and joyfully partnered and promoted other ministries.

Lisa Espineli Chinn: First Woman and Former International Student ISM Director (2000-2014)

Lisa Espineli first came to the United States in 1970 on a study leave from InterVarsity Christian Fellowship of the Philippines. She enrolled as a graduate student in Communications at Wheaton Graduate School. Soon after arriving, she was connected with InterVarsity/USA and worked as a volunteer helping to pioneer the student work at the College of DuPage in 1971. After graduation, she worked among international students in Philadelphia as an intern with Young Son at Philadelphia House. In 1973, she returned to the Philippines to resume her work with IVCF and to take on new responsibilities.

Six years later, Espineli returned to the USA and served as Intervarsity/USA campus staff in the Washington, DC area. In 1981, she married Leiton E. Chinn, an ISI staff member. Upon completing three years of her InterVarsity campus work commitment, she joined her husband

---

[95] Hale, "Appreciating Our Past."

with ISI. They settled and started a family in Fairfax Virginia, and in 1985 launched their church's ministry among international students called T.I.P.S. (Truro International Programs and Services). In 1990 they joined Interaction, Inc. (a ministry among missionary kids and international students), and later International Ministries Fellowship, led by the former ISI president, Dr. Hal Guffey, to promote ISM globally.

Espineli Chinn served as speaker at several InterVarsity ISM conferences. In July 1999, an InterVarsity director sent her a request for names to recommend for the position of InterVarsity's ISM National Director. After looking at the position description and wrestling whether to pursue it, Espineli Chinn eventually applied and went for an interview. On January 19, 2000, she was offered the position and six months later moved to Madison Wisconsin with her husband and three teenage children.

International Witnessing Communities (IWCs)

Espineli Chinn's foremost responsibility was to provide leadership for ISM's mission: To establish and advance at colleges and universities witnessing communities of international students and faculty who follow Jesus as Savior and Lord: growing in love for God, God's word, God's people of every ethnicity and culture, and God's purposes in the world.

This new vision statement, written during Hale's leadership, had to be understood clearly by ISM staff and communicated compellingly to the rest of the movement. Katie Rawson and other ISM staff wrote a helpful introductory paper on International Witnessing Communities which included its distinctives, critical success factors, and steps in establishing them.[96]

ISM groups around the country looked different from each other. Some were student-led groups; others had a strong partnership with churches, were multi-cultural, and trans-generational. Under Espineli Chinn's leadership, three ISM Models of Ministry were introduced:

1. *International Witnessing Community* – A predominantly international student-led fellowship with a focus on reaching and equipping international students.

2. *Integrated Model* – A fellowship of American and international students seeking to form one witnessing community with shared ownership, responsibilities, leadership, and vision.

3. *Collaborative Model* – An ongoing collaboration of staff and volunteers from various para-church organizations/churches

---

[96] Katie Rawson, Julia Thorne, and Tom Lawrence, "International Witnessing Communities: An Introduction for InterVarsity Staff," (Lisa Espineli Chinn's Personal Archives), late 90s.

(ranging from a handful of churches to a city-wide network) to offer a larger number of services and activities.[97]

All models embrace the goals of welcome and hospitality, evangelism with cultural sensitivity, discipleship and Christian formation, and sending internationals as world changers.

Entering Another Culture

Being a cross-cultural missionary from the Philippines to US college students, Espineli Chinn knew that learning another culture took a considerable amount of time observing, listening, and asking questions. These basic cross-cultural competencies were called on when she re-entered InterVarsity. She observed and listened. She discovered the unwritten rules at the National Service Center. Espineli Chinn tried to understand who made decisions and who were the influential people in this corporate culture. She learned what it meant to be a spiritual and an organizational leader, as well as how to lead as an Asian-American woman. Her first major assignment was teaching the Scriptures at the fall Regional Directors' meeting.

Putting ISM on the InterVarsity Map

Espineli Chinn quickly realized that one of her responsibilities was to be the ISM ambassador to the whole movement and beyond and put ISM on the InterVarsity map. With numerous initiatives and legitimate focused groups on campus, area directors and regional directors could only do so much. How do you influence the whole movement to embrace outreach among internationals? The answer: One staff at a time. One area director at a time. One region at a time.

She wanted to demonstrate to the whole movement that she was a team player, and a servant. Once the door opened for her to be invited by other regions to speak, she took on these responsibilities with a sense of urgency, stewardship, and service. Even if they did not invite her to speak on international students, she used international student illustrations, when appropriate, in her talks. In the end, the regions got to know her, her heart, and her call to reach international students. In one region, her conference talks led to conversations that resulted in an explosive growth in interest and later, in staff serving internationals in that location.[98] At the end of her fourth year on the job, her supervisor wrote, "You have

---

[97] Eva Liu Glick, Paul Holt, Ron Riesinger, Heidi Chew, and Lisa Espineli Chinn "ISM Models: An Overview," (ism.intervarsity.org) May 8, 2013.

[98] In 2004, ten ISM staff were serving in the Southern California Region; Lisa Espineli Chinn's Report to the Collegiate Ministry Leadership Team (CMLT), February 25, 2004.

achieved the primary goal we wanted: ISM is no longer on the side of the road."[99]

At Urbana '03 she was one of two Bible teachers and the first female ever asked to expound the Bible. Her phrase, *Yes, Your Majesty,* became a signature statement for that convention. Three years later she was asked to give the commitment talk at Urbana '06.

Spearheading, pioneering prime mover

One of the helpful ways that InterVarsity served its leaders at that time, was to assist them by discovering their strengths and gifts through SIMA – a non-psychological, qualitative process for clearly identifying a person's innate giftedness – their motivated strengths, interests, contextual circumstances, preferred roles, and motivational drives. Espineli Chinn's SIMA summary included "She is a spearheading, pioneering prime mover. Lisa is the type of leader who brings new life to an old organization."

During her tenure as ISM National Director, Espineli Chinn spearheaded many new projects:

1. *International Students Track (IST) at Urbana* was introduced at Urbana '03. This acceptance-only residential track replaced the International student conference after Urbana (Post-Urbana conference). The integrated track featured two afternoon plenary sessions, seminars specific to international students' needs, country prayer groups in the evening, and numerous opportunities for ISM staff and students to process the Urbana experience. All four ISTs, under her leadership, were transformative and strategic in international students' lives.

2. *INK conferences:* One of her early dreams was to start a Reentry Institute for select international students planning to return home. In 2002, several ISM leaders from other organizations gathered together. She shared the idea of a conference she called Internationals for Gods' Kingdom (INK) that would address the reentry issues in a conference setting. She directed the first INK conference with the theme: *Equipping Students for Life's Decisions and Transitions* at Wheaton College in 2004, concurrent with the ACMI annual conference. Its main thrust was to help international students with their Post Academic Transitions (PAT) and what it meant to live as Kingdom citizens as they transition into a career, back home, or into another country. It was in collaboration with Navigators, ISM, and Chi Alpha. Succeeding conferences were led by different ministries: Chi Alpha, ISI, and International

---

[99] Roger Anderson, Performance Review for 2003-2004, Lisa Espineli Chinn's Personal Archives.

Friendships, Inc. (IFI).

3. *I-GIG:* The buzz word in InterVarsity in the early 2000's was *GIGs* (Groups Investigating God), evangelistic Bible study small groups. Espineli Chinn gathered a team of Bible study writers led by Janet Payne, an ISM staff, to put together an international student version which became known as the *I-GIG.* It was specifically designed for Americans and international college students to be able to lead a series of Bible studies with their international student friends.

4. *ISM at a Glance:* Looking for ways to engage with InterVarsity directors about ISM, Espineli Chinn created *ISM at a Glance,* a one-page regional summary of schools where international students are, how many internationals are involved in their chapters, a comparative look at the past year, and how their ISM work has progressed. This simple tool gave a regional director a quick glance at how they were doing in reaching international students. Encouraged by *ISM at a Glance,* the Asian American Ministries developed their own version – *AAM at a Glance.*

5. *In Touch with ISM:* To communicate regularly and faster, Espineli Chinn introduced *In Touch with ISM,* an email newsletter sent every two months to all staff, volunteers, staff directors, and select external recipients. This was an improved version of her first email communique, *ISM Family News.*

6. *National ISM Staff Conference:* For the first five years of Espineli Chinn's tenure as ISM National Director, ISM staff around the country did not have a regular staff conference, since scheduling any event was always a challenge in an already full staff school calendar. Instead, in 2002 and 2005 they gathered for a day or two prior to a National Staff Conference for fellowship, sharing of ISM work, and prayer. ISM staff met each other at Urbana, IST, and at the National Staff Conference every three years. Espineli Chinn thought another gathering was needed to bring solidarity, community, identity, learning, training, and spiritual input. In January 2006, Espineli Chinn brought all the ISM staff and volunteers together in San Diego California for the very first *ISM National Staff Conference.* She led three of these national conferences and her successor continued the tradition in 2015.

7. *Big Ten Initiative (BTI)* is a list of the top ten priority schools that ISM should focus on. It started as a simple list of priority schools for ISM. Hale, who served as Research and Resource Person, included in the list additional information: a profile of international student population, a brief history of InterVarsity

presence on that campus, what InterVarsity and other groups are doing in reaching international students, supportive churches, and world changers among its international student alumni. On the list were the following universities: Texas, Harvard, Michigan, Ohio State, Wisconsin, California (Berkeley), Massachusetts Institute of Technology (MIT), Stanford, Columbia, and Minnesota.

On paper, it was a compelling tool to rally the staff directors to put their resources and support this initiative. Unfortunately, it did not find traction among staff directors, who were already overwhelmed with their own area and regional priorities, not to mention the other IVCF focused ministries knocking at their doors for attention and action, e.g. Greek Ministry, Asian American Ministry, Black Campus Ministry, Nurses, etc.

However, in 2006, a generous donor expressed interest in supporting new ISM chapter plants in the country. After a rigorous application process under the National Chapter Planting Strategy *over a dozen* ISM chapters were started around the country. The *BTI* is still a valuable document which can be updated periodically.

8. *Customs and Culture: A Reentry Simulation Game:* In the mid-80s, Espineli Chinn developed this game that featured a lively and interactive exchange between a returning international student and a Customs Agent. It was produced by the ISM department in 2005 and became a popular resource used by other movements in New Zealand, Australia, and the UK.

9. *Crossing Culture: Here and Now Friendships with International Students:* Paul Little's booklet, *Guide to International Friendship* had been widely used for many years and needed to be updated. With funding available and in short notice, Espineli Chinn wrote *Crossing Cultures Here and Now: Friendships with International Students,* in time for distribution to all delegates at Urbana '06 (17,000). The booklet has served the department for many years and in July 2017, an expanded and updated edition was released by the department with the title: *Friendships with International Students: Crossing Cultures Here and Now* by Lisa Espineli Chinn and Brian Hart.

10. *Coming to America/Returning Home to Your Country:* This booklet describes the two sides of transition for international students. Espineli Chinn purposely left out any Christian reference to make it available on secular campuses. Since its publication in 2011, staff, volunteers, and other organization have purchased

copies to give to their incoming international students.

11. *Back Home*: In 2011 Espineli Chinn wrote a thirty-day devotional guide to address the different feelings and issues that confront a returnee. The booklet is also helpful for Study Abroad students and short-term mission participants. Its latest edition was released in July 2017.

12. *Think Home* was originally written by Espineli Chinn in 1984 while serving with her husband with ISI. This pioneering publication for reentry of Christian international students inspired other reentry publications by various organizations, adaptations, and has been translated into several languages. After acquiring the copyright from ISI in 2008, a 2011 edition was published by the ISM department. In cooperation with ISI, *Think Home* has been given to international students in at least two Urbana Mission Conventions.

ISM Leadership Team

Without a team of dedicated and gifted ISM staff, Espineli Chinn would not have been able to move the ISM vision forward. Her Leadership Team was composed of ISM Area Directors and ISM Regional champions, including Heidi Chew, Eva Glick, Paul Holt, Collete Michal, Sarah Mitchell, Katie Rawson, Ron Riesinger, and Terrell Smith in the field.

At the National Service Center, Brian Hart replaced Hale as the ISM Resource Specialist in 2005. Espineli Chinn later promoted him as the ISM Associate Director of Communications. Less than a year later, Lucy Hsu joined the ISM Department team serving as Espineli Chinn's Administrative Assistant. Her experience, expertise, and passion for internationals made her the ideal person for the job. Espineli Chinn called her ISM team in Madison Wisconsin her *dream team*. Members of her leadership team and other staff launched several international student conferences across the country.

This team in the field and at the National Service Center labored tirelessly to inform, educate, inspire, train, and equip staff and students, as well as produce resources for the whole movement. Espineli Chinn said at the first ISM conference in 2006, "God has given me a leadership team of colleagues who care for one another and who work hard at a common vision. Companion in leadership is a gift. Burden-bearers are a must if we are to effectively serve."[100]

---

[100] Lisa Espineli Chinn, "What a Job!" Talk given at the first National ISM Staff Conference in January 2006.

Structural Challenges

In the InterVarsity/USA organizational set up, the ISM director in Madison does not directly supervise every ISM staff in the country, except those working for the department at the National Service Center.[101] The campus staff are supervised by directors on the field. The role of ISM Regional Directors/Champions is to influence the area and region. ISM Area Directors in a region can fully supervise their staff but still need to work closely with the region for a unified vision and direction. Therefore, these complex relationships call for clear communication of job responsibilities and expectations with a spirit of trust plus a common commitment to the InterVarsity vision. A team of staff directors and non-line regional coordinators worked on addressing the challenge of matrix management. Both Espineli Chinn and her leadership team learned how to be team players as well as ISM champions.

Finding creative solutions to organizational hurdles helped advance ISM. For example, InterVarsity provides an annual training opportunity for their staff called NISET (National Institute for Staff Education and Training) which is included in the staff's budget. Eager to combine the goals of NISET with ACMI's annual training conference, Espineli Chinn negotiated accepting their ACMI attendance and an additional three days of focused ISM training as a legitimate NISET course. The ISM department enjoyed this arrangement for four years until NISET changed its focus.

The Internet in 2000

Like many ministries world-wide, the rapid growth of the internet impacted the way ministry was going to be done. Questions moved from, *do you have a website?* to *how attractive, accessible, and interactive is your website? How much are you willing to invest in a state-of-the-art website? How do we take advantage of the web in promoting our publications? How long do we keep printing hard copies?*

In 2000 the InterVarsity/USA's IT (Information Technology) department helped develop the ISM website. Ned Hale served as ISM Web Manager, a job that harnessed his love for history and research. By February 1, 2002, ISM's new website was launched with over 500 articles, photos, news, and announcements of events and conferences.

To print or put it on line? That was the next question to answer in relation to *Internationals on Campus (IOC)*, the printed journal of the department. It became fiscally responsible to begin putting it on line. The last printed *IOC* publication was the 2008-2009 issue on *Reaching South*

---

[101] This is true of other ministries like Greek, Nurses, Arts, Athletes, Asian American, Black Student ministries.

Asians.

The ISM website has since undergone many changes and needed compliance with the national InterVarsity branding. Today the website is attractive and accessible, filled with helpful resources, arranged in easy-to-find topics. While the website is the go-to place for information and on-line resources, the ISM department continues to produce printed materials, and sell resources and other products.

Consultations and International Student Conferences

In the early years of Espineli Chinn's tenure, she was invited to different ISM regional consultations. These meetings brought her face-to-face with campus staff who shared about ISM opportunities and challenges on their campuses. Through case studies, she understood the issues the staff and the region faced as they sought to advance the work among international students.

One significant and historic consultation was a meeting of select staff from the Graduate and Faculty Ministry (GFM) and ISM on November 15, 2004. Both Cam Anderson, the GFM Director, and Espineli Chinn recognized the significant overlap in the students they were serving.

After drawing from recent national policies in international education, post 9-11, and a brief history of ISM in InterVarsity, Espineli Chinn concluded her opening talk,

> I want us to see God leading us into this new day of unique opportunities and cooperation. . . Our work with International graduate students is a call to our movement and the church as a whole, to actively participate in the world God has brought to our door, embracing and loving those who are different from us, temporarily borrowing their eyes in order to see a world much bigger than ours, and humbly offering them God's gift of new life in Christ. The programs we put in place today will determine how serious we are about loving people of every ethnicity and culture. Our work with international graduate students prepares us for a multicultural world and raises the bar for what it means to be God's global citizens.[102]

The two ministries worked practical applications of the partnership, including encouraging attendance in each other's events. Seed planting. Trust building. Communication. Years later, through continued communication and relational investments, GFM appointed Michael Gehrling, the first ISM GFM Coordinator in 2014.

---

[102] Lisa Espineli Chinn, "A New Day for Ministry Among International Students and Scholars: The Impact of Politics on the Academy." Opening talk at the ISM/GFM Consultation, November 15, 2004.

Leadership Changes

In the fourteen years that Espineli Chinn led the ISM Department, she served under two presidents, Dr. Steve Hayner (2000-2001) and Dr. Alec Hill (2001-2014), and three supervisors. Her first supervisor was Roger Anderson, National Field Director, who was instrumental in setting up Espineli Chinn for wider influence in the movement by recommending strategic people, events, and conversations to engage with to advance the ISM vision. She learned from his skillful and discerning leadership.

In 2004, the new Strategic Ministries Department (SMD) was formed to house the ISM, Greek Ministry, NCF, Evangelism, and Leadership and Training Department. Barney Ford, a senior leader in InterVarsity was named Vice-President for Strategic Ministries. Ford led this team for four years with humility, sensitivity, and strength as he sought various ways to advocate and access resources for the department. In the Fall of 2008, Paul Tokunaga became the new Vice-President for Strategic Ministries. He also served as National Coordinator of the Asian American Ministries. Under his leadership, he opened other avenues of growth through the ISM *Daniel Project,* [103] which Espineli Chinn directed. In preparation for this responsibility, Tokunaga sent Espineli Chinn to an elite leadership training course with the Center for Creative Leadership in Greensboro North Carolina. Espineli Chinn moved with each change of leadership with flexibility to win over each new supervisor with the compelling ISM vision.

In 2016, Tom Lin, another seasoned staff, became the new InterVarsity President and under his leadership a new organizational structure was rolled out. The SMD was dissolved to give way to a new department: *Focused Ministries.* This department included all the ministries among international students, athletes, Greeks, arts students, nurses, Asian Americans, Black Campus Ministry, Latino, and native Americans under the leadership of Joe Ho, former Asian American Ministries Director.

IFES and World Assemblies

World Assemblies are triennial gatherings for IFES national movements. Espineli Chinn represented ISM at five World Assemblies, regularly leading a seminar on ISM and engaging in robust conversations about international students with global colleagues. In the fall of 2002, she went to Singapore and Malaysia to lead ISM seminars with Ron Riesinger, ISM Coordinator in the Northwest, and to respond to the growing number of international students in the area. She also spoke at an IFES conference in New Zealand and attended a conference of the Australian Fellowship of

---

[103] The Daniel Project is the premier Leadership Training program in InterVarsity.

Evangelical Students.

Many IFES movements were spearheading outreach to international students around the world. Staff members of European movements came to a number of ISM consultations where Espineli Chinn was speaking. Her reentry Book, *Think Home,* was adapted and translated by several IFES movements.

Growth and Goodwill

Espineli Chinn's dream of attracting younger staff was realized. Young ISM staff included Asian American staff who found in ISM a ministry that affirmed and utilized their own cultural history and ethnicity. Several non-Americans and former international students joined the staff: Jovin Adjeitey (Ghana), Bok Chew (Malaysia), Heidi Chew (Germany), and Adri Fonteijn (Netherlands). Espineli Chinn served as Program Director of the 2014 triennial National Staff Conference during her last year as ISM Director. This assignment created additional goodwill for ISM from the whole movement.

For fourteen years, Espineli Chinn led the ISM department. During that period, ISM specialist staff grew from fifty to one hundred thirty-six, a 172% increase. International students involved in InterVarsity increased by 112% from 2280 students in 2000 to 4829 in 2014. Paul Tokunaga, her supervisor, summarized her tenure this way, "I continue to live with awe and wonder at the great staff I have the privilege to supervise. . . To watch you in action is to observe an artist, a prophet, a shepherd, a leader of leaders."[104]

Marc Papai ISM Director, 2014 to the present

Marc Papai worked for eight years as a chemical engineer before joining staff, later served as the Ohio Division Director of the Great Lakes East Region, and picked up the baton of ISM Department's leadership in July 2014. Papai was one of the early advocates for ISM who spoke of it in this way, "I challenge you to think of a more strategic group of people to influence for the gospel, or a single ministry that encompasses so much of what we as InterVarsity staff hold dear: witness to the nations, multi-ethnic relationships, evangelism, real partnership with local churches, and loving God's purposes in the world."[105]

God had prepared Papai for this new role. In his application for the job, he wrote,

I have been up close to ISM for the whole 26 years with InterVarsity,

---

[104] Paul Tokunga, Performance Review of Lisa Espineli Chinn, 2014.
[105] What *If?* An ISM Brochure.

from a GIG I began with a Chinese student, two weeks into my first year on staff in 1987, to leading internationals to Christ, through building Grad/ISM chapters at 2 schools, to hiring ISM staff in my division, to speaking at ISM events, to advocating for it among many audiences, to fostering ISM work among the churches I have been a part of.[106]

As he began his new role, he was introduced not only to the staff of InterVarsity, but to the broader ISM community at the ACMI annual conference in Atlanta Georgia in June 2014. He has been pleasantly surprised by the spirit of partnership among ISM leaders in other organizations.

Papai leads with a vision and is eager to help staff maintain a healthy and vibrant spiritual life as they engage in ministry. Espineli Chinn writes of her successor, "He has a solid leadership track and a pastor's heart. I count on his diligence in listening to God's voice as he enters his new role. Under his leadership I am confident that ISM will experience new areas of growth and expansion."[107]

Papai has identified five key initiatives under his leadership:[108]

1. **Ministry to High Identity Religious Students –** this includes students from Muslim and Hindu backgrounds, meeting them in serious and respectful conversations, like "Peace Feasts" where groups of Christians and Muslims gather for a meal, tea, and conversation about their faiths.

2. **Integration of ISM across InterVarsity –** IV has over 1000 chapters in the US, and there are international students on every one of the campuses represented. Relationship, cultural understanding, hospitality and respect, the character and mission of Jesus to disciple the nations—are values **all** of InterVarsity cherishes, and so helping more of those chapters launch ISM mission among their friends is the focus of this initiative.

3. **Reentry Preparation –** We long to see the mission of Jesus grow around the world, and international graduates who are well prepared vocationally and spiritually will serve this end beyond any other ministry we can do in the US.

Papai launched a Reentry Project in 2016. It was a year-long project for a select number of gifted international students to understand the critical factors for successful reentry. The project addressed how to sustain their faith through spiritual formation, cross cultural leadership, and fulfilling

---

[106] Paul Tokunaga, announcement of the new ISM Director, Marc Papai, May 15, 2014
[107] Lisa Espineli Chinn, "Passing the Baton," June 2014 Prayer Letter.
[108] Marc Papai, email to Lisa Espineli Chinn, April 18, 2017.

the Lord's calling courageously in family, workplace, community, and church. In June 2017, the first cohort graduated. Successive cohorts are being planned.

4. **Leadership Development** – Jesus' strategy in expanding His mission was to prepare ordinary people to pursue extraordinary character and leadership in community. IV is developing a pathway for students, who begin far from Christ, to become "big sisters and brothers" to others—leaders who can shepherd and shape their younger siblings for their own work of shepherding and shaping others into faith and service.

5. **Resources** – InterVarsity is committed to creating and sharing the very best resources—digital, video, print—to assist others in doing effective ministry among internationals. We are currently focusing on "bite size" resources to help students and volunteers who know almost nothing about ISM to begin with a few easy steps. These new resources are called 3X3 which address ten different topics on ministry among international students (3 important facts to know, 3 common mistakes to avoid, and 3 suggested activities to try on campus). We also are expanding our video production to better tell the amazing stories of internationals.

Papai has picked up the baton of ISM leadership with ease, humility, and confidence. He is responsibly building on the past and is fulfilling his dreams and those of his predecessors.

Conclusion

This history traces the thread of commitment by InterVarsity/USA to international student ministry. The values of personal relationships, Bible study, evangelism, prayer, hospitality, service, leadership development, community, volunteers, conferences, events, resources, innovation, partnership, organizational resilience and will, and gifted and devoted staff are strongly woven in the ISM ministry fabric.

For seventy-six years, InterVarsity/USA has been true to its primary calling to reach university students with the Gospel. Reaching international students is a part of its DNA. God called various leaders at different times in its history to lead and advocate for this ministry. Through leadership and organizational changes and challenges, shifting campus realities, campus access battles, and global uncertainties, InterVarsity is committed to reach the world for God's Kingdom through a flourishing international student ministry.

BIBLIOGRAPHY

Adeney, David. *China: Christian Students Face Revolution.* Downers Grove, IL: InterVarsity Press. 1973.

Anderson, Roger. Performance Review for 2003-2004. Lisa Espineli Chinn's Personal Archives.

Armitage, Carolyn. *Reaching for the Goal: The Life Story of David Adeney.* Wheaton, IL: Harold Shaw Publishers. 1993.

Bieler, Stacey. *The History of International Student Ministry in InterVarsity Christian Fellowship-USA, 1944-1980 – USA.* Unpublished. 2009.

Chinn, Leiton Edward. *Global Diasporas in Mission,* Regnum Edinburgh Centenary Series, Vol. 23. 2014.

Espineli Chinn, Lisa. "A New Day for Ministry Among International Students and Scholars: The Impact of Politics on the Academy." Opening talk at the ISM/GFM Consultation. November 15, 2004.

Espineli Chinn, Lisa. "Passing the Baton." Prayer Letter. June 2014.

Espineli Chinn, Lisa. Report to the Collegiate Ministry Leadership Team (CMLT). February 25, 2004.

Espineli Chinn, Lisa. "What a Job!" Talk at the National ISM Staff Conference. January 2006.

Finley, Bob. *Reformation in Foreign Missions.* Charlottesville, VA: Christian Aid Mission. 2010.

Glick, Eva Liu, Paul Holt, Ron Riesinger, Heidi Chew and Lisa Espineli Chinn, "ISM Models: An Overview." May 8, 2013. <*ism.intervarsity.org*>

Hunt, Keith and Gladys. *For Christ and the University.* Downers Grove, IL: InterVarsity Press. 1991.

Hale, Ned. "Appreciating Our Past, God's Sovereign Work." Plenary address, ACMI conference, Wheaton College, Wheaton Illinois. May 28, 2003.

Hale, Ned. "Reflections on Houseparties for International Students." <*ism.intervarsity.org*>

Kuroda, Setsu. "The Re-Creation of God's Family Through Reconciliation," *Internationals on Campus.* Spring. 1994.

Papai, Marc. Email to Lisa Espineli Chinn. April 18, 2017.

MacLeod, A. Donald. *C. Stacey Woods and the Evangelical Rediscovery of the University.* Downers Grove, IL: InterVarsity Press. 2007.

Rawson, Katie, Julia Thorne, Tom Lawrence. "International Witnessing Communities: An Introduction for InterVarsity Staff." From Lisa

Espineli Chinn's Personal Archives. Late 1990s.

Smith, Terrell. "Conference Brings International Students Together, and to Christ." InterVarsity Conference. Fall, 1994.

Thompson, Mary, Ed. *Unofficial Ambassadors: The Story of International Service.* New York, NY: International Student Service. 1982.

Tokunga, Paul. Announcement of the new ISM Director, Marc Papai. May 15, 2014.

Tokunga, Paul. Performance Review of Lisa Espineli Chinn. 2014.

Wagner, Fred. "History of ISM in Portland." Article in Espineli Chinn archives.

What If? ISM Brochure. Circa 2002.

Woods, C. Stacey. *The Growth of a Work of God: The Story of the Early Days of InterVarsity Christian Fellowship.* Downers Grove, IL: InterVarsity Press. 1978.

CHAPTER 7
THE GLOBAL ISM MOVEMENT EMERGING FROM DIASPORA MISSIONS ON CAMPUSES: FROM JOHN R. MOTT TO "LAUSANNE"[1]

Leiton Edward Chinn

Preface: The International Student Ministry (ISM) movement began in the early 20th Century in the United States by mission visionary John R. Mott and is growing globally, more notably in the early 21st century, via the Lausanne Movement. The following Regional overviews of the worldwide expansion of ministry among students from other countries incorporates relevant publications by the author.

International Student Ministry (ISM) as a Strategic Diaspora Mission

International students and scholars represent the diaspora category of those who voluntarily leave their homeland to reside in a host country, usually temporarily, for educational and professional advancement. Ministry among international students is highly strategic for numerous reasons, the most obvious of which is that tertiary students will be the future leaders of the world and influence every sphere of society. The United States Department of State's Bureau of Educational and Cultural Affairs lists hundreds of world leaders today who studied in the USA. Many church and mission leaders have become Christians and were discipled while studying in another country and have returned home to contribute to the expansion of God's kingdom in their homeland and region. International students are a global mission field that is already present on our campuses, in our communities, and often in our churches. International Student Ministry (ISM) is a classic example of *"glocal"* missions, of global missions locally, and provides the opportunity for world missions at home and in our homes. International students who come from a context that is resistant to or ignorant about Christianity may

---

[1] This paper is an updated and revised version of an earlier publication by the author: "Diaspora Missions on Campuses: John R. Mott and a Centennial Overview of the International Student Ministry Movement in North America," (revised, updated edition from *Global Diasporas and Mission*, Regnum Edinburgh Series, Vol 23, 2014, permission granted by publisher).

appreciate the freedom to explore the Bible and learn of Jesus Christ. All members of a Christian fellowship or church, from children to grandparents, can engage in mutual cross-cultural friendship, extending sincere hospitality. Equally important are the reciprocal benefits of intercultural learning from international scholars who may also provide missional perspectives about their homeland and culture. A tremendous benefit of ISM is the amount of funding not having to be spent or provided for in a budget to "send" missionaries to the multitude of nations represented by a group of international students at nearby campuses. Pastors of local congregations with ISM can attest that it is certainly one of the best values for missions because of the extremely low costs associated with it and the tremendous potential for global impact by church members. Additionally, ISM transcends personal mission involvement beyond prayer, financial support, and encouragement of missionaries, to actually being a missionary, all without leaving home. This opportunity has blessed many who had felt called to traditional missionary service earlier in life, yet did not go abroad. Another strategic aspect of ISM is that Christian students who return home may serve as ready-made missionaries to their own people, either as market-place witnesses or as professional Christian workers. Returnees could also provide valuable networking connections and advocacy for further mission partnership endeavors in their homeland on behalf of Christians in their former host-country of study, or elsewhere.

A large majority of Christians will not be called to relocate to another country to engage in Christian service, rather to remain at home. Nevertheless, remaining at home does not negate the opportunity to be involved in reaching the world that God brings to nearby campuses. Each year more and more international students are arriving on more campuses around the world. In 2013 there were over 4.3 million tertiary students studying in another country, and since 2000, the number of international students increased by 77% for an average annual growth rate of 6.6%.[2] Projected growth of the international student population for 2025 is 8 million.[3] As the number of globally mobile students increase, the opportunities to be involved in ISM continue to grow. Jesus told the disciples to lift their eyes to the harvest fields ripe for harvest; so too are the multinational fields on our campuses ready for cultivation and harvest. However, our churches, ministries, and laborers for the harvest must have eyes to see international students, open hearts and a hospitable spirit to welcome with genuine friendship, a willingness to pray for and serve them, courage to appropriately share the love of God with them, and a

---

[2] OECD (2011), *Education at a Glance 2013: Highlights,* (OECD Publishing), 3.
[3] "Revolutions Ahead in International Student Mobility," (University World News, April 2017).

desire to encourage them to be transformative agents for the welfare of their nations and the world, by and with the grace of God.

John R. Mott: Unrecognized Visionary and Founder of the ISM Movement

John Raleigh Mott's stellar leadership role as Chair of the famous 1910 World Missionary Conference (WMC) in Edinburgh Scotland has been recounted in association with the four global mission events commemorating the centennial of Edinburgh 1910: Edinburgh 2010; Tokyo 2010; Cape Town 2010; and Boston 2010. Church historians and students of mission remember the additional missional leadership achievements of John R. Mott that are listed in his biography written when he received the 1946 Nobel Peace Prize: that of serving as the first chairman of the Student Volunteer Movement for Foreign Missions (SVMFM); chair of the International Missionary Council; first general secretary of the World's Student Christian Federation (WSCF); national secretary of the Intercollegiate YMCA, and several other leadership positions.[4] What is not mentioned in that biography nor in some other biographies, and what is generally not known by most mission enthusiasts, is that John R. Mott was the visionary who launched the first national Christian service ministry for international students, called the Committee on Friendly Relations Among Foreign Students, or, CFR.

What is amazing is that he undertook creating the CFR in April of 1911, a month after returning from extensive evangelistic meetings in Europe and Egypt, and in the midst of very heavy demands to chair the Continuation Committee of the 1910 WMC, which was in addition to his other simultaneous leadership roles. It should be noted that Mott's calling and passion was to promote the expansion of mission mobilization through student movements in the USA and globally, primarily through his long-term leadership with the SVMFM, the WSCF, and the YMCA and its International Committee. His resolute focus was on "Carrying the Gospel to All the Non-Christian World," which was the title of his keynote address and of the Report of Commission I, which he chaired, of the 1910 WMC.[5] Mott's gaze was outward from America to the other nations, and he traveled extensively overseas to raise up indigenous student missionary endeavors. So how did it come about that Mott would even consider starting a new ministry or service in the USA, and to such a minority

---

[4] Frederick W. Haberman, ed., *Nobel Lectures, Peace 1926-1950,* (Amsterdam: Elsevier Publishing Company, 1972).
[5] World Missionary Conference 1910, *Report of Commission I, Carrying the Gospel to All the Non-Christian World,* (Edinburgh and London: Oliphant, Anderson, & Ferrier; New York, Chicago, and Toronto: Fleming H Revell, 1910).

population of students? The establishment of the CFR was clearly the intervention of the sovereign and providential act of God that led Mott to adapt to the American context, some preliminary ideas he had in 1907, of raising funds for establishing Christian hostels in Japan to not only serve Japanese students, but also the students from China, Korea, and other Asian nations at the Imperial University in Tokyo.[6] The seed idea of raising funds to benefit international students was planted in John R. Mott's mind. In 1909 Mott helped to organize a service agency for Chinese students in the USA and he provided funds from the Foreign Division of the YMCA. This very likely captured the thinking and interest of John R. Mott, and he set out to spread the message of the need to serve the increasing number of foreign students in the USA.[7] In April, 1911, while Mott was meeting in New York with Cleveland Dodge, chairman of the International Committee of the YMCA, he spoke of the need to raise funds to help foreign students. Dodge offered to introduce Mott to Andrew Carnegie that afternoon, and as a result, Carnegie made a gift of $10,000 and challenged Dodge to match it, which he did. On the way back to Dodge's home they met a friend who also committed $10,000. The following night Mott was sharing the story of God's provision in a committee meeting, and a member contributed another $8,000. Thus, in two days nearly all the funds necessary to start the ministry among international students was begun, and the CFR was birthed.[8] Supplemental support came from the YMCA's International Committee.

Within a few years the CRF produced a handbook for foreign students, which lists a variety of foundational services that remain as essential good works of ISMs a century later.[9] Besides the actual services rendered by the volunteers of the CFR, many of whom were recruited from churches via local YMCAs, the CFR motivated and substantially assisted other partners in the cause of caring for foreign students, with the result being the eventual establishment of numerous organizations and agencies.[10] Two such organizations that are indebted to the CFR are 1) NAFSA: Association of International Educators and 2) the Institute of International Education.[11]

---

[6] Basil Mathews, *John R. Mott: World Citizen,* (New York and London: Harper & Brothers, 1934), 412.

[7] Mary A. Thompson (ed.), *Unofficial Ambassadors: The Story of International Student Service,* (New York: International Student Service, 1982), 22.

[8] Thompson, *Unofficial Ambassadors,* 23.

[9] Charles D. Hurrey, *Educational Guide: A Handbook of Useful Information for Foreign Students in the United States of America,* (New York: The Committee on Friendly Relations Among Foreign Students, 1917), 7.

[10] Thompson, *Unofficial Ambassadors,* 14, 32, and 89-112.

[11] NAFSA was originally called National Association of Foreign Student Advisors. Later it was changed to the National Association of Foreign Student Affairs. It currently goes by NAFSA: Association of International Educators.

The CFR changed its name to International Student Services (ISS) in 1965, and after five decades, its magnanimous services and secondment of personnel had laid broad foundations for the care and service of students from abroad and the healthy beginnings of the ISM movement in North America.

Before continuing with a brief overview of the development of the ISM movement in North America, it would be insightful to obtain a glimpse of the growing vision John R. Mott had for ministry among international students. A cursory review of some of the publications by and about John R. Mott as well as published records of some of his speeches and papers reveal an increasing awareness of the gradually growing presence and needs of foreign-born scholars prior to and after the advent of the twentieth century. There were few foreign-born students before 1900 and Mott's references about them were scarce. As the numbers increased in the new century, so did Mott's recognition of the new challenge and mission opportunity. His observations and comments about international students were found in at least 15 publications. The space limitations of this study do not allow an exhaustive chronological demonstration of Mott's notice of and subsequent response to the expanding reality of the world's future leadership being educated in other countries. However, here are a few examples of excerpts about or by Mott related to foreign students:
It was undoubtedly out of this conference (Dwight L. Moody's summer conference in 1886 at Mt. Hermon/Northfield, MA) that the idea of a student volunteer organization to assist foreign students in the United States grew in the mind of Mott...But it was not to come to fruition for more than twenty-five years.[12]

Shortly after the formation of the World's Student Christian Federation in Sweden in 1895 during which Mott was named General Secretary, he wrote that the second goal of the Federation was "to grapple successfully with the problem of the spiritual welfare of the large number of foreign students in different countries."[13]

After two previous trips to China had seen minimal response to his evangelistic messages in 1896 and 1901, Mott was surprised at the large turnout of students in Hong Kong in 1906. He noticed that on the platform of the largest theater in the country, there were fifty leading officials of the province, and that most had returned from studies in Japan or America. On a trip to Japan around the same time, he found that nearly all the professors at the Imperial University in Tokyo had attained degrees in

---

[12] Thompson, *Unofficial Ambassadors*, 18.
[13] Robert C. Mackie and Others, *Layman Extraordinary: John R. Mott 1865-1955*, (New York: Associated Press, 1965), 30.

Europe or America.[14]

In 1907 Mott wrote, "I have no hesitation in saying that I consider that this first generation of modern Chinese students (in America) presents to us the greatest opportunity that I have ever known. This first wave...will furnish a vastly disproportionate share of the leaders of the New China. I maintain that nothing could be more important than Christianizing these men...I am haunted with solicitude lest we miss this absolutely unique opportunity."[15]

In an address given at the Student Volunteer Missionary Union Conference in Liverpool, England in 1908, Mott said, "Our hearts have been touched by the appeal of Dr. Datta this evening concerning Indian students in Britain. But possibly we have not been aware of the...scores of Indian students in Tokyo...nearly 700 Korean students there, also not a few students from the Philippines and Siam. There have been as many as 15,000 students there at one time from China. Without doubt Japan is leading the Orient educationally."[16]

Also, in a 1908 report on The Chinese Student Migration to Tokyo, Mott mentions that

> The Young Men's Christian Association Movement of China and Japan was the first agency to recognize the urgent need of putting forth special efforts to help these young men who were thrown as strangers in the midst of a strange city...the YMCA could do more in one year in Tokyo to reach the future leaders of China than could be done in China by all the missionaries in that country...Without doubt, the key to China is in Tokyo, and that key is in the hands of the Chinese students who are to furnish the leaders of that mighty nation.[17]

Mott's chairman's Report at the Sixth International Convention of the SVMFM in Rochester, New York in 1910 cites, "One opportunity, which comes to most of us but which many have overlooked, is that presented by the large and increasing number of students among us from Oriental and other non-Christian lands...These foreign students are in position to do more than some missionaries to extend the domain of Christ among their countrymen."[18]

The detrimental effects of negative experiences by international students are mentioned in Mott's brief referral to foreign students in his

---

[14] John R. Mott, *The Present World Situation*, (New York: Student Volunteer Movement for Foreign Missions, 1914), 45-49.

[15] Mathews, *John R. Mott*, 416.

[16] *Addresses and Papers of John R. Mott*, 6 vols., (New York: Associated Press, 1946), I.329; hereafter *APJRM* I.

[17] *Addresses and Papers of John R. Mott*, 6 vols., (The World's Student Christian Federation: New York: Associated Press, 1947), II.549-555.

[18] *APJRM*, I.139.

chairman's Report of Commission I for the 1910 WMC: "On their return, some of them as teachers, editors, and Government officials constitute a great barrier to the spread of the Gospel. This has been notably true of many Chinese and Korean students on their return from Japan."[19]

In February 1911, two months before organizing the CRF, Mott was on an extensive evangelistic tour of Europe, and declined an invitation to meet Germany's Kaiser at the Palace. Instead, he chose to "give this time to the universities of Switzerland...the fact that more than half of them (students) were from Eastern Europe, – Bulgarians, Serbs, Romanians, Czechs, and above all Russians...with a dominant misconception that Christianity must everywhere be synonymous with government oppression...a matter of forms and ceremonies and superstitions."[20]

At the Seventh International Convention of the SVMFM meeting in Kansas City in 1914, chairman Mott reminds the delegates that international students in North America who "consecrate their lives to Christ's cause could do far more to the advancement of His Kingdom among their peers than an equal number of foreign missionaries," and that relating with foreign students will "make more vivid and real to us the meaning of the missionary enterprise."[21]

Also in 1914 Mott penned a comprehensive rationale for ISM and included, "The best agency for dealing with foreign students is that of the Christian Student Movements... efficient and fruitful as has been their work in the past, the time has come when these organizations should plan more comprehensively to influence for Christ this important class of students....Possibly no one thing can be done by Christian forces which will do more to accomplish our great end."[22]

Further commendations for involvement in ISM by John R. Mott are found in his reports and addresses at the SVMFM Conventions in Des Moines Iowa (1920), Detroit Michigan (1928), and Indianapolis Indiana (1936).

Post-World War II Expansion of Nationwide ISMs in North America

After the launch of the CFR in 1911 there was about a 40-year hiatus in the development of other national ISMs. The lone exception was the initial directive, in 1944, by the board of InterVarsity USA for its staff to include international students in their campus outreach. In addition to its General Secretary, C. Stacey Woods, (who was himself a former international

---

[19] World Missionary Conference 1910, 24.
[20] Mathews, *John R. Mott*, 165.
[21] *APJRM*, I.166.
[22] Mott, *The Present World Situation*, 140-46.

student from Australia at Wheaton College), two of the early InterVarsity USA leadership staff with overseas experience and a mission's responsibility, Christy Wilson and David Adeney, sought to increase the level of awareness for ISM. Adeney became the first Director of ISM for InterVarsity USA in 1952, and by the following year was engaging in partnerships with CFR.[23] InterVarsity Canada began its ISM in 1952.

The next national ISM to form was International Students Inc (ISI) in 1953 under the leadership of Bob Finley, who was forced out of missionary service in China after the Communist revolution in 1949. Finley noticed that many of the revolutionary Chinese leaders had become communist while studying abroad and they returned as instrumental leaders of the revolution.[24]

The impact of the returned Chinese student leaders from studying abroad was foundational in his vision that international students in America could be influential Christian leaders upon return to their homelands, and this potential contributed to his establishing ISI.

The decadal growth and starting years of other national ISMs are summarized as follows:

Period	International Student Ministries and Their Starting Years
1950s	Southern Baptist Convention (1955)
1960s	Ambassadors for Christ with focus on Chinese (1963); Campus Crusade for Christ (1968, now called Cru; suspended in mid-70s and re-started in 1983 as Bridges International)
1970s	Navigators (1977); International Friendships Inc. (1979)
1980s	Association of Christians Ministering among Internationals (1981); Reformed University Fellowship-International (PCA denomination) (1983); International Student Ministries Canada (1984); China Outreach Ministries (1988); Chi Alpha (Assemblies of God) (1989)

---

[23] Stacey Bieler, "The History of International Student Ministry in InterVarsity USA 1944-81," (unpublished paper, 2011), available at Resources on the website of the Association of Christians Ministering among Internationals: www.acmi-ism.org
[24] Bob Finley, *Reformation in Foreign Missions,* (Charlottesville, VA: Christian Aid Mission, 2010), 34.

1990s	Horizons International (1990); Japanese Christian Fellowship Network specializing in Returnee ministry (1990); InterFACE Ministries (1991); ISM Inc (Lutheran Church Missouri Synod) (1996)

The Historical Development of the International Student Ministry Movement in the USA is a paper by this author detailing various ISMs from the 1950s to 1979.

A significant advance in the ISM movement in North America began through the catalytic network of ISM workers and annual conferences of the Association of Christian Ministries to Internationals (ACMI, a.k.a. Association of Christians Ministering among Internationals) established in 1981. This author served as President of ACMI from 1999 to 2008, during which period leaders of ISMs from other countries were invited to the annual ACMI conferences and the international participants were granted complimentary membership in the Association. In subsequent years the ACMI Board decided that ACMI's identity would expand beyond a North American network to a global connection of members.

In 1911 when John R. Mott started the Committee on Friendly Relations among Foreign Students there were only 4,856 foreign students in the United States.[25] A century later in 2011, there were 723,277.[26] The *Open Doors 2018* annual census of the Institute of International Education reported 1,094,792 international students at US institutions, of which 363,340 came from China and 196,271 from India. What are some missiological implications that these students will be among the leaders of the next two major powers in the world, as well as the two most populated nations?

Canada was projected to have 450,000 international students by 2022.[27] This goal was surpassed in 2018 with over 572,000 students which represented a 16% jump from 2017. In 2018 International Student Ministries Canada (ISMC) had 600+ staff and volunteers serving at 52 campuses in 20 cities.

The opportunities for engaging in diaspora missions on North American campuses have never been as great as they are now. The question is, will the Church actually see them, and if so, how will the people of God respond? A century ago John R. Mott had his eyes fixed on the world, not only out there beyond the seas, but also right here where

---

[25] "Quick Studies: A Brief History of the 20th Century and NAFSA, Selected Milestones Along the Way to the Golden Anniversary," *International Educator,* 8:2-3, Spring, 1998, 16.
[26] Patricia Chow and Rajika Bhandari, "Fast Facts," *Open Doors 2011: Report on International Educational Exchange,* (Washington DC: Institute of International Education, 2011).
[27] ICEF *Monitor,* July 18, 2017.

students from other nations were coming ashore and enrolling in local colleges and universities. He saw them and did what he could. May we do the same.

Expansion of ISM in Europe:

The following overview of national or major ISMs in Europe is gleaned out of *ISM: From Blind Spot to Vision*,[28] reports by European leaders of the International Fellowship of Evangelical Students (IFES), and Friends International of the U.K.

United Kingdom:

UCCF: the Christian Unions (part of the IFES movement)

Freddy Crittenden pioneered overseas student ministry in the post-World War II era and served as the first Overseas Students' Secretary of the InterVarsity Fellowship in 1959, until 1973.[29]

In the 1980s there were a few scattered UCCF ISMs. A UCCF International Student office was in London, yet there was nothing coordinated, e.g. no training or sharing of ideas/resources. It was in this context that Max and Pat Kershaw (missionaries with International Students Inc) came from the US and encouraged the establishment of a UK ISM, initially called International Student Christian Services, later changed to Friends International. UCCF warmly welcomed the idea of a new ministry among foreign students. Together, UCCF and ISCS decided that UCCF would continue to work on campuses through the CUs, and ISCS would be church based. It was a very good relationship as many CUs were delighted to have this specific help. Many Friends International staff and volunteers had a CU/UCCF background. Indeed, in most places where Friends International established new international student ministries the key supporters in the churches tended to be "grown up" CU members who had a continuing heart for International students.[30] The first National Director of ISCS was Gordon Showell-Rogers, who had returned to the UK after serving with IFES in Austria[31] (www.uccf.org.uk).

Churches

In 1963 John Stott's All Souls, Langham Place, became the first church

---

[28] Leiton E. Chinn, *International Student Ministry: From Blind-Spot to Vision*, unpublished paper for the Lausanne Diaspora Strategies Consultation, Manila, 2009, updated August 2017.
[29] Catherine Weston, *Mission Possible: The Story of Friends International*, (Friends International, 2006), 5.
[30] Report from Gwyneth Haden, former UCCF staff, currently with Friends International, August 2017.
[31] Report from Lindsay Brown, with IFES for over 30 years, serving variously as European Regional Secretary, International General Secretary, and other capacities, August 2017.

to appoint an ISM staff in the U.K. Starting in the latter 80s more churches became involved, primarily through the ministry of Friends International. International Students Christian Services (ISCS); now called Friends International

- 1985 (Catherine Weston's *Mission Impossible: The Story of Friends International*) has an excellent history of ISM beginnings with the IVF/CU/UCCF to the birth of ISCS/Friends International in 1985, and its development up to 2006
- 70 staff at about 35 cities (of which some have multiple campuses)
- www.friendsinternational.org.uk

Overseas Missionary Fellowship (OMF)

- 1988
- Eight "Diaspora" staff doing ISM with Chinese, Japanese, Thai
- www.omf.org/omf/uk/omf_at_work/omf_at_work_in_the_uk

Navigators

- 2001
- 10 staff
- www.navigators.co.uk/ism

Germany:

SMD (part of IFES)

- 1970s
- In the 1980s Terrell Smith, of IVCF-USA, was seconded to SMD to develop groups working with internationals in 20+ cities in Germany.[32]
- Three staff
- www.international.smd.org/en

OMF

- 1988
- Five staff reaching Chinese, Japanese
- www.omf.org/omf/deutschland/asien

Switzerland:

VBG (IFES)

- 1990s
- Two staff plus leaders in three cities
- www.evbg.ch/isa

---

[32] Lindsay Brown report

Netherlands:

IFES

- 1988 various IFES campus ministries began reaching international students; formed a platform to coordinate ISMs in 1991
- 10 staff, many volunteers in about 15 cities
- www.ifes-ism.nl

OMF

- 2008
- One staff; Chinese
- www.omf.org/omf/nederland/azie_info

Finland:

Partnership between IFES, International Christian Union and International Church in Helsinki

France:

Un Coeur Pour le Monde

- 11 staff
- www.uncoeurpourlemonde.org

IFES Europe Initiatives: see: www.ism-ifeseurope.org

Italy, Portugal, Austria, Poland, Ukraine, Spain, Belgium, Ireland, Czech Republic, and other countries of Europe had or have IFES ISM.

The earliest Europe-wide ISM meetings, held at Mittersill in Austria, were driven by Lindsay Brown, as General Secretary of the IFES Europe region.[33] When Mittersill became too small IFES and ISCS ran triennial conferences at Bischofsheim on the East German border in the 90s.[34] Currently IFES holds ISM consultations in different locations in Europe, such as Poland, Czech Republic, and Germany.

Expansion in Africa:

Besides South Africa as the leading receiving country of international students in the continent, there is increasing interest for ISM in Kenya and Ghana.

South Africa

Bridge (University of Stellenbosch, 3,000 international students)

- 2000
- Two full-time couples, 20 part-time volunteers
- www.sun.ac.za/bridge

---

[33] Report from Gordon Showell-Rogers, August 2017.
[34] Gwyneth Hayden report.

Ibero/Latin America

Currently ISM is at the pre-emergent stage.

Expansion in Asia-Pacific

This region not only sends the largest number of international students, it is growing as a destination region as well. Numerous reports identify China as becoming a leading destination of foreign students and scholars.[35] The following summary of ISMs in the Asia-Pacific region is from this author's updated, unpublished paper, *ISM: From Blind-Spot to Vision*, 2017.

Philippines:

Diliman Bible Church & Diliman Campus Bible Church, Manila
- the Outreach to International Students (OIS) began in 1982 and ministers to students at the University of the Philippines

FOCUS, University of the Philippines Los Banos & RICE Institute
- couple churches involved at UPLB and RICE Research Institute in mid-70s-80s, then formed FOCUS in 1987
- One full-time volunteer staff, 10 part-time staff from four churches

Union Church, Manila, has some ISM engagement

InterVarsity Christian Fellowship (IVCF) has had fluctuating ISM involvement since 1980s; no ISM staff currently, though one may be added by 2020

Korea:

Scientists & Engineers Members, International, Daejeon City
Cooperative outreach to international scientists and students
- 1995
- Two full-time, 21 part-time staff, 120 volunteer teachers, 20 locations
- www.semintl.org

International Student Fellowship (ISF)
- 1997
- 80 staff
- www.isfkorea.org

InterVarsity Fellowship (IVF)
- began in local cities in 2002, then nationally in 2007
- One full-time, three part-time staff, several volunteer student leaders

---

[35] Leiton E. Chinn, "International Student Ministry: The Most Strategic Yet Least Expensive Global Mission Opportunity Arises in Asia," *Globalization and Mission*, Timothy K. Park and Steve K. Eom, eds., (East West Center for Missions Research and Development, 2017), 457.

- http://club.cyworld.com/ismivf (for members only)

KOSTA (Korean Students Abroad); ministry among Korean international students by Korean churches; name changed to Evangelical Fellowship of Korean Students International; annual conferences in many countries

- began in 1986 in Washington DC
- www.kosta.org

Singapore:

FOCUS, initially a reunion fellowship of alumni who attended the FOCUS ministry of Park Street Church, Boston, MA; now has outreach to international students

- probably started in 70s
- One volunteer director

Fellowship of Evangelical Students (FES)

- 11 staff integrating ISM as part of the campus staff ministry role; provided leadership for National ISM Consultations in 2006 and 2007; logistical support for the Lausanne Asia-Pacific Regional ISM Leaders Forum in 2010 and 2015
- also, staff for Chinese students and Indonesian students
- www.fessingapore.org

Malaysia:

First Baptist Church, Kuala Lumpur

- late 1990s
- ISM Committee with 20 workers; hosted the first conference in Malaysia for international students in April 2009, with 110 participants from at least 16 countries
- www.fbc.com.my/ism

Fellowship of Evangelical Students (FES)

- has had full-time and part-time staff assigned for ISM
- www.fes.org.my

Australia:

Australian Fellowship of Evangelical Students (AFES)

- outreach to international students at least by the 1960s
- 1998--first dedicated staff for ISM; ISM called "FOCUS"
- 53 full-time and part-time staff; 18 Apprentices at 28 campuses
- www.afes.org.au/focus

Overseas Christian Fellowship (OCF)

- International students in Sydney invited international students from Melbourne and Adelaide to join them for an Easter camp in

1958. This led to formation of OCF in 1959 and the 50th Annual Convention was held in Malacca, Malaysia.
- Since its inception, OCF has been a student-led movement, which now has 15 OCF Centres throughout Australia
- www.ocfaustralia.org

Navigators
- 1980
- 12 staff
- www.navigators.org.au (link to "ministries")

OMF
- 1988
- Three staff; Japanese, Thai
- http://sites.google.com/site/reachthaioz/

New Zealand:

ISM NZ evolved from Navigator ISM activity starting in the late 60s that developed in the 70s-80s; blessed to spin-off as new entity in 2000
- 25 staff
- www.ism.org.nz

Tertiary Students Christian Fellowship (TSCF)
- ISM began in 1959 as Overseas Christian Fellowship (OCF), OCF dissolved in New Zealand and the work came under TSCF
- All TSCF staff work with international students, thus there are 10 staff
- www.tscf.org.nz

OMF
- 1988
- Three staff; Chinese, Japanese
- www.omf.org/omf/new_zealand/kiwiana/diaspora_and_bamboo

India:

Friends of International Students/Union of Evangelical Students India (FIS-UESI)
- Some ISM work began in 1992, but FIS department began in 1994
- www.fisindia.org; contact: fisuesi@hotmail.com

International Student Friendship
- (InterServe); Pune; Emmanuel Benjamin
- findemmanuel@gmail.com

Japan:

OMF

- 1988
- Two staff, Chinese
- www.omf.org/omf/japan/resources/japanese_diaspora_ministry
  _resources

IFES (KGK) has 6 staff on about 6 campuses

A long-time-missionary reports that there is no specific ISM organization in Japan that he is aware of, however the increasing number of international students is a field waiting for harvest, and there are few laborers.

Growth of International Student Mobility: Japan is not alone as a country with a growing field of international students white unto harvest. More and more developing and developed nations are seeing an increase in international students. While the US continues to be the country of choice for international students, there has been a shift away from the US to other regions of the world, ever since the more restrictive entry requirements took effect after September 11, 2001 and increased in 2017. Whereas the majority of students from Asia were selecting North America or Europe, there has been a growing trend for Asians to remain within the Asia-Pacific region. More Asian nations are adopting a national policy to attract international students for economic, political, and other national interests. The number of international students is dynamic and affected by various factors.

Data gleaned in 2018 from primary sources on international student mobility (Project Atlas of the Institute of International Education; ICEF Monitor; the PIE News; and NAFSA: Association of International Educators) provides an overview of numbers of international students and some countries' recruiting goals:

GLOBAL: In 2018 there were over 5 million international students world-wide.

REGIONAL: Europe is the top destination region, hosting 48% of all international students. North America is the second most attractive region for foreign students, with 21% of the global total, followed by Asia with 18%.

NATIONAL:

Australia: 693,000 in 2018
Azerbaijan: 5,000 in 2017
Canada: 572,415 in 2018
China: 489,000 in 2017; goal of 500,000 for 2020
Denmark: 34,000 in 2017
Egypt: 53,000 in 2017; plans to expand to 200,000

Finland: 20,000 in 2017

France: 343,000 in 2018; goal for 500,000 by 2027

Germany: 359,000 in 2017; surpassed goal to host 350,000 students by 2020

India: 47,500 in 2017; a *Study in India* program goal for 200,000 by 2023

Indonesia: 5,700 in 2016

Ireland: 33,000 regular foreign students enrolled in 2015; goal of 44,000 by 2019/20; there were 129,300 short-term international students at English Language Teaching centers in 2017, with a goal of 132,500 by the first half of 2020

Japan: 267,000 in 2017; *Global 30 Project's* goal of 300,000 by 2020

Jordan: 47,000 in 2016; goal of 70,000 by 2020

Korea: 142,000 in 2018; goal of 200,000 by 2023

Malaysia: 135,000 in 2014; changing the initial target of hosting 200,000 international students by 2020, to 250,000 by 2025

Malta: English Language Teaching (ELT) centers had 87,000 foreign students in 2017

New Zealand: 106,000 in 2017

Netherlands: 122,000 combined EU and Non-EU international students in 2017

Norway: 10,600 in 2015

Philippines: a government policy change resulted in dramatic increase from 26,000 to 61,000 between 2011-12

While visiting Manila in the mid-80s, I read on the front page of the local newspaper that the largest number of Bhutanese students outside of Bhutan, were studying in the Philippines. A strategic missions opportunity existed, as Bhutan is the only official Buddhist kingdom in the world, and Christians face restrictions and persecution there.

Russia: 220,000 in 2018; goal is 310,000 by 2020 and 710,000 by 2025

Singapore: projected growth to 150,000 in 2015

Spain: attracted 309,000 students to study the Spanish language in 2016

Slovakia: 11,100 in 2013

Taiwan: 127,000 in 2018; goal of 150,000 by 2020

Thailand: 22,000 international students

Turkey: goal of 200,000 by 2023

United Arab Emirates: 33,600 in 2016

United Kingdom: 458,490 international students enrolled in universities in 2018 with a goal of 600,000 by 2030; there were another 497,000 international students enrolled in the 400+ English Language Training centers in 2018

United States: 1,094,800 in 2017

Global Expansion of ISM via the Lausanne Network: The following is from *ISM: From Blind-Spot to Vision*:

I was curious to see if the concept of ISM was mentioned at the 1974

International Congress on World Evangelization, the progenitor of the Lausanne Committee for World Evangelization. Among the vast array of topics and articles by 110 contributing authors contained in the Congress's compendium, *Let the Earth Hear His Voice,* the article most likely to address ISM is Michael Cassidy's "Evangelization Among College & University Students." The exhaustive article covering a wide range of issues and items related to collegiate ministry, contained a brief recommendation in the section on "Christian Strategy for the Modern Campus," *"Committed Christians in a university town can use their homes in effective outreach, not just through discussion evenings, but in friendly caring. This ministry can be particularly meaningful to international Third World students studying in First World countries."* There may not have been much further mention of ISM at that historic gathering or in the compendium.

ISM was not part of the agenda or discussion groups I attended at the Conference on World Evangelization (COWE) at Pattaya in 1980, nor do I know if ISM was talked about in Manila at Lausanne II in 1989.
In 2001 I received a survey from Dr. Peter Brierley, Lausanne Researcher, asking for input about cutting edge evangelism for the upcoming Lausanne 2004 Forum. I recommended the strategic reality of the growing Diaspora movement, and the need to address the matter of permanent resident peoples (immigrants and refugees) and temporary resident groups, e.g. international students. How wonderful that the 2004 Forum did include the new topic and issue groups for Diaspora and International Students.

As the Forum convener for the International Student Ministries Issue Group, which included 24 ISM leaders representing 12 countries, I challenged some leaders to conduct a national ISM consultation. Yvonne Choo, acting General Secretary of the FES ministry in Singapore, hosted two Singapore National ISM Consultations in 2006 and 2007.
The primary issue which the 2004 ISM group desired to address concerned the challenges of Returnees. Due to the need to focus on producing the joint Issue Group paper with the Diaspora group, (which became the Lausanne Occasional Paper #55, *Diasporas and International Students: The New People Next Door*), our group did not have time to adequately discuss reentry and returnee issues. Four years later, several of the participants met at the International Consultation About Reentry/Returnees (I-CARE'08) held in conjunction with ACMI'08 in Washington DC.
While still serving as ACMI president in 2007, I was invited to join the Lausanne International Leaders Conference in Budapest where the International Student Ministries Special Interest Committee (SIC) was inaugurated, and I was asked to serve as its Chair. An initial goal was to establish a global network of ISM leaders, and I invited ISM leaders from New Zealand, South Africa, Japan, Singapore, India, Australia, Korea,

Poland, and England to consider being part of the SIC. As president of the Canadian/US ACMI network, I represented North America on the SIC. From among the ISM SIC I appointed Richard Weston, the former national director of Friends International (U.K) to be a coordinator for networking ISMs in Europe, and Terry McGrath, the founding director of ISM New Zealand, to serve as a regional coordinator for the Asia-Pacific region.

Another goal of the ISM SIC was to host regional ISM Leaders consultations in 2009 as part of the preparation for the third Lausanne worldwide congress, *Lausanne III: Cape Town 2010*. Each regional consultation was to identify and address ISM issues that were relevant to each region's contexts. Up to now, only three regions of the world have developed multiple ministries dedicated to ISM: North America, Europe, and the Asia-Pacific region. North America has been having an annual, regional ACMI conference for over 36 years. Europe has had sporadic regional or national ISM staff conferences for over 30 years as well, hosted by the International Fellowship of Evangelical Students (IFES) and/or Friends International.

Richard Weston directed the 2009 Lausanne Greater Europe Regional ISM Leaders Consultation that was held in Amsterdam, Holland. About 30 participants came from nearly 15 countries. An IFES group of participants from Poland later convened a European IFES ISM consultation in 2010 in Poland, and its "fruit" has resulted in an increase of ISM engagement among various European IFES movements. Additional regional IFES ISM Consultations were Berlin 2014, Czech Republic 2016, and Poland 2018.

The Asia-Pacific region had not had a regional ISM Leaders consultation until the 2009 Lausanne Asia-Pacific Regional ISM Leaders Consultation was held in Singapore, under the leadership of Terry McGrath, in collaboration with the Fellowship of Evangelical Students of Singapore. About 60 ISM leaders and workers from over 15 countries participated. The second Lausanne Asia-Pacific Regional ISM Leaders gathering was also held in Singapore, in 2015.

Several of the ISM leaders who participated in the 2009 regional consultations were asked to report on the ISM movement in their countries during four sessions at the Cape Town 2010 congress, which had 4,000 evangelical leaders. The presentations were part of four Dialogue Sessions (seminars) on ISM in Europe, Asia-Pacific, North America, and South Africa.

The Lausanne ISM Global Leadership Network Facilitation Team hosted the Lausanne ISM Global Leadership Forum: *Charlotte'17*, September 11-15, 2017 at the SIM USA facilities in Charlotte North Carolina. That historic gathering was comprised of 100 participants from 25 countries and 70 organizations. Part of the agenda was the consideration of advancing opportunities for needed academic training and research in ISM by seminaries and graduate schools. Also, the need to develop Lausanne ISM Regional Facilitation Teams that would encourage national ISM developments. At the conclusion of *Charlotte'17*, the Lausanne Catalyst for ISM role was transferred from Leiton Chinn to Co-Catalysts: Emma Brewster, SIM International Coordinator for Engaging the University (based in Cape Town, South Africa); and to Dr. Yaw Perbi, President of International Student Ministries Canada, based in Montreal. A primary goal of Co-Catalysts Perbi and Brewster is the establishment of a global ISM prayer movement.

Lausanne North America established the Lausanne North America ISM Strategy Working Group in 2019.

This paper has not addressed the practical "how-tos" of doing ISM. There is a wealth of information on "best-practices" and principles, as well as publications for ISM found on ISM websites, such as those listed in this paper, and the Lausanne ISM Bibliography.

Practical ISM training conferences are also offered by a number of ISMs, including ACMI, ISI, Friends International, International Student Ministries Canada, IFES Europe/Interaction, and other organizations listed above. Additionally, two ISM video training resources incorporating global ISM leaders at the *Lausanne Global ISM Leadership Forum: Charlotte'17*, and collaboration among North American national ISMs, the *Lausanne Global Classroom on ISM* and *EveryInternational,* respectively, were produced in 2018/2019.

"The Great Blind-spot in Missions" has not completely yielded to full-vision but needs the continual application of the Holy Spirit's sight-giving touch as He develops the ISM Movement world-wide. I'm grateful that the Lausanne Movement is one of the vessels through which He is working.[36]

---

[36]

CHAPTER 8
CONVERSION IN COMMUNITY: FIVE STAGES[1]

Katie J. Rawson

Elina, a nominal Muslim woman in a Central Asian nation, wanted desperately to come to the United States for graduate school. She prayed, promising she would search for God if He enabled her to attend her first-choice university. Her prayer was answered, and she arrived at a well-known institution in the Midwest. Soon Elina met some Christians through a furniture giveaway. Although she was suspicious of their motives, she remembered her promise to look for God in the United States. Right away she connected with Esther, a volunteer in the Christian group whose three children were the same ages as her three children. The two moms began sharing about child-raising, and soon a trust relationship developed.

Elina also began attending the large group Bible studies sponsored by the fellowship and felt great peacefulness during the meetings. This peace she sensed in the community made her curious about the Christian faith. In the meantime, she was experiencing tension with the husband she had left behind. Esther challenged her to treat her husband better. Observing relationships that worked in Esther's family and in the fellowship, Elina wondered if God could transform her, and she became open to change. Throughout that whole school year Elina put into practice Esther's counsel and began to interact more gently with her husband. Seeing that following Jesus' teachings was improving her marriage, she became a sincere seeker. One night a Bible study clarified the difference between relating to God as a slave and relating to Him as Father. That insight led her to the point of conversion. She experienced the Father of Jesus as her Father and knew the indwelling presence of the Holy Spirit. Elina had found the God she promised to search for in the United States through interaction with a shalom community.

Five Stages or Thresholds

Elina's journey involved five distinct stages or *thresholds*: trusting a Christian, becoming curious about Jesus, opening up to change, seeking

---

[1] Taken from *Crossing Cultures with Jesus: Sharing Good News with Sensitivity and Grace* by Katie J. Rawson. Copyright (c) 2015 by Katie J. Rawson. Used by permission of InterVarsity Press, P.O. Box 1400, Downers Grove, IL 60515, USA. **www.ivpress.com**

after God, and entering the Kingdom. In their book *I Once Was Lost*, Don Everts and Doug Schaupp describe these thresholds. Experienced evangelists in the college context, Everts and Schaupp identified these stages through two thousand interviews with postmodern people who came to Christ.[21] The five thresholds are valid cross-culturally, yet they work out differently in different cultures.

As with any Western attempt to describe relationships with rules, we will discover exceptions to the five-threshold pattern. In the journeys of some people we may discern only two or three stages, or we may see six or more! Or we may observe sudden conversions; when this happens, we need to ask what is really happening. The complete absence of conversion stages should cause a warning buzzer to go off in our minds; the growth that happens during the five thresholds is critical to transformation later.

When We Don't Discern Stages: Decision or Conversion?

My interviews of East Asian converts included a number of people who came to Christ quickly after dramatic experiences of His power; the traditional layer of their worldview mix gave them a magical view of Jesus as a powerful shaman. These did not understand the true nature of God or of relationship with Him. Conversations with these students left me feeling disturbed that our evangelism wasn't reaching deep enough to transform people.

People with traditional assumptions about God in the inner core of their worldviews can easily make a *decision* to follow Jesus as a divine miracle worker and relate to Him magically in the same way they were previously relating to local gods or ancestors. Because their hidden assumptions about the character of God and the nature of relationship with Him have not surfaced, they miss out on the dynamic, interactive relationship that our personal God desires. True *conversion* occurs when friends change their deep level assumptions about God and about relationship with Him. They will then bow to Jesus as Lord of the universe – and relate to Him in a personal way. Their deep level assumptions about the lordship of Jesus will affect all the other layers of their worldviews and result in genuine change. Figure 8.1 depicts the difference between a surface-level decision and core-level conversion.

---

[1] Don Everts, and Doug Schaupp, I Once Was Lost: What Postmodern Skeptics Taught Us About Their Path to Jesus, (Downers Grove, IL: InterVarsity Press, 2008).

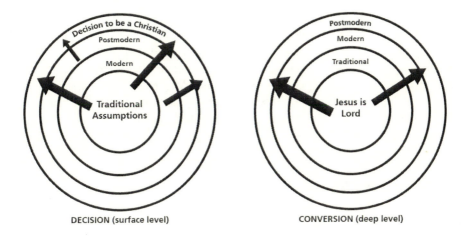

Figure 8.1. Surface-level decision versus core-level conversion

God does enable people who start out with a surface-level decision to move to the point of core-level conversion, however that requires perceptive discipling and does not always occur. Too many returnee converts to China have not given much evidence of conversion after returning home; part of the reason may be that they were not actually converted in the first place.[2] Our history of crusade-type evangelism in the United States may compound the problem, sometimes causing us to ask people to become followers of Jesus before they are ready to do so, as I did with Tao. Understanding the five thresholds will help us refrain from making such invitations too soon, stay faithful in friendship, and know how to pray and interact at different stages of our friends' journeys.

Jesus the Farmer

Jesus saw Himself as a farmer planting gospel seed. Everts and Schaupp believe His parable in Mark 4:26-29 reveals two crucial truths about evangelism:[3]

He also said, "This is what the kingdom of God is like. A man scatters seed on the ground. Night and day, whether he sleeps or gets up, the seed sprouts and grows, though he does not know how. All by itself the soil produces grain—first the stalk, then the head, then the full kernel in the head. As soon as the grain is ripe, he puts the sickle to it, because the harvest has come."

Growth is *mysterious*: some seeds we thought would grow well don't; others we were unsure of do produce a harvest. The same is true of our

[2] Justin Lee, "The Opportunity, The Tragedy, The Mission," presentation to reentry consultation, (Birmingham, UK, April, 2014).

non-Christian friends. Ultimately God is the One Who controls what happens to the seed. This truth should set us free from the urge to try to control what happens with our friends. This passage also emphasizes another truth: growth is *organic*: each seed has similar seasons of growth, and a pattern can be discerned. We can recognize those seasons (seed, stalk, head, full kernel, and ripeness) and know when to reap a harvest.[3] Understanding the stages people usually go through on the way to commitment will enable us to be helpful guides through each part of the journey.

The Five Thresholds in Cross-cultural Context

The five thresholds play out differently in each cultural context because the reasons for distrust and cultural strongholds to be overcome are different. Community normally plays a greater role in the conversion process of non-Westerners. Individuals must come to trust an entire group, whether it is a campus fellowship or small group of some kind. These groups need to build trust with the communities of the individuals they attract, asking about and caring for family and friends near and far. As groups draw people from a certain cultural background, group leaders should prayerfully reflect on the conversion process for that cultural group. The sidebar "Five Thresholds in Cross-cultural Evangelism" contains some questions to aid that reflection. I suggest a few answers to these questions later. I recommend you do your own prayerful research and thinking. Discussing these questions in leadership meetings can help you discover how to relate fruitfully to people being drawn in your group.

Five Thresholds in Cross-cultural Evangelism[4]

1. Distrust to Trust

What perceptions of Christianity or Western culture make trust difficult for this group?

What attitudes and habits build trust with this group? How can we best learn from, affirm and welcome them?

2. Apathy to Curiosity

What keeps this group from curiosity?

What role does religion or spirituality play in their culture?

What actions or questions will provoke curiosity in them?

3. Curiosity to Openness

What spiritual strongholds have we observed in this group's culture?

---

[3] Everts and Schaupp, *I Once Was Lost*, 18-23.
[4] Sarai's story is told in the video "Starting ISM: Journeying Towards Jesus," (InterVarsity, June 19, 2014), http://ism.intervarsity.org/resource/starting-ism-journeying-towards-jesus.

What reactions might they receive from their community if they converted?

Is there anything in our community that might keep them from openness?

What challenges will speak to them?

In what areas might they feel pressure to change their culture when it isn't necessary? How can we address this?

4. Openness to Seeking

Where can God's shalom bring healing to the individual or people group?

What are helpful questions to guide seekers from this group?

5. Entering the Kingdom

What indicators of readiness for commitment have we observed in this group?

What words would people from this group use to describe their conversions? What was the final decision like for them?

Note: I am indebted to Sarah Akutagawa for this material.

Threshold 1: Distrust to trust.

Stereotypes of Christianity may cause distrust of Christians and Christian groups. Often the Western culture exported by our movies and other media is seen as Christian culture. Externals such as dress and dietary habits may offend. When Sarai, a Muslim student at a Western university, became acquainted with Liz, Sarai's parents were afraid that Liz, a Christian, would corrupt their daughter with loose living. But Liz built trust with Sarai's parents by always wearing long pants and covering her arms when she visited them and speaking freely of how she honored her own parents.[4] Build relationships with Chinese through genuine, unconditional friendship. They may distrust Christians because of previous experience with high-pressure Christian groups in either Chinese or Western settings. Or they may believe that Christianity is a Western religion and be very aware of the association of missionaries with the shameful treatment of China by Western nations in the nineteenth century (see crossingculturesbook.org/chinese). So, both individuals and community must offer Chinese the security of being cared for and freedom to investigate the faith only when they become truly interested.

Barriers for Hindus are usually cultural; Christianity may be seen as a low-caste religion spread by evangelists who are greedy for money. For many years the Hindu students who came here were positive that our only motive in serving them was gaining converts. To develop trust with them we must offer authentic unconditional friendship. Authenticity involves being clear about our identity as Christ-followers and building relationships of dialogue and reciprocity.

The order of the thresholds may vary for Muslims, and the ideal is that a group – family unit or small group of friends – goes through them together so that individuals are not extracted from their communities. Trust is difficult in many Muslim societies, so be patient and take the needed time to build it. One important aspect of trust-building is making your identity as a follower of Jesus clear from the start.

If we have entered into our friends' worlds and built trust (described in previous chapters), many friends will have already passed from distrust to trust. If the community draws in new people, group members must enter their worlds, develop friendships, learn what misconceptions or past experiences cause distrust and address them. When trust with one member is built, it becomes easier to transfer trust to the community as a whole, as we saw with Elina and Esther. Participation in the community will also build trust; as non-Christians become involved in the fellowship, barriers fall away. Cooking, greeting, emceeing, or even watching over the shoes at the door allow people to feel needed and wanted in a group.

Threshold 2: Apathy to curiosity.

A person may trust Christians and even a Christian community though not be curious about their faith. Chinese may ask a lot of questions about your faith and experience, but don't mistake this kind of curiosity for deep spiritual interest. Patiently answer their questions and ask them some questions in turn. Chinese young people struggle with family of origin issues. Fellowships might offer biblically based culturally sensitive workshops on counseling topics like reconciliation with parents, building strong marriages, forgiveness, emotional health, and identity development. Asian speakers who are role models and experts in these areas can arouse curiosity. Those who struggle with the existence of God will benefit from contact with highly educated Christians who integrate the faith into their lives.[55]

Hindus may have never thought deeply about their faith; asking open-ended questions and sharing a relevant verse, story or experience may develop curiosity. Muslims may not have had a chance to discuss faith with Christians. Apologetic discussions about the divinity of Christ or reliability of Scripture will probably not be effective with them at this stage. Instead, share answers to prayer and tell stories from Scripture. With all people groups we must speak and live in ways that make them curious,

---

[5] Lu Zun'en, *Reaching the Current Generation of Chinese Students,* (Paradise, PA: Ambassadors for Christ, 2015), 1-8. Available at the AFC Bookstore website: http://afcresources.org/contents/en-us/p3888_Understanding_Current_Generation_of_Chinese.html

sharing briefly how our relationship with God affects our lives. When I mentioned to my Indian friend Raina that I wrote worship poems, I could tell that her curiosity was piqued. The poem that I shared with her later gave her insight into my devotional life, and our spiritual conversations took on a more personal tone afterward.

Threshold Three: Curiosity to Openness.

This may be the most difficult threshold of all. Changing religions can bring great dishonor on self and family, leading to death threats. Prayer for our friends is critical at this point; fear is a powerful stronghold. We should also pray *with* friends who are considering change. Jasmine, a law student, shared with her friend Ellie that she loved how Jesus interpreted the law in the stories they had been reading together. "So what do you think about following Jesus?" Ellie inquired. "I'm not sure about following Jesus. It would be very hard for me to get a job in the courts back home if I were a Christian," was Jasmine's response. Ellie helped Jasmine think clearly about the cost of following Jesus and process her fears, praying with Jasmine about them in the name of Jesus, thus opening the door for her to hear directly from God.[66]

In this threshold people begin to count the cost of following Jesus and anticipate how it would impact them and their communities. Chinese people will ask if the faith could possibly be relevant for them. At this point developing critical thinking and bringing underlying worldview assumptions to light is crucial. Discussion groups that enable the discovery of these assumptions will help them understand the change of viewpoint and behavior that following Jesus would involve (see chapter 5). Reduced job possibilities because of becoming a Christian could make them less able to honor and meet the needs of family and others in their web of relationships. But life in Jesus offers hope for healed relationships with family, friends, and self. Pray with and for Chinese students as they consider the changes following Jesus might bring.

For Muslims and Hindus, culture and religion are closely interwoven; following Jesus may feel like a betrayal of both culture and family. It is important to help people discern between spiritual necessities and cultural traits. Muslims who follow Jesus don't have to start eating pork, and vegetarian Hindus don't have to eat meat. And no one must stop honoring parents, although obeying Jesus has to come first.

Hindus may struggle with abandoning their gods, but they have infinitely more to gain in Jesus. Opening up to change may involve an experience of Jesus' power. It might be healing, answered prayer, worship

---

[6] Jasmine's story is also told in "Starting ISM: Journeying Towards Jesus," (InterVarsity, June 19, 2014), http://ism.intervarsity.org/resource/starting-ism-journeying-towards-jesus.

or other ways. Ask God to display His power and love to them. Muslims also need to experience the transforming power of Jesus. Many have shared about dreams or visions of Him, though the everyday love of Christians living out their faith in hard circumstances can also have an impact. After Muslims experience Jesus in a tangible way they will be much more open to trusting the authority of the Bible.

Threshold 4: Openness to Seeking.

In stage four people eagerly desire to learn all they can about Jesus. They need safe places to seek Him without being pressured to commitment too soon. We must carefully discern what is behind the questions people ask at this stage. The question, How can I believe in Jesus? *may* be about intellectual obstacles, though it may also be about experiencing God. In John 7:17 Jesus declares "Anyone who chooses to do the will of God will find out whether My teaching comes from God or whether I speak on My own." Based on this promise, we can encourage seekers to experiment with obeying Jesus' teaching, expecting God to reveal Himself to them. Steps of obedience like serving others or praying about daily life problems can lead to experiencing God. Ending Bible studies with next-step challenges helps seekers take concrete actions in their pursuit of God.[7] Having recent converts share their testimonies with the group is especially helpful to seekers; it gives them a picture of what change might look like for them. Much of what we do during this threshold is similar for all cultural groups, working to help them have their questions about Scripture answered and giving them opportunities to experience God.

Threshold 5: Entering the Kingdom.

At a certain point seeking can reach such a level of intensity that resolution is needed. People cannot remain seekers forever, and those who do not commit may lose their keenness to seek. Having chosen to fast in his seeking after God, Sri, the Hindu student who was part of the Indian Christian Community, was at that level of intensity the day I shared with him. Thomas and Dave had discerned that Sri was ready. They asked me to speak with him because they knew I had a great deal of experience in helping people cross the line. When we recognize that someone is close, we must extend an invitation to follow Jesus. If obstacles remain, the invitation will bring them to the surface to be addressed. If obstacles are no longer an issue, then we can help our friend enter the Kingdom.

Invitations provide opportunities for our friends to publicly respond to

---

[7] Some of these ideas come from an undated paper by Eva Liu Glick, "The Five Thresholds as They Play Out in the ISM Context," that also incorporates ideas from Dan Gonzaga.

the Spirit's wooing with surrender and commitment. Even if the Spirit has already ushered them into the Kingdom, openly confessing Jesus as their Lord seals in their hearts the reality of conversion. I often share Romans 10:9-10 with people at this point:

If you confess with your mouth Jesus *as* Lord, and believe in your heart that God raised Him from the dead, you will be saved; for with the heart a person believes, resulting in righteousness, and with the mouth he confesses, resulting in salvation. (NASB)

Joy always seems to overtake people who choose to verbally declare Jesus as Lord. I remember seeing many radiant smiles once these words tumbled out of my friends' mouths.

Giving an invitation also allows any remaining blocks to surface. Sometimes we are able to deal quickly with those blocks. People from backgrounds that emphasize merit and virtue may think that they must reach a point of perfect faith or become worthy of Jesus before following Him. The account of the father who said to Jesus, "I do believe; help me overcome my unbelief!" and then saw Jesus set his son free from a demon (Mark 9: 14-27) usually speaks powerfully to people like Sri who want to feel 100 percent prepared before making a commitment.

What should a "sinner's prayer" look like crossculturally? I hesitate to provide printed prayers because people can so easily treat them as magical, however, in general, express sin in terms of breaking relationship with and dishonoring God, and repentance in terms of coming home to God and pledging allegiance or loyalty to Jesus. Use words like "Leader" or "King" to describe Jesus' lordship. And include a request to be filled with the Holy Spirit. If at all possible, people should pray this first prayer in their heart languages. At our evangelistic retreats we always try to have a partner or two who speak Mandarin to join us for prayer times with seekers, since so many of our seekers are from China. This enables new converts to hear prayer in their heart languages and encourages worship in that language later.

How long might it take for our friends to go through all the stages? God is sovereign over conversions. Huang's story is a good example of the mysterious and organic process of coming to faith. On the bus in his Chinese city Huang was strangely attracted to a book in a stranger's hands. He looked at the title: *Holy Bible*. He was driven to read that book. He inquired about where to find such a book and, on his day off from work, took two buses to get there. So, Huang was already reading the Bible when he came to North Carolina State University to study engineering. The international student fellowship sponsored a tour of the city, and there Huang and his wife, Yan, first met Christians. They were soon part of the fellowship, and Huang was happy to discuss this book he'd been reading. Trust and curiosity developed quickly in the couple. Yan loved the women's discussion group and demonstrated a seeker's heart early on. At the March evangelistic retreat two years later, she invited Jesus into her life.

Openness to change was harder for Huang, although he met weekly with campus minister Andrew to study the Bible. Huang was active in the community, often emceeing the Friday meetings. He and Yan participated as the group cared practically for members who were moving, marrying, or having children. Members of the fellowship interceded regularly for him, and I mobilized extra prayer from a couple who support me financially. Two years later Huang and Yan attended the March retreat again; we had invited Huang to lead the Saturday hike, to be sure that he would be present. The first night Huang shared openly in his small group about what a stubborn person he was and how he would never make a decision unless he was convinced it was what he should do. Our speaker, a young Chinese pastor who had come to Christ after arriving in the United States, shared his testimony of coming to faith as a biologist, and things began to budge inside Huang. The second evening the pastor gave an invitation to follow Jesus. Finally, Huang was ready, and the pastor was happy to pray with him. Eight years after first setting eyes on the Bible he made Jesus his Lord and King. He had consistently received the Word and begun to put it into practice. Participation in the community for years helped Huang pass through the mysterious but organic journey into the Kingdom.

Personal Reflection:

1. Consider your own journey to Jesus or that of a new Christian who you know well. What stages or thresholds described in this chapter, can you discern?
2. *Lectio Divina* passages:
   - Ps 40:1-10
   - John 1:43-51
   - John 3:1-16
   - 1 Timothy 1:12-17
   - Rev 3:14-21

Group Discussion:

1. Discuss and debrief the community event that you planned from the last chapter.
2. What questions do you have about the chapter? What did you like and not like?
3. What steps or thresholds does the blind man in John 9 go through in his journey toward Jesus? How does Jesus change in his

(healed) eyes?

Group Application

Prayerfully consider your cross-cultural friendships. At what stage is each of your friends? Use the reflection questions in the "Five Thresholds in Cross-cultural Evangelism" sidebar to think through what you can do to help your friend move to the next stage. Meet your friend for coffee or dinner and experiment with some of your questions in genuine conversation.

Suggested Resources:

- *I Once Was Lost: What Postmodern Skeptics Taught Us About Their Path to Jesus* by Don Everts and Doug Schaupp. This is the book that introduces the five stages of conversion.
- *Song of a Wanderer: Beckoned by Eternity* by Cheng Li. This conversion story of a Chinese intellectual contains apologetic material especially appropriate for those with many intellectual questions.
- *Reaching the Current Generation of Chinese Students* by Ambassadors for Christ, available at http://afcresources.org/contents/en-us/p3889_Understanding_Current_Generation_of_Chinese.html. This booklet summarizes recent research on the Chinese generations. Read with a Chinese Christian friend.
- Answering Islam, answeringislam.org. A library of articles on Islam.
- *Seeking Allah, Finding Jesus* by Nabeel Qureshi. Contains helpful answers to questions.
- Yeshu Samaj, yeshusamaj.org. Material for Hindu-background seekers and disciples, written by believers from Hindu families. Includes articles, testimonies and common faith objections and answers.
- Naya Jeevan, nayajeevan.org/resources. A ministry project of Cru that focuses on welcoming the Hindu immigrant community with articles and media links to help them acclimate to life in the United States and introduce them to Jesus.

Marialena,

Blessings from God as you
seek your place in His kingdom.

Denni + Natasha
Bradford

Email to us:
kimnatalyap@gmail.com

CHAPTER 9
CONGREGATIONAL PRACTICES IN DIASPORA MISSIOLOGY INTERNATIONAL STUDENT ENGAGEMENT AMONG UNENGAGED UNREACHED PEOPLE GROUPS

Dennis C. Bradford

Abstract
Jesus declared He would build His church, and for centuries He has relocated people from their ancestral homes to distant lands. Individuals and families are moved from locations which lack an indigenous church and from territories which restrict the use of Scripture, to new homes in communities where the gospel message is preached freely. Current estimates indicate more than 215 million people live outside their country of birth. Therefore, it is imperative that the church of Jesus Christ see the sovereign hand of God in this unprecedented movement of people across the planet. Mission organizations the world over are correctly focused on evangelizing the ethnolinguistic groups which lack an indigenous/reproducing church. However, it is also instrumental for the global body of Christ to realize that many unreached peoples are currently represented on college campuses in the West. As recently as 2015, nearly one and a half million international students were registered at U.S. institutions of higher learning. And in 2014, within the state of Alabama, approximately twenty percent of international students were comprised of Northern African, Middle Eastern, Central Asian, and South Asian peoples. Many of the world's unreached peoples are comprised of these Global Affinity Groups. Some live and study within the so-called USA "Bible Belt," yet they continue to lack both access to Scripture and significant friendships with evangelicals. In some cases, they are even treated as unwelcomed guests in this supposed Christian nation. However, local churches have an opportunity to change this by reaching international students with the message of Jesus Christ. It is not necessary for the local church to embark on this task alone; it can consult with mission agencies that are knowledgeable of the people groups represented on college and university campuses and develop key relationships with international students and foreign scholars.

Introduction

Look around at the nations; look and be amazed! For I am doing something in your own day, something you wouldn't believe even if someone told you about it (Hab. 1:5, NLT).

The Great Commission passages found in the four gospel accounts and the book of Acts render the irrefutable command of Christ to His Church that she gather His "lost sheep" from among every ethnicity on earth.[1] Take for instance Matthew 28:19 (ESV) which reads: "Go therefore and make disciples of all nations." In interacting with this passage in the original language, Steven Hawthorne (2009) states that "all nations" can incline one to envision geopolitical states or "countries." However, the *ethne*, as recorded in the Greek, is the root word for ethnic. Further, Hawthorne explains that combining this word with the Greek word that means "all" is best rendered as "ethnic or cultural people group" (Hawthorne 2009, 128). This demonstrates that Christ was not speaking in generalities, rather being very specific regarding the individuals who make up His Kingdom.

This reading of the text is further clarified by the Apostle John where he writes: "After this I looked, and behold, a great multitude that no one could number, from every nation, from all tribes and people and languages, standing before the throne and before the Lamb" (Rev. 7:9, ESV). Hawthorne continues to explain that "from the viewpoint of evangelization, a 'people group' is the largest possible group within which the gospel can spread as a discipling or 'church planting movement' without encountering barriers of understanding or acceptance" (Hawthorne 2009, 128). Michael Pocock, et al. (2005, 16) further develops the meaning of *ethne* by stating that "a people are usually defined by ethnic or linguistic terms. It is estimated that there are twelve thousand distinct languages and dialects and as many as twenty-four thousand people groups in the world today. Therefore, it is understood that Christ followers will eventually come from every ethnic and/or cultural people group on Earth. Given His command in the Great Commission passages, the objective of the Church is to strategically make contact with representatives from every one of these people groups. Fortunately, much progress has occurred over the last two thousand plus years. This is confirmed by assertions that roughly twenty-seven percent of the known people groups remain un-evangelized (Lausanne Committee for World Evangelization 2004; Mandryk 2005).

Jesus also stated that He would build His church (Matt. 16:18), and for

---

[1] Jeff Lewis (2012) and other scholars hold that the Great Commission is communicated a total of five times by Jesus in Matt. 28:19, Mark 16:15, Luke 24:46-48, John 20:21, and Acts 1:8, emphasizing the level of importance the body of Christ should place on this single command.

centuries He has relocated people from their countries of birth (Acts 17:26-27), just as God moved Abraham to a distant land. Similarly to many foreign born today, throughout the church age Christ has moved individuals from countries lacking an indigenous church or access to Scripture to locations offering greater access to the gospel message (Houston, Thomson, Gidoomal, and Chinn 2005; Winter 2009). Missiologists refer to locations lacking access to Scripture as *limited access, creative access,* or *restricted nations,* due to their hostility to the Christian faith and open persecution of its adherents (The Voice of the Martyrs 2015). Today, many Western nations are experiencing what Ralph Winter (2009a) termed as the *voluntary and involuntary coming* of internationals for safety, education, and a better way of life as God brings unengaged unreached peoples—Muslim, Hindus, Buddhist, and Sikhs to the doorsteps of the church in Europe, Canada, and the United States (Winter 2009; Caleb Project 2003).

The *voluntary coming* is normally related to education and economic advancement, whereas the *involuntary* relocation occurs primarily among refugees, human trafficking victims, and those escaping conflict (Wan and Tira 2010). As the United States experiences an influx of international students, many from *creative access countries,* one might ask what strategic role local congregations can play in support of diaspora missions. Congregations can partner with and seek the consultation of mission agencies as they engage unreached peoples in their community.

The "Scattering"

The book of Acts chronicles how the Sovereign Lord uses human circumstances to allow current and future believers to cross paths as He establishes new congregations. This is also observable in the current Diaspora or scattering of peoples globally (Lausanne Committee for World Evangelization 2004). Scripture declares that God orchestrates the relocation of people in order to express His love and grace toward those estranged from Him by encouraging them to seek Him (Acts 17:26-27). God is moving family members of creative access nations so that the "hidden people" (Winter 1980) who are also referred to as *Unengaged Unreached People Groups* (UUPG) (Haney 2012, 319; Mathis 2012, 22) may hear the gospel message. Also, as one considers the events recorded in Scripture; it becomes clear that the prophecy recorded in Micah 5:2 was fulfilled by the human decision of Caesar Augustus (Luke 2:1-7) who called for a census immediately prior to the birth of Jesus. In like manner it is vital that devoted followers of Christ see the sovereign hand of God in human circumstances today.

Christ followers living in the United States, with its evangelistic history should not be surprised that a loving God would bring a remnant from the nations to her doorstep as the inclination toward pioneer mission wanes among Westerners (Koch 2009). Currently, married and single women make up two-thirds of the Western mission force (Kraft and Crossman 2009) while missionary involvement among many Western nations stagnates and shows signs of declining (Johnstone 2011; Kim 2009).[2] Most Western sending agencies (also referred to as mission agencies) report a nearly forty-five percent attrition rate among fulltime missionaries within ten years of their arrival onto the field (Lausanne Committee for World Evangelization 2004; Mandryk 2005). Therefore, the prevalence of unreached peoples moving to Western nations is actually an extension of grace on the part of Christ. Jesus directed His Church to pray that the Lord of the harvest would send workers into His harvest field and the Lord has actually moved that field within proximity to available workers. He is indeed compassionate and longsuffering (Ps. 86:15, NKJV).

Currently thirty-three percent of migrant populations live within the borders of the seven wealthiest nations (Wan and Tira 2010). And according to Galloway and Payne (2014), a significant number of immigrants seek refuge in the United States annually. Acts 17:26 states that the Creator not only made all people from one set of parents, He also determined where everyone would live in advance. However, in light of current world events, these Scripture references can challenge beliefs about God and His ability to determine in advance the circumstances of Earth and its occupants. Some may ask. "If God made us all from one set of parents, why do we not all look alike?" and "if He determined where we would each live, then what was God's involvement in the sins which contributed to the movements of the world's people over the millennia?" These legitimate questions speak to the heart of what one believes about the Creator and His sovereignty, and they exceed the scope of this paper. However, a brief response is in order.

Regarding the issue of ethnicity, recent scientific discoveries regarding the human genome offer some insight. Because research is still in its infancy, there is not complete agreement on all matters, nevertheless, according to the National Human Genome Research Institute (2007, 2), "any two people (on Earth) are more than 99% the same." Therefore, the glaring differences many people emphasize, such as race, height, weight,

---

[2] Patrick Johnstone (2011, 233, figure 8.13) looks at sending agencies from 1900 to 2010. Although the United States continues to cultivate missionaries consistent with population growth, all other North American and European countries' missionary sending capacity is declining. As of 2010, only eight Western nations remained in the top twenty mission sending nations in the world. And of those that remain, nearly all are sending less numerically than in the past. Of note, Sweden is currently sending less than in 1960 and the UK is slightly under its 1900 numbers.

intelligence, etc., are quite minute in comparison to what humans have in common. Touching briefly on the issue of God's dominion and the atrocities committed on Earth, J.I. Packer (1961) offers assistance when he addressed the intersection of three realities: God's sovereignty, human responsibility, and the Christian's duty to evangelize. Packer takes great care to explain that God is sovereign and will accomplish His end with or without human cooperation. He goes on to explain that sin does not have the capacity to either surprise God or thwart His plans. Packer concludes by stating that every human is totally responsible for their individual actions while God super-rules over human activities to accomplish His will.

Now, to return to the topic of the Unengaged Unreached People Groups (UUPG): the Church should both send missionaries to distant lands and engage the unreached living within her borders (Galloway and Payne 2014). As human capacity increases to both discern God's leading and understand the world around us, the Church has a responsibility to follow the commands of Christ to the pinnacle of that understanding. Traditionally the global mission thrust has been concentrated toward the geographic regions of the world where Jesus has not been named (Galloway and Payne 2014). A paradigm shift in the global approach to missions is now before the Church. Precisely as in 1974 when speaking before his peers in Lausanne Switzerland, Ralph Winter drew attention to what he termed "hidden people," (Winter 1980) leading to a refocusing on UUPG. Given the expanding understanding of God's purposes associated with diaspora, the Church should now place these same global families under a microscope to see where members are actually living and engage them everywhere (Wan 2007).

In like manner, Galloway and Payne (2014) cite Terry Sharp of the International Mission Board, who compels believers not to squander the opportunity which the Lord is granting the Church in America and to realize that the very people groups most evangelicals believe must be reached before Christ will return are currently flooding Western nations as international students, immigrants, and refugees. The Heavenly Father, like any loving parent is throwing a slow pitch right across the base and encouraging His child, the Western Church, by saying "it is okay if you miss, just take a swing." Today, significant diaspora can be found in communities throughout the United States. Church leaders upon hearing this should not fear inadequacy or feel overwhelmed. Instead, they should develop strategic partnerships with mission agencies to focus their combined efforts.

Diaspora Missions

Missiologist Enoch Wan is one of many in the world calling attention to the mass migration of people. Estimates are that from 214-to-232 million (Pocock 2015) people currently live outside their place of birth. Wan (2007) is encouraging the global Body of Christ to build relationships with unreached peoples where they are. He frequently uses his family's story of coming to faith in Christ after migrating from China to Canada as an example of the strategic nature of diaspora missions. Unlike foreign missions, reaching the diaspora does not require years of professional training; it relies heavily upon hospitality and welcoming. Nor should diaspora missions be viewed as an alternative to pioneer missions. Instead of replacing foreign missions, they should be viewed as supplements to the traditional approach (Wan and Tira 2010).

According to the Student and Exchange Visitor Information System (2015), some 1.4 million international students were registered at U.S. institutions of higher education. Additionally, nearly thirty percent of all Science, Technology, Engineer, and Math (STEM) professionals are immigrants to the United States (Lausanne Committee for World Evangelization 2004). This growing reality moved Ed Stetzer, director of LifeWay Research, to assert that the nations are living among us, without ever hearing the gospel message (Lowery 2010). Local churches have an opportunity to reach these individuals with the message of Jesus Christ (Phillips and Eaton 2010). Unreached peoples are more open to the gospel message during times of transition when they are away from home and being exposed to new concepts and aspects of life (Rankin 2015). Therefore, diaspora missions offer local congregations a tremendous opportunity to contribute to the Great Commission.

Christianity is often associated with Western society in the rest of the world. For these and other cultural reasons, many non-Western believers refer to themselves as "follower, devotee and/or disciple" of Christ (Lausanne Committee for World Evangelization 2004). Cultural sensitivity is important when sharing the gospel message with diaspora individuals. For this reason, emphasis should be placed on relationship building and not on seeking conversion. Evangelicals should concentrate on developing healthy holistic relationships, learning the customs, and addressing the felt needs of immigrants. This personal approach can open the door to enduring relationships (Wan and Tira 2010). Additionally, Jerry Rankin (2015) suggests that viewing the American society as a melting pot or focusing on assimilation is not helpful to evangelism. He recommends viewing culture as a salad bowl comprised of various components whose distinctness adds value. When members of a host country approach or receive others in this manner, it conveys both acceptance of the guest and humility on the part of the host.

Missiologists also estimate that many international students will return to their countries of birth and assume significant roles of leadership and influence during their lifetimes (Payne 2012; Pocock 2015). The U.S. State Department appears to agree given their assertion that some 300 current or former world leaders have studied at U.S. institutions (Wolfgang 2012). Also, foreign born believers in Christ are free to return to their counties of birth and immediately share the gospel message with family and friends in places where missionaries are forbidden to travel. However, not everyone hearing a clear gospel presentation will embrace its message. Therefore, the goal in building relationships with internationals should be multipronged. In the case of nonbelievers who obtain influential positions within their respective counties, relationships established and maintained with Christians in the West can prove beneficial to Christ followers abroad.

If healthy respectful relationships endure, influential non-Christian friends in creative access countries can benefit the cause of Christ in innumerable ways. Within the secular world, much is accomplished out of allegiance to friends; and the church should learn from that example. Christ, in Luke 16:8, noted how wise or shrewd the children of the world are in dealing with their own kind. Believers should build enduring relationships with internationals of all faiths, realizing that some will become devoted to Christ, while others will not. Upon developing deep trusting relationships, individuals occupying influential positions in creative access countries can be called upon to use their influence to benefit the church in their geographic area. Only a trusted friend[3] would have the capacity to make such a request of an influential person. Politicians and leaders of industry often appeal to personal acquaintances of international origin to make decisions which benefit the requestor's personal interest. What prevents followers of Christ from making similar requests?

These favors can be called upon in a protracted manner by seeking strategic adjustments to a nation's policies or during times of crisis, as when believers are being persecuted. Relationships of this nature could lead to Christian aid workers and/or university professors receiving permission to work in a creative access county or may result in the easing of restrictions on minority religious groups in general or converts to Christianity in particular. Developing and maintaining trusting

---

[3] William R. Yount, (2012, 442) advises that "we build stable human relationships on a foundation of mutual trust. Trusting others wisely and establishing our own trustworthiness by the way we behave are both essential to mission success." When he recommends "trusting others wisely," he goes on to elaborate "that (one should) trust—but not too much! Trust without caution produces naiveté. Caution without trust produces suspicion."

relationships[4] with internationals could result in enormous contributions to world evangelism in both direct and indirect ways. All this may be accomplished by a member of a small congregation who surrendered to God's leading by befriending a young and possibly lonely college student who is studying thousands of miles from friends and family.

Foreign/Pioneer Missions

Mobilizing a fully trained missionary with a ministry platform is both time and resource intensive. A platform is a legitimate reason for allowing a non-citizen permission to live and work within a particular nation that normally places restrictions on visas and openly forbids Christian missions and/or evangelism (Steffen 2012). In the past, various "tent-making" (James 2012; Williams 2012)[5] opportunities have proved successful in establishing viable ministry platforms and facilitating access to nations hostile to the gospel message. Specifically, two such platforms which are well documented are Business-as-Missions and Humanitarian Aid & Relief organizations (Steffen 2012). These endeavors are often structured as Non-Governmental Organizations or NGOs (Barnett 2012). Given the overwhelming numbers of UUPG and estimates that workers in this harvest field are severely under resourced in personnel and finances, it is understandable that foreign missionaries willing to serve in this capacity are in tremendous need (About missions 2016).

Therefore, a paradigm shift in missional thinking, as mentioned above, is sorely needed. Local churches partnering with mission agencies to engage the remaining unreached both within their nation of birth and abroad among the diaspora is one such approach. Therefore, sending agencies should continue to mobilize foreign missionaries while also equipping local congregations to reach internationals living in the West. This approach would exponentially increase the global church's missional

---

[4] Lawson Lau, (1984, 76) "Mutual respect, however, involves a balanced, reciprocal relationship. Each person perceives that his or her point of view is valid and worthy of being heard. Complete acceptance of one another, rather than prejudice, forms the basis of the relationship. Each person is permitted to realize fully his or her own potential. Neither has to abandon ethical or moral principles in an arbitrary fashion. Manipulation is absent in mutual respect. They are befriended as people created in the image of God and deserving of respect. In the cross-cultural context mutual respect means that no culture is considered superior or more advanced than the other. Such respect also fosters trust. If trust is undermined, both parties will make every effort to restore the trust balance as the relationship is built on a foundation of two-way communication."

[5] Alton James (2012, 264) identifies "a term to describe the efforts of those working separate jobs to support their ministry efforts as "tentmaking," based on the apostle Paul's example of working as a tentmaker to support himself (Acts 18:3)." And Joel Williams (2012, 61-62) agrees that "Paul often supported his missionary work through his own manual labor, using his training as a tentmaker (Acts 18:1-5, cf. Acts 20:33-35, 1 Thessalonians 2:9)."

efforts.

Historically, mission agencies have traditionally focused on geographic locations (Rankin 2015) and the ethnolinguistic people within geopolitical nations. Foreign missions requires years of ministry and language training as well as cultural awareness (Holste 2012) in addition to the business or social service endeavor which the stated platform will offer to the host nation. All this is crucial in light of mistakes made in the past where the work of the stated platform was ignored, causing the Western missionary to compromise his reputation within the community he was attempting to reach (Love 2009). For example: the computer repairman who never has time to repair computers but always wants to talk with host nation people about religious matters. This person will quickly appear odd to some and suspicious to others.

The Unengaged on U.S. Soil

With these mass migrations of peoples, we may have the opportunity to reach people who were, up to this point, considered unreached — not because we went to their place but because they came to our place. In Toronto, one of the most international cities in North America, a pastor observed, "God called us to go to all nations. But we didn't go, so He's bringing all nations to us!" (Borthwick 2012, 40).

According to Paul Borthwick (2012), the United States and Canada together only make up five to six percent of the global population. Yet, these countries are experiencing the voluntary and involuntary coming (Winter 2009a)[6] of internationals for safety, education, and a better way of life. God is bringing unreached peoples — Muslims, Hindus, Buddhists, and Sikhs (Culbertson 2016), to communities, particularly within the United States, which have a history of flaunting their evangelical heritage (Nichols 2008). Payne (2012) asserts that thirteen percent of the United States population and twenty percent of Canadians are foreign-born. He goes on to cite the *Joshua Project,* which identifies fifty-three unreached people groups living within the borders of these two counties. He goes on to argue that within such ethnically diverse nations, global disciple-

---

[6] Winter (2009) describes the voluntary and involuntary coming and going of people globally, all orchestrated to accomplish the purposes of God. Historical examples of *Voluntary Going* include missionaries like William Carey and Hudson Taylor; *Involuntary Going* would include the large number of soldiers who participated in World War II, who were so impacted by the poverty and human suffering they observed that upon completing their enlistment they started nearly 150 mission agencies. Examples of *Voluntary Coming* include international students, scholars and businesspersons immigrating to the West and investing in those economies. And *Involuntary Coming* includes refugees, human trafficking victims, and those fleeing armed conflict.

making is an opportunity that local congregations should not ignore. These statistics convince us that unreached peoples are dispersed throughout both countries, and they give reasonable assurance that unreached peoples exist within easy access of many evangelical churches in the United States. Therefore, local churches have an opportunity to reach individuals who beforehand were prevented from hearing the message of Jesus Christ (Phillips and Eaton 2010). Upon learning of the suggestion for local congregations to build relationships with international students, many pastors may argue that they are already taxed to maximum capacity. As they serve their congregations daily, their members seek intervention on a host of challenges ranging from marital infidelity, divorce, or disobedient children to requiring support escaping the grip of gambling, pornography, or drug addiction. Additionally, they may contend that "many church members lack a passion for the things of God in their own lives and those of their immediate neighbors. Expecting them to commit time and energy to cross-cultural missions is simply unrealistic." Admittedly these are all legitimate and challenging concerns which many pastors face.

However, welcoming strangers, in this case international students, is not merely another task for ministers to perform; it is an *opportunity* for the average church member. The first step is to pray and remember that being kind and demonstrating hospitality does not require a seminary degree, rather simply the courage to drive to a nearby campus and ask about opportunities volunteering with international students. Let the school leadership set the agenda and be diligent to understand and comply with their policy, if any, regarding proselytizing. This is not a contradiction, rather an application of faith. Demonstrate integrity by being open and honest concerning who you are, and be respectful of stated requirements for volunteers interacting with students. Remember, God is sovereign; He is the one drawing individuals to Christ (John 6:40-46). Encourage congregational members to be willing to serve, spend time with others, and cultivate the character qualities that an international student can grow to depend upon regardless of their receptivity to the gospel message.

In addition to praying, Christ followers should also seek God's wisdom and discernment regarding all of life's affairs (Powers 2010). As one routinely reads the Bible it would be prudent to also give thought to the Sovereign Lord's involvement in the global movement of people. As Western nations in general and the United States in particular experience the influx of unreached peoples, pray: "Lord, what are you requiring of me in this situation?" and allow Him to determine your next step. Scripture is replete with examples of the scattering of peoples. Most notable are the Jews in the Old Testament and the first Christians in the New Testament. The Lord God has used and will continue to use human circumstances to bring about His sovereign will, even as He allowed the Roman census to coincide with the birth of Jesus in fulfillment of prophecy. God is at work in the lives of the scattered peoples of the world today and the church should pay attention.

Many well-meaning citizens have exclaimed that "the large numbers of foreign-born people" seeking refuge in Europe and the United States "is simply frightening." They argue that "the Islamic State (ISIS), Al-Qaeda, the Taliban, and others are taking advantage of our open door policy and putting the lives of Americans at risk." They consider it "foolish to welcome people like that" into their homes. No doubt, this calls for exceptional wisdom and prudence. Trusting God in situations like these can be significantly challenging and requires maturity and insight on the part of believers (Borthwick 2012).[7] Regrettably many church attenders in the United States are more concerned with material possessions, political agendas, or personal freedoms than the word of God and His purposes.

Consider internal criticism regarding the worldliness of the American church. Two notable Christian leaders have commented on this growing trend. Russell Moore, President of the Ethics & Religious Liberty Commission of the Southern Baptist Convention, argued in a recent interview that the political use of the word *evangelical* is "subverting the gospel of Jesus Christ" (Miller 2016). He is leveling this charge against voters and the media for using *evangelical* as a synonym for political conservatives. Likewise, Stephen Nichols, President of Reformation Bible College maintains that American society has historically recast the image of Jesus in its likeness (Nichols 2008). In other words, Nichols is positing that many self-professed Christians in America worship a god of their own making whom they call Jesus, although what they worship has little resemblance to the God of the Bible. Both these conservative Christian leaders as well as others are warning the Western Church to take stock of what they believe and to ask themselves what source material they are basing those beliefs upon. Most notably, these leaders are entreating self-identified Christians to consider what they hold as true about Christ and to compare those beliefs with what Scripture identifies as the communicable attributes of God (Grudem 1994).

In describing the communicable attributes of God, Grudem (1994) argues that conforming to the image of Christ cannot be accomplished without accurate knowledge of God. The truth regarding God, His character, and creation is contained in Scripture. Therefore, the wisdom

---

[7] Borthwick (2012, 29) in quoting Philip Jenkins, argues against the fears that Islam will become the dominate religion in Europe. He contends that proponents from these concerns fail to consider that large numbers of immigrants to Europe are African Christians fleeing Islam. The largest church in London is pastored by a Nigerian, as is the largest church Kiev Ukraine, as well as one of the five largest churches in New York City.

needed to accurately discern who to befriend comes from God alone and cannot be determined by human means. Numerous biblical passages speak of the believers' responsibility to grow in Christlikeness, identifying Christian maturity as infinitely more important than material possessions, political agenda, or personal freedoms.

College Campuses

Paul Borthwick (2012) asserts that over half the global population is of college age or younger, and notes that China's teenage population exceeds the total inhabitants of the United States. In light of these statistics, more missionary effort would wisely be focused on the world's youth. Consequently, international student ministry offers an excellent opportunity for the average congregant to actively participate in global missions.

Reflecting upon the more than 1.4 million international students currently registered at US institutions of higher education (Student and Exchange Visitor Information System 2015), Hegarty (2014, 223) argues that although "many recognize the importance of this student population, they fail to understand the scale of their influence." Hegarty is referring to their economic impact, which although important to local economies, pales in comparison to their strategic implication to the Kingdom. When statistics are discussed at the macro level, numbers can often be overwhelming. Therefore, consider the micro level impact of international students.

According to *The Open Doors Fact Sheet*, in 2015 there were approximately 7,901 international students studying within the state of Alabama (Institute of International Education 2016). Of those numbers, nearly twenty percent are Northern African/Middle Eastern or Central and South Asian Peoples. Many of the world's UUGP are comprised of these Global Affinity Groups (Rankin 2015). Additionally, for the past five years China has consistently sent the greatest number of international students to Alabama, ranging from twenty to thirty percent of the international student population annually (Institute of International Education 2016). In light of these numbers, a legitimate question to ask is: "Does Ed Stetzer's comment that although internationals are living among us, they still fail to hear the gospel message (Lowery 2010) hold true in the Bible-belt also?" Fortunately, churches can take some fairly simple and inexpensive steps to reach international students and first-generation immigrants in their communities with the good news of Jesus Christ (Lowery 2010).

Outreach Ministry and the Local Church

As stated earlier, many Americans view evangelicals as a political block instead of an expression of faith in Jesus Christ grounded in Scripture. The Center for the Study of Global Christianity (2013) at Gordon Conwell Theological Seminary offers a composite definition based partly on Jason Mandryk's handling of the word in *Operation World:*

Evangelicals are largely Protestant, Independent, or Anglican, but some are Catholic or Orthodox. Operation World defines Evangelicals as affiliated church members who hold to four qualities: grounded belief in the crucified Christ, an experience of a personal conversion, theological foundation in the Bible as the word of God, and active missionary evangelism or preaching of the gospel.

Given this definition, a goal of evangelicals would include the global propagation of the gospel message to those who have not heard it. In keeping with this approach, the U.S. Center for World Missions, through the course *Perspectives on the World Christian Movement* (2016) has identified five lifestyle practices by which an individual church member can actively support and thus participate in global missions: *Mobilize, Pray, Send, Welcome, and Go.* A brief description of each follows.

According to Clyde Meador, "God doesn't call every person to go to some other part of the country or the world to carry the gospel. There are other critical, strategic ways in which you may be called to participate in His mission" (Meador 2012, 617). Therefore, individual Christ followers can find one or more of the following applications of global missions appropriate to their life circumstances and natural abilities: (a) "Mobilization is communicating to others the compelling need and certain command to be involved in God's mission, helping them to see how they may be involved in the mission and encouraging them to put those pieces together" (Meador 2012, 619). (b) "One way that every one of us must be involved in God's mission is through prayer. God's mission is accomplished when God acts, and God acts in response to the prayers of His people. Jesus said 'the harvest is plentiful, but the workers are few. Ask the Lord of the harvest, therefore, to send out workers into his harvest field' (Luke 10:2)." (Meador 2012, 617). (c) "Those active in the practice of sending strive to complete the task by supporting the work of others. This includes providing ongoing financial support or occasional gifts, prayers, offering one's expertise at a distance, and/or making strategically timed visits to missionaries, are just a few examples. And the habit of sending involves a decision to connect our heart to God's heart by investing our treasure in His mission" (Hickman, Hawthorne and Ahrend 2009, 727). (d) "We use the word 'welcoming' as a way to describe going to people without traveling as far. Working with people who are visiting or have newly migrated to our home communities can be every bit as significant as going to distant countries. And reaching out to internationals should be a natural practice for those of us who claim to care for God's purposes to all nations" (Hickman, Hawthorne, and Ahrend 2009, 727). (e) "Many have old, or odd, stereotypes of what missionaries are like and what missionaries really do. The models and modes of cross-cultural work are changing rapidly with international commerce and communication. Business as mission, tentmaking and other creative approaches has allowed many believers to thrust themselves into strategic opportunities" (Hickman, Hawthorne, and Ahrend 2009, 726).

However, not every person of a different faith will embrace Christianity when given a chance, even as not every person who claims faith in Christ will spend eternity with Him (Matt. 7:21-23). Believers have a responsibility before Christ to obey His command and make disciples of all nations. The importance of relying on wisdom and discernment was addressed earlier. This is particularly true when attempting to understand what Scripture teaches and how one should apply those instructions to daily life. For instance, Scripture makes a distinction between "foreigners" and "strangers." Scripture forbids marrying "foreigners" (Deut. 31:16, 1 Kings 11:1-2) who are described as worshipers of foreign gods that seek to persuade believers to reject the Living God. However, a difference is discovered upon close examination of the word translated as "strangers" (Lev. 19:33-34). Although they may have previously worshiped foreign gods, believers are encouraged to develop right relationships with strangers as they embrace faith in the Living God.

Believers are urged to treat strangers with care, because God will judge the believing person who mistreats the stranger whom He drew to the believer's country or community to learn of and worship the one true God (Exod. 22:21, Lev. 19:33). Both terms, foreigners and strangers, address people of a different racial, national, and religious background, yet there is a clear distinction between the two. Believers are instructed to distance themselves from one and to treat the other as a family member. Godly insight, perspective, and context are critically important in reading Scripture because purely human reasoning results in these terms appearing indistinguishable.

In the New Testament, Paul argues in Romans 15:20 that he desires to preach Christ to those who have never heard His name before. When believers consider the example of strangers above, it becomes clear that some who will ultimately convert to Christianity do so by abandoning their former religion or faith. Christ is building His church and humanity is not only the rocks which He uses to form this church, but often are the stone implements He uses to extract the pebbles of which He is taking possession. Mission agencies are skillfully equipped to engage and make disciples of unreached peoples within their native lands. However, some of the most available of the unreached are currently studying at Western universities. For this reason, Rankin (2015) suggests that establishing partnerships between mission agencies and local churches can create significant inroads toward reaching this accessible population of future leaders.

A Collaborative Approach to International Student Engagement

Some critics would recoil at the suggestion that local congregations develop partnerships with any organization other than another church, nevertheless Ralph Winter (2009b) argues in favor of both *Modality* (local churches and denominational bodies) and *Sodality* (parachurch organizations and sending agencies) working collaboratively. A team is comprised of both defensive and offensive elements. The objective of the offense is to maintain possession of the ball and score points. The focus of the defense is to prevent the opposing team from scoring by depriving them of the ball and blocking their scoring attempts. In a similar manner, the local church is called to take the offense with the goal of making disciples for Christ while the parachurch ministry or mission agency assumes a defensive posture among the unbelieving world. The defense is seeking to halt the progression of the Enemy in the lives of individuals currently outside the community of faith. Together these two elements limit the advancement of other faiths and increase the number of potential disciples for the body of Christ.

In light of this analogy, one could argue that the average church attender lacks the skill and capacity to effectively engage international students. Many parishioners within the local church view themselves as ill-equipped to enter some cultural settings and share the gospel. However, Christ is determined to build His church as seen in Luke 14:22-24, where the Master of the banquet commands his servants to go out into the "highways and hedges and compel people to come in." This is the beauty of the Sodality; these individuals are equipped in understanding cultural differences and applying cross-cultural ministry techniques. They also understand which traditional activities within the Western church would be culturally inappropriate and even derail the progress of the gospel among certain people groups (Ward 1999). It is precisely for these reasons that a mission agency would instruct and advise local congregations in the intricacies unique to the unreached peoples living in close proximity of that local congregation.

Mission agencies can equip and mobilize local churches to engage unreached peoples within their communities. These same agencies can also provide training and serve as consultants for local congregations. They have the resident expertise that the local church needs to effectively engage internationals. Historically, the local church is well served by agencies who partner with them by providing training and orientation for those going overseas. Some agencies provide potential partners with *vision trips* to frontier areas and others provide orientation programs which introduce future partners to a geographic location (Rankin and Edens 2012). This type of interaction could be extended to congregational members who desire to serve a particular people group within their current community.

Training, orientation, and vision trips can energize individuals, families, and congregations to commit to years (if not decades) of service among internationals living in America. This consultative relationship between mission agency and local church or partnership of churches would allow the collaborative planning and support (Ward 1999) needed to successfully begin to cultivate a relationship with an international student residing in the United States. Once that individual returns home, the sending agency could follow up and continue where the local church left off. Not to discredit the education and training received by missionaries, pastors, and others in vocational ministry, but we assume too much when we believe that God "saves" someone because of what is said or done. Possibly closer to the truth is that God "saves" in spite of what is said or done by humans. Believers are required to obey our Lord and Savior. He has issued the command to go out into diverse places and compel various people to join Him (Luke 14:22-24). The only question remaining is whether His church will obey.

Summary/Conclusion

The Great Commission was given to the global Body of Christ, the Church. This mandate is for both individual believers and the Church as a whole. Therefore, encouraging local congregations to focus on both pioneer and diaspora missions is very fitting. Developing partnerships between local congregations and mission agencies to reach internationals on large and small campuses is instrumental to evangelizing UUPG. Diaspora missions, unlike foreign missions, do not require years of professional training, rather are founded on hospitality and welcoming (Wan 2007). It should not be viewed as an alternative to foreign missions, but as a supplement (Wan and Tira 2010). Focusing on diaspora missions is very appropriate for the average church member and should not be considered another responsibility for the pastoral staff. The Lord of the feast has commanded His servants to go into the highways and hedges and compel people (Luke 14:22-23) to come to His banquet. Local churches seeking ways to support both foreign and diaspora missions will greatly contribute to compelling the various peoples of Earth to join our Lord and Savior at this meal.

References

About missions. 2016. "Statistics." Accessed April 8, 2016,
http://www.aboutmissions.org/statistics.html.

Barnett, Mike. 2012. "The Global Century." *Discovering the Mission of God: Best Missional Practices for the 21st Century.* Eds. Mike Barnett and Robin Martin, 287-305. Downers Grove: InterVarsity Press.

Borthwick, Paul. 2012. *Western Christians in Global Mission: What's the Role of the North American Church?* Downers Grove: InterVarsity Press. Accessed April 20, 2016, ESBCOhost.

Center for the Study of Global Christianity. 2013. "Christianity in its Global Context, 1970-2020: Society, Religion, and Mission." Hamilton, MA: Gordon-Conwell Theological Seminary. Accessed Apr 13, 2016. http://www.gordonconwell.edu/ockenga/research/documents/2Christianityinitsglobalcontext.pdf.

Culbertson, Howard. 2016. The *Mission Mobilizer* (blog), Southern Nazarene University. Accessed April 14, 2016. https://home.snu.edu/~hculbert/thumb.htm

Galloway, Bryan and J.D. Payne. 2014. "More Than Strangers Next Door...Our Neighbors: The Peoplegroups.info Initiative to Research the Nations within the United States." Paper presented at the S. E. Regional Evangelical Missiological Society, Columbia International University, Columbia, SC, March 28-29, 2014. Accessed January 17, 2016. http://www.jdpayne.org/wp-content/uploads/2014/04/2014-SE-EMS-Paper.docx

Grudem, Wayne. 1994. *Systematic Theology: An Introduction to Biblical Doctrine.* Grand Rapids: Zondervan.

Haney, Jim. 2012. "The State of the Spread of the Gospel," *Discovering the Mission of God: Best Missional Practices for the 21st Century.* Eds. Mike Barnett and Robin Martin, 309-322. Downers Grove: InterVarsity Press.

Hawthorne, Steven C. 2009. "Mandate on the Mountain." In *Perspectives on the World Christian Movement: A Reader,* 4th ed. Eds. Ralph D. Winter and Steven C. Hawthorn, 126-131. Pasadena: William Carey Library.

Hegarty, Niall. 2014. "Where We are Now: The Presence and Importance of International Students to Universities in the United States." *Journal of International Students,* 4 no. 3, 223-235.

Hickman, Claude, Steven C. Hawthorne, and Todd Ahrend. 2009. "Life on Purpose." *Perspectives on the World Christian Movement: A Reader,* 4th ed. Eds. Ralph D. Winter and Steven C. Hawthorn, 725-730. Pasadena: William Carey Library.

Holste, J. Scott. 2012. "Finishing the Task," *Discovering the Mission of God: Best Missional Practices for the 21st Century.* Eds. Mike Barnett and Robin Martin, 323-339. Downers Grove: InterVarsity Press.

Institute of International Education. 2016. "The Open Doors Fact Sheet." Accessed April 2, 2016. http://www.iie.org/Research-and-Publications/Open-Doors/Data/Fact-Sheets-by-US-State/2015.

James, R. Alton. 2012. "Post-Reformation Missions Pioneers," *Discovering the Mission of God: Best Missional Practices for the 21st Century.* Eds. Mike Barnett and Robin Martin, 251-266. Downers Grove: InterVarsity Press.

Kim, Steve (Heung Chan). 2009. "A Newer Missions Paradigm and the Growth of Missions from the Majority World." In *Missions from the Majority World: Progress, Challenges, and Case Studies.* Eds. Enoch Wan and Michael Pocock, 1-34. Pasadena: William Carey Library.

Koch, Bruce A. 2009. "The Surging Non-Western Mission Force," *Perspectives on the World Christian Movement: A Reader*, 4th ed. Eds. Ralph D. Winter and Steven C. Hawthorn, 370. Pasadena: William Carey Library.

Kraft, Marguerite and Meg Crossman. 2009. "Women in Mission," *Perspectives on the World Christian Movement: A Reader*, 4th ed. Eds. Ralph D. Winter and Steven C. Hawthorn, 294-298. Pasadena: William Carey Library.

Krumov, Krum and Knud S. Larsen. 2013. *Cross-cultural Psychology: Why Culture Matters.* Charlotte: Information Age Publishing.

Lausanne Committee for World Evangelization. 2004. "The New People Next Door." Lausanne *Occasional Paper* No. 55. Pattaya, Thailand: Lausanne Committee for World Evangelization. Accessed December 15, 2015. https://www.lausanne.org/wp-content/uploads/2007/06/LOP55_IG26.pdf.

Lewis, Jeff. 2012. "God's Great Commissions for the Nations." *Discovering the Mission of God: Best Missional Practices for the 21st Century.* Eds. Mike Barnett and Robin Martin, 99-113. Downers Grove: InterVarsity Press.

Love, Rick. 2009. "Identity with Integrity: Apostolic Ministry in the 21st Century." *Perspectives on the World Christian Movement: A Reader*, 4th ed. Eds. Ralph D. Winter and Steven C. Hawthorn, 477-481. Pasadena: William Carey Library.

Lowery, Brooklyn. 2010. "Research: Outreach to First-Generation Immigrants Succeeding, Needs Improvement." LifeWay Research, March 29. Accessed December 20, 2015.

http://www.lifeway.com/Article/LifeWay-Research-finds-outreach-to-first-generation-immigrants-succeeding-needs-improvement.

Mandryk, Jason. 2005. "The State of the Gospel." In *Perspectives on the World Christian Movement: A Reader*, 4th ed. Eds. Ralph D. Winter and Steven C. Hawthorn, 361-368. Pasadena: William Carey Library.

———. 2010. *Operation World: The Definitive Prayer Guide to Every Nation.* 7th ed. Colorado Springs: Biblica Publishing.

Mathis, David. 2012. "Introduction: Remember, Jesus Never Lies." In *Finish the Mission: Bringing the Gospel to the Unreached and Unengaged*. Eds. John Piper and David Mathis, 13-28. Wheaton: Crossway.

Meador, Clyde. 2012. "Where Do You Fit in the Mission of God," *Discovering the Mission of God: Best Missional Practices for the 21st Century*. Eds. Mike Barnett and Robin Martin Editors, 610-621. Downers Grove: InterVarsity Press.

Miller, Emily McFarlan. 2016. "Russell Moore: Don't Call Me an 'Evangelical.'" Accessed March 30, 2016. http://www.religionnews.com/2016/02/29/russell-moore-dont-call-me-an-evangelical.

National Human Genome Research Institute. 2007. "A Guide to your Genome, National Institute of Health." *NIH Publication* No. 07-6284. Accessed April 16, 2016. https://www.genome.gov/pages/education/allaboutthehumangenomeproject/guidetoyourgenome07.pdf

Nichols, Stephen J. 2008. *Jesus Made in America: A Cultural History from the Puritans to the Passion of the Christ*. Downers Grove: InterVarsity Press.

Packer, J.I. 1961. *Evangelism and the Sovereignty of God. Downers* Grove: Inter-Varsity.

Payne, J.D. 2012. *Strangers Next Door: Immigration, Migration and Mission*. Downers Grove: InterVarsity Press.

Perspectives on the World Christian Movement. 2016. "Alumni next steps." Accessed April 15, 2016. http://www.perspectives.org/Alumni#/HTML/alumni_next_steps.htm.

Phillips, Rob and Doug Eaton. 2010. "People and Churches can Reach First-Generation Immigrants." *Facts & Trends*. Nashville: Lifeway Christian Resources, 6-8. Accessed December 20, 2015. http://factsandtrends.net/files/2013/02/2010_04Fall.pdf.

Piper, John. 1993. *Let the Nations be Glad: The Supremacy of God in Missions*. Grand Rapids: Baker Books.

Pocock, Michael, Gailyn van Rheenen, and Douglas McConnell. 2005. *The*

Changing Face of World Missions: Engaging Contemporary Issues and Trends. Grand Rapids: Baker Academic.

Pocock, Michael. 2015. "Global Migration: Where Do We Stand." *Diaspora Missions: Reflections on Reaching the Scattered Peoples of the World.* Pasadena: William Carey Library.

Powers, Philip. 2010. "Acts and Pauline Epistles." Lectures, Capital Bible Seminary, Lanham, MD, Spring 2010.

Rankin, Jerry. 2015. "Organizing to Reach the Diaspora: A Case Study of The International Mission Board, SBC; Changing its Overseas Structure from Geographic Components to Global Affinity Groups." *Diaspora Missions: Reflections on Reaching the Scattered Peoples of the World.* Pasadena: William Carey Library.

Rankin, Jerry and Mike Edens. 2012. "Church and Agency Co-Laboring," In *Discovering the Mission of God: Supplement.* Eds. Mike Barnett and Robin Martin. Downers Grove: InterVarsity Press.

Steffen, Tom. 2012. "Creative-access platforms." *Discovering the Mission of God: Best Missional Practices for the 21st Century.* Eds. Mike Barnett and Robin Martin, 517-534. Downers Grove: InterVarsity Press.

Student and Exchange Visitor Information System. 2015. "SEVIS by the Numbers: General Summary Quarterly Review." (November). Accessed April 2, 2016. https://www.ice.gov/sites/default/files/documents/Report/2015/sevis-bythenumbers-dec15.pdf.

The Voice of the Martyrs, Accessed December 20, 2015. http://www.persecution.com/public/nationsdefined.aspx.

Wan, Enoch. 2007. "Diaspora Missiology," *Occasional Bulletin of EMS* 4, no. 4, (Spring). Accessed December 20, 2015. http://ojs.globalmissiology.org/index.php/english/article/viewFile/303/848.

Wan, Enoch and Sadiri Joy Tira. 2010. "Diaspora Missiology and Missions in the Context of the Twenty-First Century." *Torch Trinity Journal.* Accessed December 20, 2015. http://www.ttgst.ac.kr/upload/ttgst_resources13/20124-254.pdf.

Ward, Ted. 1999. "Repositioning Mission Agencies for the Twenty-First Century." *International Bulletin of Missionary Research*, ProQuest Religion, 23 no. 4.

Williams, Joel F. 2012. "The Missionary Message of the New Testament." *Discovering the Mission of God: Best Missional Practices for the 21st Century.* Eds. Mike Barnett and Robin Martin Editors, 49-67. Downers Grove: InterVarsity Press.

Winter, Ralph D. 1980. "Waving the Flag for 'Hidden' People.'" *Mission Frontier,* (March). Accessed April 2, 2016. http://www.missionfrontiers.org/issue/article/waving-the-flag-for-hidden-peoples.

–––––––. 2009a. "The Kingdom Strikes Back: Ten Epochs of Redemptive History," *Perspectives on the World Christian Movement: A Reader*, 4th ed. Eds. Ralph D. Winter and Steven C. Hawthorn, 209-227. Pasadena: William Carey Library.

–––––––. 2009b. "The Two Structures of God's Redemptive Mission," *Perspectives on the World Christian Movement: A Reader*, 4th ed. Eds. Ralph D. Winter and Steven C. Hawthorn, 244-253. Pasadena: William Carey Library.

Wolfgang, Ben. 2012. "Armed with U.S. Education, Many Leaders Take on World." The Washington Times. (Sunday, August 19). Accessed April 15, 2016. http://www.washingtontimes.com/news/2012/aug/19/armed-with-us-education-many-leaders-take-on-world/?page=all.

Yount, William R. 2012. "Back to Basics." *Discovering the Mission of God: Best Missional Practices for the 21st Century*. Eds. Mike Barnett and Robin Martin Editors, 435-450. Downers Grove: InterVarsity Press

CHAPTER 10
FROM EVERY CAMPUS TO EVERY NATION: CASE STUDIES OF DIASPORA MISSION

William S Murrell

Introduction: Iranians in Turkey and Filipinos in Dubai

A few months ago, I sat down in my office in Nashville Tennessee with an Iranian man who for security reasons we'll call "Paul." We were meeting to discuss the translation of theology, Bible, and leadership courses into Farsi for young leaders in an Iranian diaspora church in Turkey. Paul, though he lives in Nashville, travels to this particular city in Turkey several times a year to baptize new believers, establish the young church in the faith, and train young men and women to lead small group Bible studies and house churches in their new city—and wherever they end up next.

A few of the members of this church (numbering around forty-five) are Muslim-background believers who fled Iran because of religious persecution or economic hardship, while many others are diasporic Iranians who have come to faith in Turkey as a result of this community of believers. There are also Farsi-speaking Kurds and Afghans who have come to faith in this community. Paul is connected to this group because several of the initial members of this diaspora church first came to faith in the house church network he started in Iran almost twenty years ago.

Whenever Paul meets with these young Iranian believers, he tells them from his own experience how God can use persecution to purify and strengthen the church, and he also tells them from his own experience how God can use diaspora churches to reach the world.

Paul was born a Shia Muslim in Iran, but he came to faith in Jesus in an evangelical charismatic Filipino diaspora church in Dubai where his Filipina wife (a Catholic turned Muslim turned Evangelical) was attending. When Paul began attending this thriving Filipino church with his wife, he began to notice that though Filipinos comprised the majority, there were people from twenty-four nations present—people from Iran, India, Sri Lanka, Pakistan, Nigeria, and Nepal. Some (especially those from the Philippines and Nigeria) were already Christians working in Dubai and looking for a church community, yet others (like those from Iran and Nepal) were from distinctly non-Christian backgrounds and came to faith in that church community.

At the time Paul was an engineer working in Dubai; nineteen months later he and his family moved back to Iran. Immediately, Paul shared the gospel with his Muslim friends and family — many of whom came to faith in Jesus within a matter of months. Paul quickly began discipling these new believers and equipping them to disciple others. This initial house church in Paul's hometown multiplied into a network of underground house churches in five different cities in Iran.

However, it was not long before the government noticed the rapidly growing Christian movement in their country.

Paul and several key leaders were arrested and questioned. Most of them were threatened and released, but Paul remained in prison for several months where he was interrogated almost daily, held in solitary confinement, and ultimately tried for apostasy — a capital offense in Iran.

Paul assumed that he would be convicted and executed, nevertheless, in his final hearing, the judge unexpectedly acquitted him of all charges. Upon release, Paul and his family (who had been under government surveillance for many months) fled the country — first spending several months being hosted by a church in Mumbai, a church which coincidentally had been planted out of the Dubai church; then traveling to Manila.

Manila was a strategic landing spot not only because his wife was Filipina but also because his home church in Dubai had been planted out of an evangelical charismatic church in Manila. It was in this church where Paul's family found a new home after many months of fleeing for their lives and where Paul was further equipped as a pastor and missionary. Though Paul wanted to return to Iran to care for the flock that had been scattered during the persecution, he was a marked man in Iran and acknowledged that he could not return home.

After several years in the Philippines, Paul and his family received asylum in the United States. Though he can never return to Iran, he has always reached out to Muslims (particularly Iranian Muslims) wherever he finds himself — whether in Manila or Nashville.

As subsequent persecutions in Iran have scattered members of the church to Turkey, Paul has taken this opportunity to serve the flock once again and to equip them to make disciples wherever they go.

Diaspora Missions in Every Nation

I recount the remarkable story of my friend Paul for two reasons. First, Paul's story is a fascinating case study in diaspora missiology. In his prolific work on the topic, Enoch Wan outlines four types of diaspora missions — missions *to, through, by and beyond,* and *with* the diaspora; each of these four types are at play in Paul's story.[1] In the Dubai church, we find strategic missions *to* diasporic Muslims working in Dubai, a nation where it is strictly illegal to reach local Emirati Muslims though less illegal to reach foreign Iranian Muslims. We also find missions *through* Iranian believers, like Paul, to Iranian Muslims, first in Dubai, then in Iran, and later in Manila, Nashville, and now Turkey. What we also find in this story is missions *by and beyond* a Filipino diaspora church in Dubai—one which was able to reach beyond its ethnic enclave and engage unreached Muslim diaspora communities in Dubai. Finally, in Paul's story we also see an example of missions *with* the diaspora, as churches in both Mumbai and Manila partnered with Paul as he sought refuge from persecution and later as he sought new opportunities for missions to the Muslim world.

I also tell this story because it has become something of a folk legend in Every Nation Churches and Ministries, the ministry where both Paul and I work. Every Nation is an evangelical charismatic church-planting organization that exists, according to its mission statement, "to honor God by establishing Christ-centered, Spirit-empowered, socially responsible churches and campus ministries in every nation."[2] While no one could have predicted Paul's remarkable trajectory, in many ways, Paul's story is a prototypical Every Nation story. Though its original founders are Americans, Every Nation has never promoted a "West to the rest" mentality in global missions. For example, in Paul's story we find an Iranian diaspora church in Turkey planted by a group of churches in Iran that were planted by a Filipino diaspora church in Dubai that was planted by a church in the Philippines.

Over the last twenty-five years since its founding in 1994, Every Nation's growth from a handful of churches in three nations to over four hundred churches in eighty one nations has been a product of multi-directional sending and receiving with its greatest missionary dynamism coming from one particular Every Nation church in Manila. This is no accident, for multi-directional missions *among* the diaspora, to use Wan's language, has been part of Every Nation's DNA from its inception.

In 1994, Rice Broocks, a campus evangelist from Nashville, Phil Bonasso, a church-planter from Los Angeles, and Steve Murrell, a cross-cultural church-planter in the Philippines, met in Murrell's home in Manila to discuss potential church plants in Singapore and Malaysia. Broocks, Bonasso, and Murrell had become friends in college through participation in a charismatic campus ministry during the Jesus Movement in the 1970s. By 1994, the ministry that connected them no longer existed, yet their

---

[1] For a summary of each type, see Enoch Wan, *Diaspora Missiology: Theory, Methodology, and Practice*, (Western Seminary: Portland, 2001), 6-8 and 129-34.
[2] See https://www.everynation.org/about/

friendship remained.

The collaborative effort that brought them together in 1994 would become another hallmark of Every Nation global missions—reaching the nations by reaching international students on the university campus. In this particular case, Bonasso and Broocks were asking Murrell to assist (from Manila) a prospective church planter in the region, a Singaporean who had been reached as a college student at the University of Southern California through Bonasso's church-based campus ministry.

Recognizing they could do more for the Kingdom together than apart, the three decided to start Every Nation in 1994. Since that day, Every Nation has planted churches and campus ministries in over eighty nations and hopes, by God's grace, to have a presence in every nation of the world by the middle of this century.

Though diaspora mission has never been an explicitly articulated mission strategy in Every Nation, in retrospect, many of the movement's most fruitful church plants over the last twenty-five years have been the result of reaching international students on university campuses and launching these diasporic Christians into mission—whether to their countries of origin or to new mission fields.

In what follows, I will give a brief history of Every Nation's work in the Philippines, followed by several case studies of churches and campus ministries that are a result of diasporic missions *through, by and beyond* Filipinos—some of whom were sent from the Philippines and others who were scattered.

Every Nation in the Philippines (and the Role of Diaspora Missions)

In the summer of 1984, a team of sixty-five American college students embarked on a one-month summer mission trip to Manila's University Belt—the epicenter of student protest and unrest in the final years of the Marcos regime. After four weeks of evangelistic outreaches, a small church of 165 college students was birthed. Steve and Deborah Murrell, some of the team leaders, were left behind to shepherd the fledgling church. First they committed to staying in the Philippines through the summer, then through the fall. Eventually, they decided to stay for good.

From its inception Murrell encouraged young Filipino disciples not only to pray for their nation but also to pray for the nations of the world.

Jun Escosar, one of the original disciples from 1984, recalls:

The vision for world missions was planted in me in the first days of my life as a Christian. In those early days, young Filipino students who were becoming believers and disciples every day were inspired to envision themselves as missionaries... We started to learn about what it meant to follow Christ by laying our hands on a tattered old National Geographic world map and interceding for the nations one by one. That became one of our earliest traditions at Victory.[3]

Escosar, who is now the director for the Every Nation School of World Missions in Manila, recalls that the mantra in the early days of the church was *a Bible and a passport*. Every disciple needed a Bible so that they could know God and His redemptive purposes for the world; every disciple needed a passport so that they could obey God and participate in His redemptive purposes in the world.

Thirty-five years later, Victory Manila, one of the founding churches of Every Nation Churches and Ministries, is a thriving discipleship-oriented church that has planted churches in ninety-nine other Philippine cities and forty-five nations around the world, including Afghanistan, Iran, Bangladesh, Cambodia, Laos, China, Spain, the United Arab Emirates, and Vietnam. Over the last three and a half decades, Victory has sent out 185 long-term cross-cultural Filipino missionaries and sends out an average of 650 short-term missionaries each year.[4]

While Victory Manila, a multi-site church of over 90,000, operates on a scale that exceeds even most megachurches in the world, its story and mission strategy have become a model for churches throughout the Every Nation world: Reach the university campus. Plant churches. Send out missionaries around the world. Wash, rinse, repeat.[5]

However, what differentiates Victory's church planting efforts from other Every Nation churches around the world (besides the scale) is the pivotal role of the Filipino diaspora — which, with over ten million Filipinos scattered in over one hundred nations, is one of the largest global diasporas in the world.[6]

In other words, though Victory's astounding missionary success in the last few decades can be attributed in large part to the church's remarkable growth and its single-minded focus on discipleship and world missions, the Philippine global diaspora has been an essential (if unplanned) aspect of this success story.

---

[3] Jun Escosar, *A Bible and a Passport* (Forthcoming, 2019), Preface (p15 in PDF draft).

[4] Escosar, *A Bible and a Passport*, Preface, 16-17 (PDF).

[5] For a detailed history of Victory Manila, see Steve Murrell, *WikiChurch: Making Discipleship Engaging, Empowering, and Viral*, (Lake Mary, FL: CharismaHouse, 2011). And for recent statistics on Victory, see Warren Bird, "Philippines: Victory Megachurch Building on Discipleship," *Outreach Magazine Online*, November 25, 2015. Accessed September 6, 2018. http://www.outreachmagazine.com/ideas/14125-philippines-victory-megachurch-building-on-discipleship.html

[6] Statistics from "Commision on Filipinos Overseas" in 2013. http://www.cfo.gov.ph/images/stories/pdf/StockEstimate2013.pdf. For more on the missional potential of the Filipino diaspora, see L. Pantoja Jr., S.J. Tira, E. Wan eds., *Scattered: The Filipino Global Presence*, (Life Change Publishing, Inc.: Manila, 2004).

I say unplanned because with few exceptions, the mission strategy of Victory and Every Nation has never been to plant Filipino diaspora churches around the world, rather to plant indigenous disciple-making churches in every nation. While some Filipino church planters and missionaries have been sent to places where many Filipinos had already been scattered (like Dubai or San Francisco), many others have been sent to places where few Filipinos were present (like Kathmandu or Tel Aviv).

Nonetheless, the ubiquitous global presence of the Filipino diaspora has often provided unexpected support and momentum for Filipino (and other Every Nation) cross-cultural missionaries in their church-planting and campus ministry efforts.

Similar to the rapid spread of the gospel along Jewish diasporic networks throughout the Mediterranean world in the West and the Indian Ocean in the East in the early decades of the Christian church, the Every Nation Philippines church-planting movement has also spread rapidly along Filipino diasporic networks around the world.

However, what is perhaps most unique is that this story is not only about the spread of the gospel *by* the Filipino diaspora but *beyond* it, as Filipinos have engaged other diasporic communities whether at home or abroad.

Nepalese in Los Baños: Missions *to* and *through* the Diaspora

Though Victory Manila, a growing megachurch in a prominent Global South metropolis, often receives attention from church-growth experts and missiologists, our case study will focus on a lesser known Victory congregation in Los Baños, a provincial college town south of Manila.

Victory Los Baños was planted in 1989 in an effort to reach students at the University of the Philippines Los Baños (UPLB). Over the years, Victory Los Baños, in partnership with Every Nation's campus ministry arm, Every Nation Campus (ENC), has seen great fruit at UPLB. Starting with thirty students in 1993, Victory Los Baños grew to over 1200 members by 2005 with over 1000 of their members being students from UPLB.[7]

UPLB is a public research university that is world renowned for its agricultural research and, in particular, its work in bioengineering high-yield strains of rice. UPLB houses the International Rice Research Institute (IRRI), which draws funding and students from all over the world.[8]

In 1995, an international student from Nepal began attending worship

---

[7] Today, Victory Los Baños still has over 1000 members, though at present only around 250 of them are students from UPLB, as many graduated in the years since the initial revival on campus. See Steve Murrell, *100 Years from Now*, (Nashville: 2013), 65-66.

[8] See https://www.irri.org/

services at Victory Los Baños. Shortly thereafter, the church began a discipleship group for international students which soon snowballed into an international student ministry. Within a few years, Victory Los Baños had engaged (through special events, discipleship groups, and worship services) students from Bhutan, Cambodia, Canada, China, India, Indonesia, Japan, Nepal, New Zealand, Pakistan, South Korea, Thailand, Timor-Leste, the United States, Liberia, Ghana, and Nigeria.

While hundreds of international students have walked through the doors of Victory Los Baños over the years, perhaps its greatest fruit has been with Nepalese students. Though there is no substantial Nepalese diaspora community in the Philippines, the International Rice Research Institute at UPLB draws a significant number of Nepalese students to study in Los Baños each year, creating a micro diaspora community on the university campus. Most of these students come from Hindu backgrounds yet have expressed varying degrees of openness to Christianity during their time in the Philippines.

Over the years, some Nepalese students have merely attended events held at the church while others have committed to following Jesus and have embarked on a process of lifelong discipleship.

As is always the case in Christian discipleship, it was through the first Nepalese disciples that Victory Los Baños has reached more and more Nepalese students over years. However, as is usually the case with international student ministry, most of these Nepalese disciples have completed their programs at UPLB and returned to their homeland.

Nevertheless, that is not the end of the story.

Filipinos in Kathmandu: Missions *by and beyond* the Diaspora

During the early years of Victory Los Baños' outreach to Nepalese students, a recent UPLB graduate and member of Victory Los Baños, we'll call "Peter," was asked by the pastor to help with the new yet growing international student ministry on campus.

Peter helped with the international student ministry first as a volunteer then from 2003 to 2005 as a campus missionary with ENC. According to Peter, his time working with international students at UPLB was deeply formative and caused him to wonder if God might be calling him to be a cross-cultural missionary outside of the Philippines.

In 2005, Peter moved to Mumbai to help with an Every Nation church plant (out of the Every Nation church in Dubai mentioned in the introduction). After three years of serving in India, Peter felt called to plant a church in Nepal.

When Peter and his wife "Esther" landed in Kathmandu in 2009, they had few contacts in the city. However, Peter had been able to reconnect with a few Nepalis who had been discipled through ENC and Victory Los Baños when they were students at UPLB in the 1990s and early 2000s. Though Peter hoped that these Nepali disciples would form the core of his church plant in Kathmandu, most of them had either joined other local churches or lived in other provinces in Nepal. Nonetheless, reconnecting with these Nepali disciples who had been reached and discipled as students in Los Baños gave Peter confidence that more Hindu-background Nepalis could be transformed by the gospel and planted in a local church.

For nine years, Peter and Esther made disciples and trained local leaders in Kathmandu. Regrettably, in the summer of 2018, they received an unexpected visit from the Nepalese immigration authorities who accused them of proselytizing and misusing their visa. They were given ten days to leave the country. Thankfully, Peter had already trained a local Nepali leadership team who were to take leadership in the church when Peter and Esther were forced to leave the country. All five of these Nepali leaders were from a Hindu background and were reached, baptized, and discipled in the Every Nation church in Kathmandu.

Today the church that Peter and Esther left one year ago is thriving under local leadership and looking to plant more churches in Nepal.

Nepalese in Abu Dhabi: Missions *with* the Diaspora

The Every Nation church in Kathmandu planted by Filipinos from Los Baños is not the only Every Nation church in Kathmandu. There is one more, though this congregation was planted out of an Every Nation church in Abu Dhabi.

While the former was the product of international student ministry at the University of Los Baños, the latter was the product of diaspora missions in Abu Dhabi. Every Nation Abu Dhabi is led by a Filipino pastor, yet the congregation mirrors the diversity of the labor force in the Arab states of the Persian Gulf. One of the most prominent diasporic groups they have reached in the last ten years are oversees workers from Nepal. In fact, the growing number of Nepalese attending the Every Nation church in Abu Dhabi necessitated the launching of a Nepalese service.

Though he did not expect to reach Nepalese people in Abu Dhabi, the pastor of the Every Nation church welcomed the opportunity to make disciples and train leaders among this diasporic people. Soon, one of the Nepalese disciples in that church felt called to return to Nepal and plant a church.

In partnership with Every Nation Abu Dhabi and the Every Nation School of World Missions in Manila, this Nepalese disciple planted a second Every Nation church in the city of Kathmandu.

Zimbabweans in Istanbul, Berlin, and Rio: Missions *with* the Diaspora (Pt 2)

This example of missions *with* the diaspora is not unusual in the Every Nation world. In Every Nation Grahamstown, we find another example of a church-based campus ministry partnering with a diasporic people on mission.

As a small university town in the Eastern Cape Province of South Africa, Grahamstown often attracts students from beyond the region. One such student was Brian, a Zimbabwean who moved first to Cape Town then to Grahamstown to study Psychology. Brian was already a Christian when he connected with Every Nation first as a student in Cape Town, then in Grahamstown where he reconnected with a fellow Zimbabwean and childhood friend, Gareth, who was the campus pastor.

During his time with Every Nation, Brian was trained in theology and missiology and participated in regional mission trips and church plants. And after a season of working in Singapore, Brian attended the Every Nation School of World Mission in Manila and moved to Istanbul to pioneer an Every Nation church plant in 2005.

Gareth, the campus pastor of Every Nation Grahamstown, eventually became the senior pastor when the founding pastors moved to plant a new church in the region. However, like his friend and fellow Zimbabwean, Gareth and his wife felt called to go—this time to plant a church in Berlin Germany in 2008. Supported and sent out from Grahamstown, Gareth's family and a small team pioneered a church plant in one of the world's most atheistic cities.

A few years later, one of the elders of the church in Grahamstown named Lester (who also happened to be a Zimbabwean), also felt called to go. In 2014, his family and a small team planted a church in Rio de Janeiro Brazil.

While this example certainly illustrates the unique missional dynamism of a particular church in a particular university town in South Africa, it also illustrates a larger principle that has been echoed throughout this essay. Diasporic peoples—particularly those that are reached as international students—are a powerful (and often underrated) mission-sending force, whether they are returning to their nation of origin or continuing in their sojourn to the next place where God, in His providence, brings them.

Conclusion: Jews in Asia Minor and Iranians in Turkey

Today, I sat down once again with Paul to hear an update about how things are going with the Iranian diaspora church in Turkey. In the last few months since we had last spoken, three new Iranian diaspora churches had been established. Two were in other cities in Turkey, and one was in a coastal city in France. All three of these new churches had their roots in churches in Iran started by Paul many years earlier.[9]

In each case the story was the same. Persecution and other migratory factors scattered Iranian believers to cities where they had friends or relatives. In their new cities, these refugee believers connected with the Iranian community — most of whom were Shia Muslims — and began sharing the gospel with their fellow Iranians. According to Paul, most of the members of these new churches are not former members of his churches in Iran. The leaders are, yet most of the members are actually diasporic Muslim background believers who came to faith after they left Iran.[10]

The Iranian diaspora church in France is Every Nation's third church plant in that nation. The first (in Marseille) was pioneered by American missionaries; the second (in Paris) by South African missionaries. This third and most recent church plant has occurred not because a mission organization (or even a local church) targeted a particular city and a particular people. Rather this church came organically (and unexpectedly) as a result of mission *with* the Iranian diaspora.

This kind of missional movement is reminiscent of the early church in the book of Acts. Persecution scattered the church in Jerusalem, and Jewish believers, initially ministering *to* the Jewish diaspora, planted churches in cities where Jesus' original disciples had never been (see Acts 8). Some of these churches, like Antioch, became places the church expanded *beyond* the diaspora, including Greeks for the first time (see Acts 11). It was also at Antioch where the church partnered *with* diasporic Jews, like Paul of Tarsus and Barnabas, to plant churches in Asia Minor and beyond.

While these varied stories of diaspora mission in the Every Nation world, particularly those facilitated through international student ministry, may represent something of a departure from conventional, western missionary narratives of the nineteenth and twentieth centuries, there is something peculiarly biblical about God using diasporic peoples in unexpected times and places in the story of redemption.

If God can use Hebrew slaves in Egypt, then He can certainly use overseas Filipino workers in Dubai. If He can reach a young Moabite woman in Bethlehem, then He can reach Nepalese students in Los Baños. If He can use young exilic Jews in Babylon, then He can use diasporic Zimbabweans in Berlin. And if He can use Paul of Tarsus to pioneer

---

[9] Interview with "Paul," April 3, 2019.
[10] Interview with "Paul," April 3, 2019.

churches across Asia Minor and the Mediterranean in the first century, then He can use "Paul" of Tehran to pioneer churches in Turkey and France in the twenty-first century.

CHAPTER 11
CONCLUSION

To the editor, the publication of this book on ISM and diaspora missions is both personally and professionally significant. He himself came to New York as an international student in January 1971 so the planning and publication of this book is personal. He has spent decades engaging in diaspora missions among Filipino, Chinese, and Vietnamese, as a missiological practitioner prior to the presentation of the diaspora and missiological paradigm, as a professional missiologist at the international gathering in April at Tokyo 2010 and in October 2010 at Cape Town 2010 (The Third Lausanne Congress on World Evangelization) in South Africa.

There are few academic papers on ISM from the perspective of diaspora missiology (see footnote below)[1] and not a book of this category. In this sense, this book is unique. It is a collection of contributions from academics and practitioners. The theoretical and theological framework of this book is a clear departure from the popular view that the fulfilment of the Great Commission of making disciples is the way to carry out our Christian "mission." In chapter 2, an alternative definition of "mission" in relational terms is proposed and extensive discussion entailed, covering aspects of Scripture, history, theology, and practice.

Not in conformity to the popular programmatic and outcome-based approach in Christian practice, the "relational paradigm" is presented in this volume for ISM to rediscover the relational characteristic of Christian faith and practice in the pluralistic and post-modernist era of the 21st century. This book is not merely another title on ISM; this title is

---

[1] Papers by Leition Chin on ISM from the perspective of diaspora missiology:
"International students: a strategic component of diaspora missions & the Great Commission," Asia Missions Association, posted June 22, 2016, accessed May 2019, **http://www.asiamissions.net/international-students-a-strategic-component-of-diaspora-missions-the-great-commission/**
"Reflections on Reaching the International Student Diaspora in North America," *Global Missiology* Vol 4, No 11, 2014,
http://ojs.globalmissiology.org/index.php/english/article/view/1684
Leiton Edward Chinn & Lisa Espineli Chinn, "Agents of diaspora missions in and from the academic world," in *Scatted and Gathered: A Global Compendium of Diaspora Missiology,* eds. Sadiri Joy Tira and Testsunnao Yamamori, Regnum Books International, 2016:228-241.
Papers BY OTHERS:
J. Hun KIM "Diaspora missiology and Lausanne diaspora evangelical movement with a case study on Korean diaspora mission in Eurasia," Asia Missions Association, Posted April 1, 2019, accessed May 2019, **http://www.asiamissions.net/diaspora-missiology-and-lausanne-diaspora-evangelical-movement-with-a-case-study-on-korean-diaspora-mission-in-eurasia/**
Phil Jones, "International Students in China—an Unreached Diaspora," *China Source*, October 6, 2017, accessed May 2019, **https://www.chinasource.org/blog/posts/international-students-in-china-an-unreached-diaspora**

theoretically and theologically variant to popular writings. It is a continuation of what was presented by the editor of this book at Tokyo 2010 and LCWE 2010[2] as an integration of the diaspora missiological paradigm and the relational paradigm.

A Biblical and theological foundation for ISM was covered in Chapter 4. Case studies of international students were presented in Chapter 3 and reflections on ISM were included in Chapter 5. Chapters 6 and 7 form a unit covering the history and development of ISM by Leiton and Lisa Chinn (with Stacey Bieler) – a couple whose life-long careers have been devoted to ISM. They combined firsthand experience and extensive research to produce two outstanding chapters with both diachronic and synchronic perspectives as well as institutional (InterVarsity and ISM) and global scopes. Chapter 8 is an attempt to enable readers to understand the five stages of conversion in community in cross-cultural evangelism. The strategy proposed in Chapter 9 eludes the concept of "unreached people groups" in traditional missiology. Congregational practices in diaspora missiology engaging international students locally is a good illustration of the contrast of two paradigms: traditional vis-à-vis diaspora.

Chapter 10 presents case studies of diaspora mission with Every Nation illustrating all four types of diaspora missions in the context of ISM: missions *to, through, by and beyond,* and *with* the diaspora. The stories recorded and reported are very telling, showing why and how the diaspora missiological paradigm is so very relevant for the new reality in comparison to a traditional missiological paradigm.

---

[2] Figure 10 in Chapter 2 was first introduced for both occasions; links for video presentations:
- **Tokyo 2010** – Plenary Session Video   (paper in pdf file, pages 92-100)
- **Cape Town 2010** – "Multiplex" Session Video   (paper in digital format)

APPENDIX 1 - "STARS" APPROACH OF INTEGRATIVE RESEARCH

Inter-disciplinary research in missiology combines and integrates biblical study, theology, anthropology, demographics, statistics, etc., in order to achieve a high degree of coherence or unity in research and for the practice of Christian mission. As evangelicals, we are not to be sold out to the newest theory or pragmatic efficiency. Nor should we engage in unreserved contextualization, such as multiple forms of liberation theology (e.g. feminist theology of the west, "*minjung* theology of Korea," C.S. Song's "third eye theology"). The diagrams below emerged from personal research, professional publications and two-decades-long coaching of doctoral dissertations. If inter-disciplinary research in missiological studies is conducted by following the five-steps according to priority, then it will be characteristically evangelical, doctrinally sound, and theologically grounded.

Wan's Way of Integrative Research ("STARS")[1]

CRITERIA	*	EXPLANATION
1. Scripturally Sound	S	Not proof-text; rather the "whole counsel of God" (Acts 20:26-27)
2. Theologically Supported	T	Not simply pragmatism/expedience; but sound theology
3. Analytically Coherent	A	Not to be self-contradictory; rather, to be coherent
4. Relevantly Contextual	R	Not to be out of place; rather, fitting for the context
5. Strategically Practical	S	Not only good in theory; also, can be strategically put into practice

Listed below are simple explanations of each of the five points in the table:

1. Scripturally Sound

As evangelicals, Scripture is to be the basis and guide of Christian faith and practice. It is axiomatic for evangelical Protestants based on the conviction of "*sola scriptura.*"

---

[1] Enoch Wan, "Inter-disciplinary and Integrative Missiological Research: the 'What,' 'Why,' and 'How,'" July 2017, www.GlobalMissiology.org

2. Theologically Supported

A base of pragmatism/expedience is insufficient; rather, sound theology is essential and required.

3. Analytically Coherent

Not to be self-contradictory; rather to be both consistent and coherent.

4. Relevantly Contextual

Not to be out of place; rather, required to be fitting for the context.

5. Strategically Practical

It is good to have scriptural/theological support with coherent theory and cultural relevance, which may be strategically put into practice.

Comparisons between "Biblical" and Scriptural"[2]

#	BIBLICAL	SCRIPTURAL
1	Descriptive: Recorded/reported in the Bible	Prescriptive: Prescribed by the Incarnate & "enscriptured" Word
2	Precedent in the Bible	Principle of "the whole counsel of God"
3	Particular: time and place specific	Universal: transcending time & space
4	culturally & contextually specific	Neither culturally nor contextually specific

For a detailed discussion of the "STARS" approach, please check out the following pieces previously published:

- Enoch Wan, "Core Values of Mission Organization in the Cultural Context of the 21st Century," *Global Missiology,* January 2009, www.GlobalMissiology.org/
- Enoch Wan, "Inter-disciplinary and Integrative Missiological Research: the 'What,' 'Why,' and 'How,'" July 2017, **www.GlobalMissiology.org**

---

[2] Enoch Wan, ""Core Values of Mission Organization in the Cultural Context of the 21st Century," "Featured Article" January 2009:6-7, **www.GlobalMissiology.org**

APPENDIX 2 - COMPARISON OF TWO COGNITIVE PATTERN/PROCESS

- The table below (Wan 1999:34-35) is a comparison of American (with European backdrop) and Chinese (with Asian background) cognitive pattern/processes.

Ameri-European & Sino-Asian Cognitive Patterns/Processes

AREA		AMERI-EUROPEAN	SINO-ASIAN
P A T T E R N	1. General	-low-context	-high-context
	2. Perception: 2.1 nature 2.2 self 2.3 other	-material, mechanistic -separate from nature -equality, individualism	-organic, organismic -integrate with nature -hierarchy, communal
	3.Conception: 3.1 deity 3.2 self 3.3 truth 3.4 knowledge 3.5 time	-monotheism, atheism -independent, unique -Bible/rational-relative -"a priori"/"a posteri" -lineal	-polytheism, animism -member of a group -naturalism, humanism -intuitive, introspective -cyclical
	4. Preference: 4.1 personal 4.2 social 4.3 goal	-achievement/autonomy -egalitarian/voluntary -diversity/self-actualization	-ascription/inter-dependence -hierarchy/inequality -unity/group-solidarity
	5. Predisposition: 5.1 individual & social 5.2 ethical 5.3 goal	-doing/program -competition -guilt/universal justice /proselytization -change/effort-optimism	-being/people -cooperation -shame/situational justice /reconciliation/syncretism -equilibrium/conservatism /relation-optimism
P R O C E S S	1. time-management	-mono-chronic	-poly-chronic
	2. logic	-inductive	-deductive
	3. methodology	-empirical, causative (obj.)	-intuitive/introspective
	4. tendency	-quantitative, mathematical	-qualitative, ontological
	5. approach	-analytical	-analogical/relational
	6. operation	-dialectic/duality /directive/aggressive	-correlational/holistic /non-directive
	7. direction	-teleological, future	-historical/retrospective

For detailed discussion of this type of comparative study for the contextual Sino-theology, see Wan 1999:34-35.

Made in United States
North Haven, CT
29 June 2025

70203173R00111